Y0-AQQ-500

A superb analysis of unparalleled clarity, José De Gregorio's *How Latin America Weathered the Global Financial Crisis* is essential reading for those who seek to understand Latin America's recent evolution, prospects, and challenges.

Agustín Carstens, Governor, Banco de México

Latin America stands out as a good performer in the current global economic crisis. José De Gregorio, an exceptionally accomplished economist and policymaker, analyzes why its record was different this time. He provides a convincing and important explanation of how and why good policies, consistently implemented, work—and why a little luck in the form of improved terms of trade also helps.

Stanley Fischer, Council on Foreign Relations, former governor of the Bank of Israel, and former top official at the International Monetary Fund and World Bank

De Gregorio's book offers brilliant insight into how sound macro-financial policies in good times mitigate vulnerabilities and support sustainable development. The book conveys a heartening message about Latin America's ability to outperform in the face of formidable challenges. It also delivers a finely nuanced message for consolidating long-term growth and prosperity: vigilance and preparedness on the macro-financial front and decisively advancing a social progress agenda to alleviate inequality and accelerate social integration.

Luis Alberto Moreno, President, Inter-American Development Bank

Latin America did poorly during the Asian crisis. But it weathered the global financial crisis much better. Why? José De Gregorio, who had a first row seat as governor of the Bank of Chile, gives a detailed and convincing answer: Most Latin American countries learned their lessons, and this time, they had their macroeconomic house in order. It is nice to know that old truths are sometimes right.... An important book.

Olivier Blanchard, Chief Economist, International Monetary Fund

A definitive analysis of Latin America's resilience after the recent global financial crisis from a leading academic researcher and former top policymaker. De Gregorio traces the history of the region's chronic financial instability and asks when, where, and why instability might return in the coming decade. An elegant synthesis of theory and practice. Must reading for scholars, students, and policymakers interested in the Latin American experience and its lessons for the rest of the world.

Kenneth S. Rogoff, Thomas D. Cabot Professor of Public Policy, Harvard University

MIX
Paper from
responsible sources
FSC www.fsc.org **FSC® C005010**

Peterson Institute for
International Economics

HOW
LATIN
AMERICA
WEATHERED
THE GLOBAL
FINANCIAL
CRISIS

José De Gregorio

WASHINGTON, DC
JANUARY 2014

José De Gregorio, visiting fellow at the Peterson Institute for International Economics, is full professor in the Department of Economics at the Universidad de Chile. He was governor of the Central Bank of Chile from 2007 until 2011. Before that he was vice-governor from 2003 and member of the bank's board from 2001. During 2000 and 2001, De Gregorio was minister of the combined portfolios of economy, mining, and energy.

Between 1997 and 2000 he was professor and head of postgraduate programs at the Center of Applied Economics at the University of Chile. He also served on the executive of the Latin American Doctoral Program in Economics. From 1994 to 1997, he was coordinator of economic policy at the Ministry of Finance, Chile. From 1990 to 1994 he worked as an economist in the research department of the International Monetary Fund (IMF). He has been a visiting scholar at the IMF and the World Bank and visiting professor at the Anderson School, University of California, Los Angeles. He is on the board of and advisor to several private companies. He is also a consultant to international organizations.

De Gregorio has received a number of honors and awards, including Central Banker of the Year in Latin America for 2008, awarded by *The Banker*, a member of the *Financial Times* editorial group. He was also named Distinguished Industrial Engineer of 2007 by the Industrial Engineering–Universidad de Chile Alumni Association and Economist of the Year by the newspaper *El Mercurio* in 2011, among others.

He has a degree in civil engineering and a master's degree in engineering from the University of Chile, where he received the Marcos Orrego Puelma award for the best graduate of his year. He obtained a PhD in economics from MIT in 1990. He has published two books and more than 100 articles in international academic reviews and books on issues including monetary policy, exchange rates, international finance, and economic growth. He has served as a referee and member of editorial boards for several academic journals. He is also a member of the Executive Committee of the Latin American and Caribbean Economic Association.

PETERSON INSTITUTE FOR INTERNATIONAL ECONOMICS
1750 Massachusetts Avenue, NW
Washington, DC 20036-1903
(202) 328-9000   FAX: (202) 659-3225
www.piie.com

Adam S. Posen, *President*
Steven R. Weisman, *Editorial and Publications Director*

Graphics typesetted by MidAtlantic Publishing Services
Cover design by Fletcher Design
Printing by Versa Press, Inc.

Printed in the United States of America
16   15   14   5   4   3   2   1

Library of Congress Cataloging-in-Publication Data
De Gregorio, José.
   How Latin America weathered the global financial crisis / Jose De Gregorio.
      pages cm
   ISBN 978-0-88132-678-9
   1. Latin America—Economic policy. 2. Monetary policy—Latin America. 3. Financial crises—Latin America. 4. Global Financial Crisis, 2008-2009. I. Title.
   HC125.D3695 2013
   330.98'00411—dc23

                                  2013023860

To my parents

Contents

Tables

Figures

Preface

The global financial and economic crisis of 2008–09 rallied countries around the world to a dramatic and coordinated response. Despite these efforts, Europe and the United States have suffered their worst economic downturns in 75 years. There were also fears at the time of the turmoil that developing regions like Latin America, which had experienced a number of crises of its own in recent decades, would be even worse affected. Instead, to the surprise of many experts, the emerging markets, including those in Latin America, suffered only limited damage. Latin America's performance has been better than its performance during not only its debt crisis of the 1980s but also the Asian crisis of the 1990s.

In this important book, José De Gregorio, former governor of the Central Bank of Chile and visiting fellow at the Peterson Institute for International Economics, explains why the emerging markets did well in surviving the crisis. As he notes, the global crisis has not ended, and it is too early to say that the story for Latin America has reached its conclusion. But the region's economic resilience has been striking. The book focuses mainly on the seven largest economies of the region—Argentina, Brazil, Chile, Colombia, Mexico, Peru, and Venezuela—which together comprise more than 90 percent of regional output. De Gregorio argues that strong performance during the crisis resulted from sound macroeconomic and financial policies before the crisis. These countries' accomplishments allowed them to undertake significant monetary and fiscal expansion in the context of robust financial systems.

More specifically, the Latin American nations under study were able to maintain flexible inflation targeting regimes and utilize exchange rate flexibility. Their banking systems were strong, well regulated, and fairly simple to understand. They had high levels of international reserves, which helped to deter attacks on their currencies and addressed potential shortages of foreign financing. De Gregorio acknowledges that there was also an element of luck. Latin America's terms of trade were improving over this period; investors around the world did not run away from the region. But even external financial conditions are influenced by domestic economic policies as well, as he shows.

There are also disparities within the region that amplify his argument. Brazil, Chile, Colombia, Mexico, and Peru have all done better in their macroeconomic and financial management than Argentina and Venezuela, in part because of high prices for commodities like soybean and oil. Many problems remain in the latter two countries, including high inflation rates, monetary policy that is not independent, and rigid exchange rate regimes. There are also tensions in foreign exchange markets resulting from losses of reserves and black market exchange rates.

Thus the most important lesson De Gregorio draws from recent Latin American experience is the simplest: Good macroeconomic management and strong financial systems can mitigate a large shock caused by external factors. Another lesson is that the countries in the region that have integrated more with the rest of the world have benefited from doing so, though he warns that integration must be prudent, not "unfettered." He concludes that the effort to achieve stability and resilience, however, is never-ending. His book takes us far in understanding what has worked better than in the past, so that emerging markets can draw on their own successes in meeting future challenges.

This book has grown out of the Peterson Institute's ongoing commitment to addressing issues of concern to globalizing economies throughout the world. As part of that commitment, the Institute has inaugurated a new series of lectures by policy leaders with economic expertise in emerging markets, supported by the Sunrise Foundation. We are proud that De Gregorio delivered the inaugural lecture in that series in September 2012. The second Sunrise Foundation lecture at the Peterson Institute was given by Simeon Djankov, then finance minister of Bulgaria, in February 2013.

Developments in Latin America have been of major interest at the Peterson Institute since its inception. This book follows other important Institute studies, including by John Williamson (*Prospects for Adjustment in Argentina, Brazil, and Mexico: Responding to the Debt Crisis*; *The Progress of Policy Reform in Latin America*; *Latin American Adjustment: How Much Has Happened?* and *After the Washington Consensus: Restarting Growth and Reform in Latin America* edited with Pedro-Pablo Kuczynski); Michael Mussa (*Argentina and the Fund: From Triumph to Tragedy*); and Jeffrey Schott (*Prospects for Free Trade in the Americas* and *Trade Relations between Colombia and the United States*).

The Peterson Institute for International Economics is a private, nonprofit institution for rigorous, intellectually open and honest study and discussion of international economic policy. Its purpose is to identify and analyze important issues to making globalization beneficial and sustainable for the people of the United States and the world and then to develop and communicate practical new approaches for dealing with them. The Institute is completely nonpartisan.

The Institute's work is funded by a highly diverse group of philanthropic foundations, private corporations, and interested individuals, as well as income on its capital fund. About 35 percent of the Institute's resources in our latest fiscal year were provided by contributors from outside the United States. For a list of Institute supporters, see www.piie.com/supporters. We are grateful to the Sunrise Foundation, and to its founder and President Antoine van Agtmael, for its generous support of this book project, as well as for the lecture on which it was based.

The Executive Committee of the Institute's Board of Directors bears overall responsibility for the Institute's direction, gives general guidance and approval to its research program, and evaluates its performance in pursuit of its mission. The Institute's President is responsible for the identification of topics that are likely to become important over the medium term (one to three years) that should be addressed Institute scholars. This rolling agenda is set in close consultation with the Institute's research staff and Board of Directors, as well as its other stakeholders. The President makes the final decision to publish any individual Institute study, following independent internal and external review of the work.

The Institute hopes that its research and other activities will contribute to building a stronger foundation for international economic policy around the world. We invite readers of these publications to let us know how they think we can best accomplish this objective.

ADAM S. POSEN
President
January 2014

Acknowledgments

The idea of writing this book was born when I gave the first Sunrise Emerging Markets Lecture at the Peterson Institute for International Economics (PIIE) in September 2012. However, the ideas contained here have been evolving for many years—in particular since I had the opportunity to be the governor of the Central Bank of Chile during the global financial crisis, the most severe since the Great Depression.

Many new issues were raised as result of the economic and financial collapse in advanced economies. But, also, the resilience of emerging-market economies, in particular Latin America, is worth highlighting. Latin America has managed to amplify every external crisis it faced, but this time was different, perhaps for the first time. The good performance of Latin American countries during the global financial crisis is unprecedented, at least in the last half century.

The adoption of sound macroeconomic policies, built in part during a time of favorable international conditions and with the lessons learned after so many experiences of gross mismanagement, was key to this performance. The crisis is not over, there is heterogeneity within the region, and new challenges have emerged, but it is a good time to take stock of the central features of these policies and the lessons for the future. Latin America will continue facing internal and external shocks, but having sound macroeconomic policies is key to addressing those challenges successfully.

While I was governor of the Central Bank of Chile I benefited enormously from the collaboration of a superb staff and members of the Board. It was great to work in an intellectually challenging environment and with people who understood the critical role that good policies play in the well-being of the Chilean people. They helped me to craft many of the ideas contained in this book. Among many collaborators I would like to thank Luis Felipe Céspedes, Rodrigo Cifuentes, Beltrán de Ramón, Mariana García, Luis Oscar Herrera, Felipe Labbé, Sergio Lehmann, Igal Magendzo, Christopher Neilson, Enrique Orellana, Claudio Raddatz, Claudio Soto, and Andrea Tokman. Special thanks to Kevin Cowan and Pablo García, who not only were some of my closest colleagues during the global financial crisis but also provided valuable inputs and comments to this book.

My visits to the International Monetary Fund and the PIIE since I left the bank have been extremely productive. I have benefited from many discussions and presentations of parts of this work in both places. The PIIE provided a very stimulating environment to work. I am very thankful to Eduardo Borensztein, Ted Truman, and Alejandro Werner, who provided valuable comments to the entire book. I also enjoyed discussions in several areas covered in this book with Joseph Gagnon, Sebastian Edwards, Eduardo Levy-Yeyati, and Rodrigo Valdes. During 2012 I had the opportunity to work closely with Marcus Brunnermeier, Philip Lane, Eswar Prasad, Hélène Rey, and Hyun Song Shin on international financial issues, which shaped many of my ideas on this area. I have learned a lot from them.

I thank Fred Bergsten, Adam Posen, and Steve Weisman for all the support in producing this book and Madona Devasahayam for great, and patient, editorial assistance. I thank José Tomás De Gregorio, Bastián Gallardo, and Marc Hinterschweiger for valuable research assistance.

My wife, Sol, and four children, Soledad, José Tomás, Victoria, and Manuela, have been very supportive during this entire project. They were very encouraging while I had to spend Chile's summer in Washington, DC's winter, while I worked hard until late hours and weekends, and while I was a bit distracted from things other than writing. Without their care and support it would not have been possible to undertake this project.

JOSÉ DE GREGORIO

Latin America

1

Introduction

Latin America's robust economic performance in the wake of the global financial crisis of 2008-09—the worst crisis since the Great Depression—is unprecedented. Other global crises during the postwar period caused significant downturns in most emerging-market economies, including those in Latin America, which generally took the largest hit. While Latin American and other emerging-market economies around the world suffered during the recent crisis, and although some endured sizable contractions in 2009, overall, they have been surprisingly resilient: The damage was limited, and their recoveries have been very strong. Even against the relative strength of other emerging-market economies, Latin America's performance has been surprisingly robust. It has performed better than during other recent crises that affected all economies in the region, notably the Latin American debt crisis of the 1980s and the 1997-98 Asian financial crisis. Growth in the region has almost paralleled the success of emerging Asia and has outstripped that of the advanced economies (figure 1.1).

In this book I examine the factors underlying Latin America's impressive economic performance during the global financial crisis. The focus is on the region's seven largest economies, which are referred to as the LA-7 and account for more than 90 percent of the region's output: Argentina, Brazil, Chile, Colombia, Mexico, Peru, and Venezuela.[1] These are the only countries

---

1. The data used here are from the International Monetary Fund's *World Economic Outlook* (WEO) database. The WEO tracks data for the Latin American and Caribbean (LAC) region, which includes 32 countries—the LA-7 and the 25 other countries in the WEO's LAC region: Antigua and Barbuda, the Bahamas, Barbados, Belize, Bolivia, Costa Rica, Dominica, Dominican Republic, Ecuador, El Salvador, Grenada, Guatemala, Guyana, Haiti, Honduras, Jamaica, Nicaragua, Panama, Paraguay, St. Kitts and Nevis, St. Lucia, St. Vincent and the Grenadines, Suriname, Trinidad and Tobago, and Uruguay.

Figure 1.1   GDP during debt crisis, Asian crisis, and global financial crisis: Latin America, emerging Asia, and advanced economies

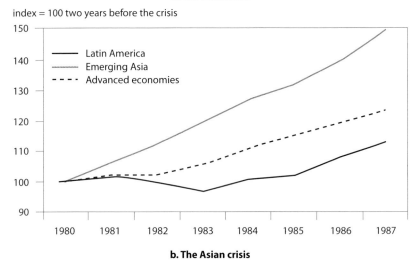

a. The debt crisis

index = 100 two years before the crisis

Legend:
— Latin America
⋯ Emerging Asia
- - - Advanced economies

(x-axis: 1980, 1981, 1982, 1983, 1984, 1985, 1986, 1987)

b. The Asian crisis

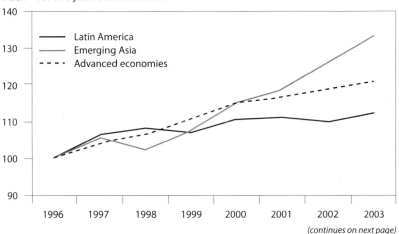

index = 100 two years before the crisis

Legend:
— Latin America
— Emerging Asia
- - - Advanced economies

(x-axis: 1996, 1997, 1998, 1999, 2000, 2001, 2002, 2003)

(continues on next page)

with GDP of over $100 billion. Most of my discussion is concentrated on this group of countries, since it allows more focus and is the most relevant from a global point of view. These countries have also been the poster children of previous crises, high inflation, financial crises, and macroeconomic misman-agement. All these countries have faced serious economic problems of varying degrees and at different periods.

The book reviews recent regional and country-specific experiences, de-scribes the main features of these economies' macroeconomic and financial

Figure 1.1   GDP during debt crisis, Asian crisis, and global financial crisis: Latin America, emerging Asia, and advanced economies *(continued)*

c. The global financial crisis

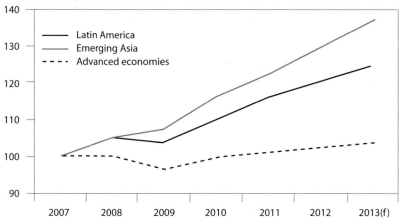

f = forecast

Note: Latin America: Argentina, Brazil, Chile, Colombia, Mexico, Peru, and Venezuela; emerging Asia: China, India, Indonesia, Korea, Malaysia, the Philippines, and Thailand; advanced economies: 41 countries as defined by the International Monetary Fund.

Source: IMF (2013a).

policies, explores why the region fared so much better during this crisis than during previous crises, and extracts lessons for how best to preserve stability and promote sustained growth.

The analysis here shows that Latin America's strong economic performance in the wake of the crisis is the result of good macroeconomic and financial policies, which allowed for significant monetary and fiscal expansion and a resilient financial system. It is also the result of good international conditions. Specifically, the terms of trade—the ratio of export prices to import prices—have been very favorable for Latin America since the mid-2000s, and overall global financial conditions have been positive for emerging markets as a whole. This contrasts with the Latin American debt crisis and the Asian financial crisis, when terms of trade declined and external conditions deteriorated for the region.

The relative importance of good policies versus good luck is different for the various countries of the region because the ultimate effects of external conditions largely depend on domestic policies. Potential vulnerabilities such as a sudden stop in capital inflows, a disruption of international trade or financial flows, or fluctuations in commodity prices, can be mitigated by sound domestic policies.

Brazil, Chile, Colombia, Mexico, and Peru have significantly strengthened their macroeconomic, financial, and regulatory management and have become more financially integrated into the global economy, all of which improved their resilience during the crisis. This was not true of Argentina and Venezuela. Both, as well as the other countries, benefited from high commodity prices (soybeans for Argentina and oil for Venezuela), which enabled them to perform well before and during the crisis and to implement expansionary policies. But both countries have high inflation rates, lack an independent monetary policy, and are hampered by rigid exchange rate regimes, and these policy weaknesses have recently begun to bite, specifically through the foreign exchange markets, producing significant black-market premiums and massive reserve losses that threaten their stability and growth.

High commodity prices are the result of good economic performance in emerging markets, in particular the impressive growth in China. Things would have been different if the decline in commodity prices observed in late 2008 had persisted. However, good macroeconomic policies still could have alleviated the effects of bad external conditions if they had persisted. Experience shows that good macroeconomic management and strong financial systems can significantly mitigate a deterioration in the external environment. Chile offers an example. Copper is quite important in the Chilean economy and in 2012 represented 12 percent of GDP and 54 percent of exports. Hence, it is one of the most exposed countries to the commodity cycle. Good policies helped Chile to grow moderately in the early 2000s, when real copper prices were lower than at any other time since the Great Depression, and to avoid an unsustainable boom in the face of the record-high copper prices of recent years. Chile's dependence on copper price fluctuations has declined over time, despite the importance of copper in economic activity and exports.

Recent macroeconomic reform and favorable external conditions may have helped the region's performance in the wake of the crisis, but additional reforms will be necessary to improve these economies' potential output and spur sustainable growth over the long term.

The risks to the region linger from the global financial crisis. Advanced economies have not fully recovered from the crisis and face serious problems, including lackluster growth, high unemployment, incomplete financial reforms, and, in the euro area, a need to bolster economic and monetary union. At the same time, the advanced economies have only limited policy space to address these problems through traditional approaches such as expansionary fiscal policies. Several euro area member countries have faced sovereign debt crises, which intensified in mid-2011 and have been only partly resolved by intervention by the European Union, the European Central Bank (ECB), and the International Monetary Fund (IMF)—the so-called troika behind the recent bailouts. A number of EU banks remain weak, and bank deleveraging may further weaken growth. Japan, the United Kingdom, and the United States continue their efforts to bolster growth by keeping interest rates near the zero lower bound through the use of unconventional monetary policy. In contrast, activity in most emerging-market economies has already reached full capacity. In fact, many of these economies have recently faced challenges associated with relatively strong growth that may threaten their economic and financial stability, in particular, strong currencies and large capital inflows. With such risks still prevalent, securing long-term growth and financial stability is an important policy concern for Latin America.

Latin America from a Global Perspective

Table 1.1 provides a snapshot of current economic data for the LA-7, which account for more than 90 percent of the region's GDP. These countries all have a long tradition of poor economic performance. Throughout the postwar period until the 1980s or 1990s, depending on the country,[2] they were characterized by a number of factors that hampered growth: weak institutions, high inflation, unsustainable fiscal policies, exchange rate rigidities, high inequality, and low openness to trade (De Gregorio and Lee 2004).[3]

To different degrees and at different periods, all of these countries have faced serious economic problems. The debt crisis that began in 1982 had its origins in the adjustment in the United States to high inflation following the oil shocks of the 1970s, which induced the Federal Reserve to sharply tighten monetary policy. Latin American governments owed high levels of external debt to US banks, and the steep rise in US interest rates made the debt burden unsustainable. The Mexican government defaulted on its debt in August 1982, which set off a regional crisis. The crisis also owed much to macroeconomic mismanagement. For example, Chile had huge financial end external imbalances that led to a massive devaluation and the abandonment if its fixed exchange rate regime in June 1982. This initiated a deep economic and financial crisis, which would have taken place regardless of the Fed monetary policy adjustment, although effects would have been less dramatic without the negative external shock.

The abundance of international capital since the early 1990s and the lessons learned from the mismanagement before the debt crisis provided the impetus for reform. The success of Chile, in particular in the context of the return to democracy, was also an example in the region to push for reforms.

The 1980s were a lost decade for Latin America, with a sharp decline in relative income during the first half of the decade. In 1985 GDP had recovered to its precrisis levels, but advanced economies and Asia had GDP growth of 15 and 30 percent, respectively, above their 1980 levels.

---

2. Reforms in different countries have come at different times. For example, in Chile, the early reformer, the opening up of the economy and the liberalization of domestic prices took place in the 1970s, while inflation stabilization came only in the 1990s.

3. Weak institutions are key to understanding the stagnation in Latin America. See the persuasive account of Acemoglu and Robinson (2012).

Table 1.1 Basic indicators for the seven largest Latin American countries, 2012

| Country | GDP (billions of US dollars) | GDP per capita | | Share of Latin American GDP (percent) | Population (millions) |
		US dollars	PPP US dollars		
Argentina	475	11,576	18,112	8.2	41
Brazil	2,396	12,079	11,875	41.6	198
Chile	268	15,410	18,419	4.7	17
Colombia	366	7,855	10,792	6.3	47
Mexico	1,177	10,247	15,312	20.4	115
Peru	199	6,530	10,719	3.5	30
Venezuela	382	12,956	13,616	6.6	30

PPP = purchasing power parity
Source: IMF (2012d).

Certainly macroeconomic mismanagement led to crisis and slow growth, and mistakes could have been avoided. However, most of the macroeconomic reforms were undertaken in the 1990s, and benefits came almost a decade later. There is always trial and error; ex post we obviously have a better understanding of what went wrong. Nevertheless, not only has good performance been the result of current policies but also a path has been built over time by learning from mistakes.

Indeed, the first five, out of ten, recommendations of the so-called Washington Consensus, quite unfairly discredited as being unable to promote growth, refer to broad macroeconomic principles, in particular geared to sound fiscal policies and competitive exchange rate (Williamson 1990).[4] The latter was a response to artificially overvalued currencies that were central to economic malaise in the region. Of course, the recommendations are insufficient, so the list is quite incomplete. The region is in a development stage where new challenges to foster economic progress have to be addressed. Indeed, issues such as poverty alleviation and social inclusion should be a top priority and were not in the Washington Consensus list. Despite being incomplete, most recommendations of the Washington Consensus have been followed and have paid off, in particular opening up of the economy and consolidating macroeconomic stability.

The reforms of the late 1980s and early 1990s did produce stronger growth, but the pace of growth was not fast enough to make up for lost ground and, despite positive growth, the 1990s were a period of continued income stagna-

---

4. See also the recent review and revision in Fischer (2012).

Figure 1.2 Per capita GDP of Latin America, emerging Asia, and emerging Europe as a percent of US per capita GDP, 1980–2012

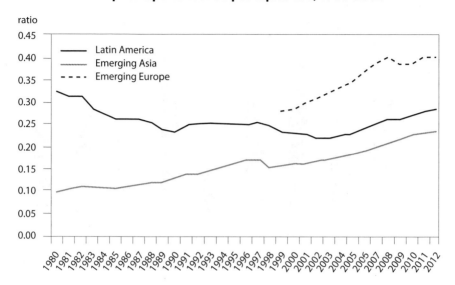

Note: Latin America: Argentina, Brazil, Chile, Colombia, Mexico, Peru, and Venezuela; emerging Asia: China, India, Indonesia, Korea, Malaysia, the Philippines, and Thailand; emerging Europe: Czech Republic, Hungary, Latvia, Lithuania, Poland, and Romania.

Source: IMF (2013a).

tion for the region in relation to both other emerging-market and advanced economies.

Figure 1.2 shows that growth, on average, tracked growth rates in the United States, until the slowdown attendant to the Asian financial crisis of 1997–98 and early 2000s. However, it is important to separate out the cyclical growth patterns to identify the long-term results of the reforms. Figure 1.3 shows average growth by decade since the 1980s. Chile, the earliest reformer, enjoyed its highest growth during the 1990s. In the other countries, most of the macroeconomic reforms occurred during the 1990s—including granting independence to central banks, consolidating fiscal policy, taking the first steps toward exchange rate flexibility, and other structural reforms—and these countries enjoyed the benefits almost a decade later.[5]

Figure 1.4 shows the growth experiences of the LA-7 in more detail by showing GDP per capita by country compared with the United States.[6] Chile

---

5. See Edwards (2010) for further discussion of macroeconomic progress during the 1990s and early 2000s.

6. Caution must be taken in comparing annual GDP per capita with that of the United States because these data are very sensitive to exchange rate fluctuations.

Figure 1.3 Growth in Latin America, 1981–2010

average per decade (percent)

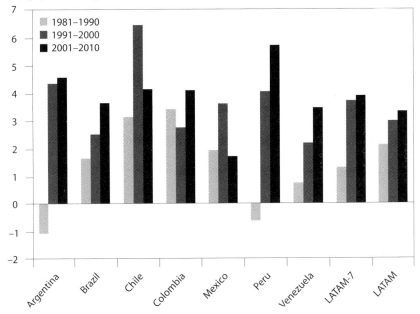

Note: The figures are simple annual averages across decades. The figure for the seven Latin American countries (LATAM-7) is the simple average and for Latin America (LATAM) is the weighted average from the IMF's *World Economic Outlook*.

Source: IMF (2012d).

and Peru have made important income gains, while Mexico's income per capita has remained relatively stable relative to income in the United States since 1994, after the so-called Tequila crisis. Income in Venezuela declined on a relative basis until 2004, when oil prices started to rise. Argentina experienced a sharp fall in income with the convertibility crisis of 2001–02 but has experienced a significant recovery since then.[7] Income in Brazil and Colombia started to grow faster than in the United States after a slight decline during the early 2000s. In 1990, the richest among the LA-7 were Mexico and Venezuela, but by 2012, they had been overtaken by Argentina and Chile. Argentina and Venezuela experienced the most rapid growth during the commodity price boom from 2004 until 2008. These countries are examples of the benefits of good luck in weathering the recent crisis, but they also demonstrate the

7. Argentina's official statistics have been considered unreliable since about 2007. In fact, the IMF has called on Argentina to adopt remedial measures to address data quality, particularly for inflation figures. Official estimates put inflation at about 10 percent, but others estimate it at around 25 percent. Similarly, current GDP estimates could be overvalued by about 15 percent.

Figure 1.4   Per capita GDP of Latin American countries as percent of US per capita GDP, 1990–2012

a. Argentina, Brazil, Chile, and Colombia

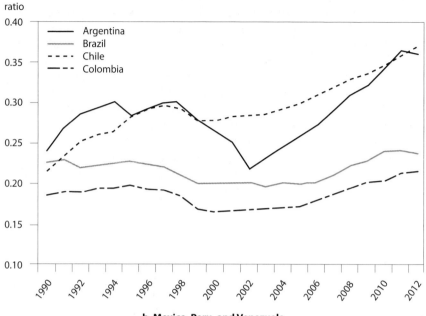

b. Mexico, Peru, and Venezuela

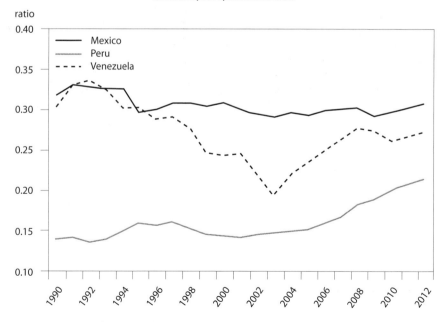

Source: IMF (2013a).

perils of being too dependent on external conditions, as discussed in detail in chapter 2.

More recent reform measures, some of which were adopted after the Asian crisis, created the policy space that helped the region respond to the global financial crisis. These reforms, mostly on the macroeconomic front, have stabilized inflation and consolidated public finances. One of the key early reforms, around 1990, was to grant independence to and mandate accountability by the central banks. To various degrees, central banks have been tasked with controlling inflation and have not been allowed to finance government budget deficits. The central banks in Brazil, Chile, Colombia, Mexico, and Peru adopted flexible inflation targets and, in an environment of low inflation, this permitted them to respond aggressively to the deterioration of the global economy by loosening monetary policy (e.g., lowering policy rates). In terms of fiscal policy, better policy has prevailed, which took advantage of the good external conditions. Most countries have run prudent fiscal policies, with limited budget deficits and in several cases surpluses as a result of the commodity price boom. However, less progress has been made on fiscal institutions, not only in the region but in emerging markets in general, with the exception of Chile with the application of a fiscal rule founded on solid economic principles.

There is a long history of populist experiments in Latin America to address the serious economic inequality and low growth that have characterized the region. By populist policies I mean policies oriented to solve many of the serious inequality problems, by means of fiscally unsustainable measures and widespread distortions.[8] These distortions did not efficiently tackle the social problems, although intentions may have been commendable. In other cases, populist policies end up giving special privileges to interest groups, which are not the right targets from a social point of view, on the one hand, and hinder economic growth on the other.

There was a resurgence of populism in the region during the 1980s, with leaders such as Raúl Alfonsín in Argentina, José Sarney in Brazil, and Alan García in Peru, and a renewed wave during the early 2000s, with the emergence of Hugo Chávez in Venezuela and Néstor Kirchner in Argentina. The region is not free from populism; the road ahead should decisively promote social progress in a sustainable way and ensure that these policies are not detrimental to long-term economic growth and macroeconomic stability.[9]

---

8. Massive trade protection, price controls, and widespread subsidies have characterized these episodes.

9. Dornbusch and Edwards (1991) is the classical reference for the macroeconomics of populism in Latin America.

Latin America Compared with Other Emerging-Market Economies

Figure 1.2 shows the disparate growth performances of selected Asian, Latin American, and European emerging-market economies, and the experience of these three groups highlights some of the factors that explain Latin America's recent resilience.[10] The countries in each group are the following:

- Latin America: LA-7 (Argentina, Brazil, Chile, Colombia, Mexico, Peru, and Venezuela). These countries accounted for 91 percent of the LAC region's economy and 8 percent of world GDP in 2012.

- Emerging Asia: China, India, Indonesia, Korea, Malaysia, the Philippines, and Thailand. These countries accounted for 19 percent of world GDP in 2012, and 7 percent when China is excluded.

- Emerging Europe: Czech Republic, Hungary, Latvia, Lithuania, Poland, and Romania. These countries accounted for only 2 percent of global GDP in 2012.

The question of weighting the sample of Latin American countries is quite important. If the average is weighted by the GDP of each country, the evidence for Latin America comes mostly from Brazil and Mexico, obscuring the rest of the countries. In contrast, if all 32 Latin American and Caribbean countries are equally weighted, then Brazil and Mexico are each only 1/32 of the average, which clearly minimizes their impact. A good compromise is to take a few countries and apply the same weight to all of them. This is what I will do with the seven Latin American countries I study in this book.

The Asian countries included here experienced persistent growth since the early 1980s, which was only briefly interrupted during the Asian crisis. GDP per capita was 10 percent of US GDP per capita in 1980 and had grown to 23 percent in 2012. In 1980 the LA-7 had GDP per capita of 32 percent of the US level but only 29 percent in 2012, a decline that was more marked during the debt crisis and during the late 1990s and early 2000s. Growth recovered during the second half of the 2000s.[11] Growth in the included emerging European countries was significant after the adoption of the euro but has stalled since the start of the global financial crisis in 2008. This group of countries appears to have initially experienced overheating and unsustainable growth—performance not too different from that of Latin America during the debt crisis of the 1980s.

---

10. GDP per capita is calculated as the simple average across the selected countries in each region. This does not provide an indication of the relative importance of each region from a global perspective, but it does provide a better comparison of the average performance of each region.

11. Arithmetically, in per capita terms Latin America grew 31 percent more than the United States between 2002 and 2012.

Was This Crisis Different for Latin America?

In the past, global crises have had very significant negative effects in Latin America. The recent crisis stands in stark contrast, which can be seen by comparing the economic performance of the group of Asian emerging-market economies discussed above, the LA-7, and the advanced economies during three recent international crises: the debt crisis of the 1980s, the Asian crisis of 1997–98, and the recent global financial crisis (see figure 1.1).[12] The level of GDP for each region is set equal to 100 two years before the start of each crisis (1980, 1996, and 2007).[13]

The debt crisis hit Latin America particularly hard. If the recession in the United States in the late 1970s were considered a flu, the effects on Latin America were more like pneumonia. The region's economies were ill equipped to deal with the slowdown in the United States and in global trade or with the tightening of US monetary policy and the rise in interest rates in 1981. High levels of external debt, wide current account deficits, large fiscal deficits in some cases, poorly regulated financial markets, and general macroeconomic mismanagement led to a sharp contraction when US capital stopped flowing into the region. Exchange rate regimes had been semirigid before the crisis, but once the rigidity was abandoned, the region's currencies experienced significant devaluations. By 1987, the region's GDP was only 10 percent higher than in 1980 and GDP per capita remained stagnant. Meanwhile, Asian GDP had grown by 50 percent and advanced economies' GDP by 23 percent.

It is not surprising that Latin America performed poorly during the debt crisis, which was centered in the region. But when Asian countries were the epicenter of the crisis that spread through all emerging-market economies in 1997–98, their subsequent recovery was also much stronger than that of the Latin American economies. In 2003, five years after the crisis, GDP in Asia was more than 30 percent higher than the precrisis level, lower than the 50 percent increase in the five years after the debt crisis but still remarkable. Latin America, in contrast, stagnated. The initial decline was greater in Asia, but over the medium term, Latin America performed as poorly as after the debt crisis despite the fact that the initial contraction was less severe.

One reason is that the problems in Latin America were due not only to the Asian crisis but also to serious economic mismanagement. There was a convertibility crisis in Argentina in 2001, a currency crisis in Brazil in 1999, and a banking crisis in Colombia in 1999. The other countries in the region were un-

---

12. All data come from the WEO database, and "advanced economies" include those defined as such in this database, which weights by size. For Latin American and Asian countries, the average growth rate is calculated for each year and used to construct the index. The WEO definition contains 41 countries in the advanced economies group. Korea and the Czech Republic are classified as advanced economies, but they are kept in the Asian and emerging Europe samples here, respectively.

13. I assume the year of the largest decline in GDP to be the year the crisis started. The index is constructed using simple average growth rates.

able to implement vigorous expansionary policies to engineer a rapid recovery. Indeed, Latin American economies had become used to pursuing procyclical macroeconomic policies, to a large extent because of their reluctance to adopt flexible exchange rates—"fear of floating"—which led them to tighten monetary policy and reduce access to international financial markets, which further impeded fiscal expansion. These issues are discussed in more depth in subsequent chapters.

The recent crisis was different for Latin America—quite different. Four years after the crisis, Latin America's GDP is expected to be about 25 percent higher than the precrisis level, twice the growth achieved five years after the other two crises. Latin America's recovery still lags Asia's, although it is similar if China and India are excluded from the Asian group.

Saying that this time is different, especially when risks are still on the horizon, could be interpreted as an exaggeration. As Reinhart and Rogoff (2009) document, all crises are similar and go through similar phases. Indeed the global financial crisis had a strong credit boom, a softening of the financial conditions, supervisory negligence, and all the ingredients needed to cause a financial collapse. Nothing of this is new in Latin America. The recurrent financial crises in the region are quite similar to the recent one in the advanced world. Sometimes it was of fiscal origin, other times it was private. Regardless of the source, the crises were deep. The global crisis has not ended, therefore, we cannot say the story is over for Latin America, but the resilience has been astonishing. This time has been different, so far.

What Explains Latin America's Resilience?

The remainder of this book examines the factors underlying the strong performance of Latin America in the wake of the global financial crisis and identifies some important challenges and risks that lie ahead. In short, Latin America was resilient because of good macroeconomic policies, strong financial systems, and a bit of luck.[14]

1. Improved macroeconomic policy frameworks and good initial conditions generated enough policy space to allow the implementation of strong monetary and fiscal stimulus. The adoption of flexible inflation targeting regimes helped improve the success of monetary policy.

2. A cornerstone of the improved macroeconomic framework is exchange rate flexibility. Although several countries have used a combination of exchange rate intervention and capital controls to mitigate the appreciation of their currencies, for the most part and, more important, at crucial times, exchange rates have been allowed to float and thereby to act as shock absorbers.

---

14. Paraphrasing Rudiger Dornbusch's book, *Keys to Prosperity: Free Markets, Sound Money and a Bit of Luck* (Dornbusch 2000).

3. Strong, well-regulated, and fairly simple financial systems prevented exchange rate depreciations from causing a financial collapse. The strength of the financial systems meant that lending could resume as soon as conditions improved. A well-regulated financial system, with an appropriate macroeconomic framework, has been key to avoiding the perils of capital inflows.

4. High levels of international reserves played an important role in deterring attacks on the region's currencies. The reserves also provided a cushion to buffer the effects of any shortages of foreign financing.

5. It was a bit of good luck that most Latin American countries, which are exporters of primary commodities, enjoyed very good terms of trade: Commodity prices boomed during the second half of the 2000s and bounced back to very high levels after the sharp decline experienced during the crisis.

Overview of the Book

The chapters in this book examine each of these factors and identify some of the associated challenges that will need to be overcome in order to solidify the region's resilience, ensure sustainable growth for the long term, and tackle inequality to broaden the spread of prosperity.

Chapter 2 sets the stage by reviewing the favorable international environment for Latin America before the start of the global financial crisis, particularly the evolution of terms of trade. The benefits of terms of trade improvements were not equal for all countries in the region and were particularly strong for Argentina, Chile, Peru, and Venezuela. Moreover, Mexico and some countries in Central America suffered an important negative external shock from the expansion of manufacturing in China. The chapter reviews how improved fiscal and monetary policy positioned various countries to take advantage of good luck, overcome external shocks, and pursue expansionary policies during the crisis. The chapter examines the role of flexible inflation targets in monetary policy and the adoption by some countries of countercyclical fiscal policies, which helped to mitigate the effects of the external shocks.

Chapter 3 examines two very important factors underlying Latin America's recent success: flexible exchange rates and accumulation of international reserves. Most Latin American economies have overcome their traditional fear of floating. The extent of floating varies from country to country, and there has been foreign exchange rate intervention to build up reserves and avoid excessive appreciation of currencies. But these countries did not stubbornly defend an unrealistic value for the currencies, as in many previous episodes. The chapter reviews how anchoring inflation rates and strengthening their financial resilience has allowed these countries to overcome fear of floating, as large fluctuations of exchange rates have muted effects on financial stability and limited pass-through to inflation.

These economies also built up significant international reserve holdings before the crisis. Their use of these reserves during the crisis was limited, but they acted as a deterrent to currency speculation and sudden stops of foreign credit.

Chapter 4 discusses how improved financial systems and a focus on financial stability helped prevent serious disruptions during the crisis. The chapter reviews the origins of the financial crisis and how Latin America's cautious approach to financial innovation helped the region escape financial problems and avoid the credit booms that occurred in the advanced economies and emerging Europe. The chapter also discusses the role of new macroprudential tools in ensuring financial stability and the interactions between such tools and monetary policy.

A very important source of financial risk in emerging markets is capital flows, discussed in chapter 5. During the early 1990s, net capital inflows to emerging markets financed a widening of current account deficits. This was not the case in the years before the crisis, when most emerging-market economies had current account surpluses. Instead, these economies used inflows to accumulate reserves. The type of inflows to Latin America has changed as well, and this has reduced the attendant volatility and financial risks. Before the debt crisis, most flows to Latin America were in the form of bank credit, but the composition has been changing and now includes more foreign direct investment. Latin America has also become more financially integrated into the global economy, which made it more resilient. Despite a sharp decline in bank cross-border credit at the peak of the crisis, capital flows quickly resumed. Chapter 5 also examines the issue of how best to manage capital inflows to improve financial stability, an important question in emerging markets. The chapter explores the benefits and risks of exchange rate intervention or the use of capital controls. It argues that exchange rate intervention must be exceptional and preferably undertaken on a rule based on avoiding "intervention addiction," which ends up introducing inefficient rigidities.

Chapter 6 summarizes the main findings of the analysis in the book and some further challenges to fostering growth and prosperity in Latin America. These include the quality of institutions, high levels of inequality, and the need to promote social integration.

2

A Favorable International Environment and Effective Monetary and Fiscal Policies

Leading into the global financial crisis of 2008-09, Latin America faced an extremely positive international economic environment, in particular favorable terms of trade (the price of exports over imports), which are a key determinant of exchange rates and business cycle fluctuations in Latin America. The surge of commodity prices in the second half of the 2000s was a very positive development for Latin American commodity exporters—the "good luck" component of Latin America's resilience to the global financial crisis. Moreover, the region's trading partners were experiencing high growth before the crisis, and access to international finance was fluid and relatively low cost. These countries also had the policy space and better policy frameworks to conduct expansionary policies once the crisis began. The combination of enough policy space and efficient policy frameworks were key to mitigating the effects of crisis (Kose and Prasad 2010).

Latin American policymakers' ability to conduct expansionary macroeconomic policies rested upon sound initial macroeconomic positions. Fiscal accounts were healthy. Levels of public debt were relatively low. Countries that saved some of the windfall gains from high terms of trade had resources to spend during the downturn. Other countries were able to borrow to finance fiscal expansion without serious constraints. In addition, commodity prices quickly rose again after a sharp reversal at the peak of the crisis, providing further fiscal policy space.

On the monetary side, having inflation under control allowed for a loosening of monetary policy. The sharp rise of commodity prices during the buildup to the crisis caused inflation to increase, but the subsequent slowdown put enough downward pressure on prices to allow for interest rate cuts. The pass-through of exchange rate to inflation was much more muted than during previous crises, primarily because of increased exchange rate flexibility.

Rather than transferring turmoil from the international economy to domestic economic activity and employment, as in past crises, exchange rates served as a shock absorber.

This chapter first examines the positive international environment that Latin America enjoyed before the crisis and in particular the very high terms of trade. Although strong commodity prices put the region in a strong position to face the crisis, the commodity price shock also created serious challenges on the inflation front before the crisis and delayed the loosening of monetary policy. Furthermore, commodity prices are also one of the region's main risks, because a decline in the terms of trade can have serious consequences. These can be mitigated by building buffers through fiscal prudence, letting the exchange rate float, and keeping space for monetary policy maneuver. The chapter then reviews recent inflation developments, some common problems and challenges, the role of inflation targets in conducting monetary policy, and the effect of commodity prices on inflation. It reviews recent progress in fiscal policy and the expansionary fiscal policies that helped mitigate the impact of the global financial crisis. The fiscal expansions were unprecedented, and while they did not prevent recession, they did limit the repercussions of the crisis and, following only a mild downturn, set the stage for a quick and long-lasting recovery.

Good Luck and Terms of Trade

The commodity price boom of the 2000s had repercussions all around the region, given that most Latin American countries are commodity exporters. There has been much discussion about the causes of the steep rise in commodity prices during the 2000s, including the financialization of commodities, but the strongest determinant was strong growth in China and other emerging-market economies, which increased demand in the face of an inflexible supply (Bluedorn et al. 2012). Figure 2.1 traces the evolution of commodity prices since 2000. At the start of the decade, commodity prices had fallen to historic lows, in the wake of the Asian crisis and the dot-com bust in the United States. They rose sharply starting in 2004–05, and on the eve of the crisis, they had nearly tripled or quadrupled from their levels at the beginning of the decade. There was a sharp downturn during the crisis, but prices quickly recovered to near-record levels.

While Argentina and Brazil export soybeans, Brazil and Colombia export coffee. Oil is an important export for Colombia and Mexico, but above all for Ecuador and Venezuela. Minerals are the main exports for Bolivia, Chile, and Peru; in the latter two, these are overwhelmingly copper. The countries more exposed to commodity prices are Chile and Venezuela: In Chile copper accounts for about 50 percent of exports, while in Venezuela oil accounts for about 90 percent of exports.

With the rise in commodity prices, the region's economies enjoyed significant terms of trade gains before the global financial crisis. Terms of trade are perhaps the most evident positive external development for emerging markets.

Figure 2.1 Global commodity prices, 2000–2012

index, period average = 100

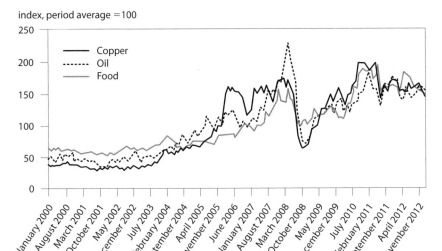

Note: Food prices are a simple average of wheat, corn, sugar, coffee, and soybeans.

Source: Bloomberg.

It is also where the good economic conditions of trade partners should reflect: better prices for exports. But financial conditions were also very favorable. Therefore, good conditions for trade, such as high terms of trade as well as improved market access, and good financial conditions, such as abundant access to financing at low costs, characterized the external environment for emerging-market economies in the years before the global financial crisis. On the other hand, the rise in commodity prices also increased the price of imports. For example, oil prices have been a negative shock in countries with no production of oil; the same has been true for food and minerals.

Tracking changes in the terms of trade helps identify the macroeconomic impact of commodity price changes. Figure 2.2 shows the terms of trade for the LA-7 using the International Monetary Fund's *World Economic Outlook* (WEO) database. Unlike other measures, these terms of trade data are adjusted by the importance of trade in the countries' GDP. This is important because fluctuations in the relative prices of exports and imports matter more if the economy is relatively open to trade than if it is relatively closed.[1] The bars represent the maximum and minimum values from 1980 to 2010. Average terms of trade

1. The graph is similar using terms of trade data series from the World Bank and from the Economic Commission for Latin America and the Caribbean, although the vertical axis covers a smaller range in this graph. The data are constructed using the rate of change of terms of trade, which is computed as the rate of change in the price of exports times the share of exports in GDP minus the rate of change in the price of imports times the share of imports in GDP.

Figure 2.2 Terms of trade, Latin America, 1980–2010

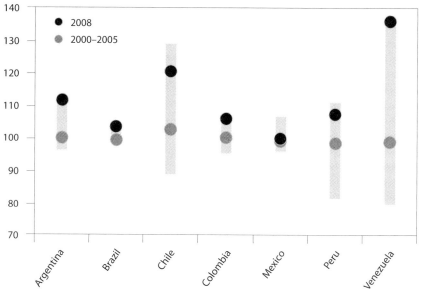

index, period average = 100

Note: The bars represent the maximum and minimum values in the 30-year period from 1980 to 2010. The dots are the average terms of trade for 2000–2005 and its value before the crisis.

Source: International Monetary Fund, *World Economic Outlook* database.

have been normalized to the period average, which is equal to 100. The two circles represent the average terms of trade for 2000–05 and the value before the crisis. As shown, the terms of trade for most of these countries were at or close to their 30-year maximum at the beginning of the global financial crisis. The magnitude of the positive effect is more significant for Chile and especially Venezuela. However, Brazil, Colombia, and especially Mexico did not enjoy large terms of trade gains, and they still had good economic performance. This heterogeneity suggests that effective policies played a role in increasing their resilience to the effects of the global financial crisis.

Another point worth emphasizing is that the terms of trade were very low after the Asian crisis until 2004, when they started to rise. Terms of trade were also very low during the debt crisis of the 1980s and indeed were at their minimum in Argentina, Brazil, and Chile. Therefore, during both the Asian crisis and the debt crisis, the decline in the terms of trade further aggravated already poor economic performance in the region. This time was different: Latin American countries had favorable terms of trade when the global financial crisis arrived and again enjoyed favorable terms of trade soon thereafter.

Some years ago, the Inter-American Development Bank emphasized that good performance in the region before the crisis was mostly good luck. To quote from that report:

> [This report seeks] to examine whether Latin America's performance and fundamentals are as sound as they appear at first sight. We will argue that "not all that glitters is gold" and that maybe "this time" is not necessarily that different. After all, it is often the case that fragilities are both generated and easily missed in good times. (IDB 2008, 1)

The 2008 report also recognized some significant progress, but it emphasized the risks the region would face if the external environment deteriorated, and these risks remain relevant. However, fewer people are crediting the region's strong economic performance primarily to good luck (i.e., beneficial terms of trade) as the region has continued to perform quite remarkably during and after the crisis (IDB 2012).

Some recent studies show that sound policies, and not just positive terms of trade, help explain the improved resilience of emerging-market economies in general and Latin America in particular. Mendoza (1995) calibrates an equilibrium model to demonstrate that about half of business cycle fluctuations are due to terms of trade shocks and that the level of economic growth and its fluctuations are affected not only by the terms of trade level but also by its variability. Aguiar and Gopinath (2007) find that fluctuations in emerging markets are mostly due to changes in long-term growth rather than shocks around a smooth trend. They attribute this to recurrent changes in policy regimes, which impact the way the terms of trade are transmitted to the rest of the economy.

Abiad et al. (2012) analyze the resilience of more than 100 economies over 60 years. Rather than looking only at growth and volatility, they also examine the characteristics of the business cycle, the length and strength of expansions, and the speed and steepness of recoveries. They find that expansions have grown longer and recessions have become shallower and shorter.

The evidence in Abiad et al. (2012) confirms that the greater resilience of emerging markets to internal and external shocks is a recent phenomenon, in particular in Latin America, and coincides with a period during which policy frameworks have improved and policy space has expanded. The external shocks examined include terms of trade deterioration, changes in world growth, uncertainty, and sudden stops of capital. The domestic shocks included banking crises and credit booms. The study attributes about 60 percent of the increased resilience of emerging-market economies to better policies and the rest to diminished external and domestic shocks.

The case of Chile supports the view that terms of trade are less important drivers of the business cycle in the region than in the past. Terms of trade are quite important to Chilean economy, and Chile has made a great deal of progress in fundamental reforms and improving its macroeconomic policy framework. The Chilean economy has generally gone into recession when the price of copper has collapsed and has boomed when the price has been high. A number of studies attributed Chile's strong growth from the mid-1980s to the late 1990s to copper exports (Calvo and Mendoza 1998, Spilimbergo 1999). However, things have definitely changed in the 2000s, and copper prices are no longer the main drivers of the business cycle. During the three years from 2000 through 2002, when the copper price dropped to its lowest three-year average real price since the Great Depression, Chile's economy grew at 3.4 percent. In contrast, from 2004 to 2007, when the price of copper rose sharply, the economy grew at an average of 6 percent and did not experience a sharp boom as in the past. The business cycle has been moderated by sound policies, including the application of a fiscal rule, which requires that windfalls from copper exports are saved, and an inflation targeting regime with flexible exchange rates.[2]

Another important case is Mexico. As noted, Mexico did not enjoy a terms of trade boom like most other countries in the region, because the bulk of its exports are manufactures. Moreover, Mexico was negatively affected by the strong growth of China's manufacturing exports, especially after China's accession to the World Trade Organization in 2001. Indeed, China's export development significantly reduced the dynamism of Mexico's exports to the United States that followed implementation of the North American Free Trade Agreement (NAFTA). By 2008, more than 80 percent of Mexico's exports went to the United States, and so the Mexican economy contracted sharply during the global financial crisis. Total exports fell by about 10 percent in real terms during the crisis, and output fell by more than 6 percent in 2009. However, Mexico recovered to an average growth rate of 4.4 percent in 2010–12, despite having an anemic neighbor to the north. This is another example of how important macroeconomic and financial policies, adopted after the Tequila crisis, were in overcoming the global financial crisis, since for Mexico, the "good luck" component was not relevant.

In addition to positive terms of trade and strong policies, the region has benefited from supportive international financial conditions. Figure 2.3 tracks international short- and long-term interest rates (panel a) and the sovereign risk premium for Brazil, Chile, Colombia, Mexico, and Peru (panel b).[3] Unlike in previous crises, when the region's risk premiums rose sharply, during the global financial crisis they increased fairly mildly and only during the peak of the crisis (the third quarter of 2008 through the second quarter of 2009). Risk premiums increased by about 400 to 500 basis points for Brazil, Colombia, Mexico, and Peru, and by 200 to 300 basis points for Chile. In comparison, risk premiums for these countries were well above 500 basis points during the

---

2. For further discussions of the role of copper in the Chilean economy, see De Gregorio and Labbé (2011).

3. Argentina and Venezuela have been excluded. They have had risk premium averaging about 1,000 basis points since the start of the global financial crisis.

Figure 2.3　International financial conditions

a. Interest rates, 1996–2012

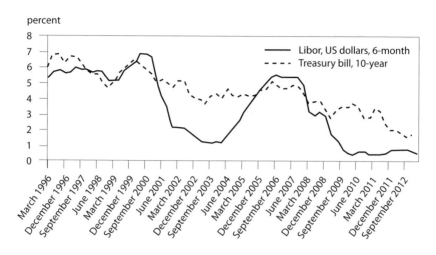

percent

Legend:
— Libor, US dollars, 6-month
--- Treasury bill, 10-year

b. Sovereign risk premium, 2005–13

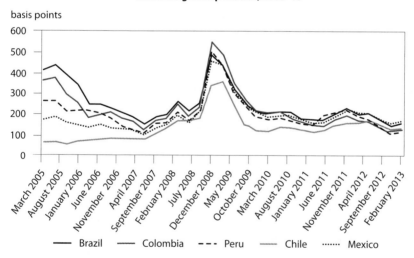

basis points

Legend: —— Brazil　—— Colombia　--- Peru　—— Chile　⋯⋯ Mexico

Libor = London interbank offered rate

Note: Argentina and Venezuela are excluded from panel (b) because they have had a risk premium averaging about 1,000 basis points since the global financial crisis began.

Source: Bloomberg.

Asian crisis, except for Chile, which already had a history of strong fiscal policy. Because risk premiums depend on perceptions of risk, they are supported by good macroeconomic conditions and sound policies (internal factors), in addition to international interest rates and the risk appetite of foreign investors (external factors).

During the worst part of the crisis, financial conditions deteriorated in the region because of a flight to safety by international investors and increased uncertainty. And the global recession also resulted in a sharp, but short-lived, decline in the region's terms of trade. These external factors largely underlie the recession in Latin American countries in 2009. What explains the region's quick and strong recovery is the implementation of good policies, to which we now turn.

Controlling Inflation

The Latin America and Caribbean region has historically had the highest inflation rate in the world. All LA-7 countries had two- or three-digit inflation rates during most of the postwar period, including several periods of very high inflation and some hyperinflations. Indeed, all but a few Latin American countries have been on the brink of hyperinflation in recent decades.[4] Colombia is the only LA-7 country that did not experience inflation above 100 percent a year since 1970, and all had two-digit average inflation rates during the 1980s (figure 2.4). High inflation clearly has been a widespread problem among countries large and small. According to the *World Economic Outlook*, average annual inflation in Latin America and the Caribbean reached one digit only in 1999.

High inflation has decisively hindered growth in the region (De Gregorio 1992), but it is also a symptom of the institutional weaknesses that make it difficult to implement appropriate macroeconomic policies, including weak tax collection systems or weak central banks (Fischer 1993, De Gregorio 1993). Inflation affects growth through a number of channels, and in turn inflation can be affected by other underlying problems. Inflation raises transaction costs as people avoid the use of money and devote excessive effort and resources to avoid the costs of inflation. Firms often hedge against future inflation rather than devoting resources to more productive activities. Inflation also mirrors and exacerbates social tensions and inequality.

Causes of Inflation

Economic theory identifies two main causes of inflation. One reason is fiscal imbalances. Inflation is a tax, and under a weak tax system authorities often have to rely on seigniorage (the difference between the value of money and the

---

4. Cagan (1956) defines hyperinflation as 50 percent a month, which leads to a rate of 13,000 percent a year. Extreme inflation is defined as 1,000 percent a year—15 to 20 percent a month (see Dornbusch et al. 1990).

Figure 2.4 Inflation in Latin America, 1981–2012

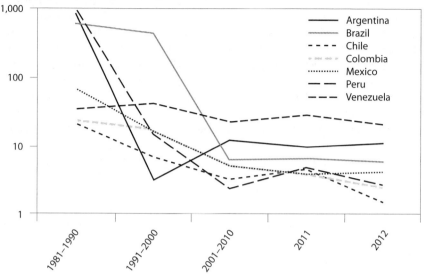

percent, log scale, end-of-year average

Note: The scale in this figure is logarithmic, which is the only way to represent inflation in Latin America during the last 30 years. Bolivia also had inflation above 1,000 percent during a hyperinflation in the mid-1980s. For scale reasons Peru was set at 1,000 percent, but its average for the decade was 1,300 percent.

Source: International Monetary Fund, *World Economic Outlook* database.

cost of producing it). In this scenario, inflation results from the government spending more than it can finance through regular taxation. High collection costs, such as a broad informal economy or widespread corruption, or political conflicts that excessively increase government expenditure may cause the government to use monetary financing. The way to reduce inflation is through fiscal consolidation.

The Latin American experiences with hyperinflation were all intimately tied to fiscal imbalances. When seigniorage requirements are greater than what can be stably financed with money creation, authorities may need to keep accelerating the rate of money growth to finance the budget, which causes accelerating inflation rates (Kiguel 1989, Bruno and Fischer 1990).

A modern fiscal source of inflation is "fiscal dominance," a situation in which monetary policy cannot anchor inflation because it is dominated by fiscal needs (Woodford 2003)—for example, the central bank announces an inflation target that cannot be achieved because inflation is too low to meet fiscal requirements. Although the government may be able to avoid financing fiscal needs by borrowing instead of increasing the money supply, the buildup of public debt will also cause inflation. This phenomenon was described by Sargent and Wallace (1981), who called it unpleasant monetarist arithmetic and emphasized that it is not necessary to undertake money financing of the budget in order for fiscal imbalances to cause inflation. The anticipation of future monetization is sufficient to create inflation pressure, as long as regular taxes are not an option.

Another cause of inflation in Latin America is inflation bias, first explained by Barro and Gordon (1983). Stated simply, central banks have incentives to keep unemployment below its full employment level, and a way to do this is through an unexpected increase in inflation. This induces a spurt of economic activity. When the public recognizes this incentive, and anticipates the increase in inflation when forming expectations, the central bank is forced to maintain inflation above its optimal level. This generates an inflationary bias. Weak public finances can also create an inflation bias because unexpected inflation also reduces the burden of public debt. To combat inflation bias, the discretion of monetary authorities to spur inflation must be limited in some way.

Tackling Inflation Inertia

The appropriate policy response to inflation caused by either fiscal imbalances or inflation bias is to build credible institutions with a clear and credible anti-inflation commitment. The most important policies are to grant independence to the central bank, make low inflation its legal mandate, and prevent money financing of the budget. Many countries around the world, and particularly in Latin America, have pursued these reforms since the early 1990s.

Eliminating the sources of inflation is not sufficient, however, to ensure low inflation, even in an economy with sound fundamentals. Inertia in the price-setting mechanism can propagate inflation and increase the costs of reducing inflation. In Latin America, the long history of high inflation made indexation a pervasive feature of price- and wage-setting behavior. And inflation adjustments were used to manage the exchange rate, feeding past inflation back into current prices. When an economy becomes trapped in a high-inflation equilibrium, inflation can become indeterminate, in the sense that inflation today is what it was yesterday, and inflationary shocks therefore have a permanent effect and there is no nominal anchor.

The decline in inertia comes only after inflation is reduced in a credible form; starting the other way around is very unlikely to succeed, as demonstrated by the failed attempts at stabilization in Latin American during the 1980s. The so-called heterodox programs sought mainly to eliminate inertia but failed to eliminate the root causes of inflation and ended up causing severe inflation outbreaks. Examples include the Austral plan in Argentina, the Cruzado plan in Brazil, and the Inti plan in Peru. They relied on monetary reforms that introduced an indexed new currency and were complemented by incomes policies that froze some key prices.

Some other countries have used the exchange rate to anchor inflation and eliminate inertia, for example, Chile and Mexico. Chile had a fixed exchange rate from 1979 to 1982, which collapsed during the debt crisis, and Mexico launched a crawling peg in the early 1990s that ended with the Mexican crisis of 1994.[5] In both cases, the promise of a fixed or semifixed exchange rate caused a rapid increase in foreign borrowing for activities in the nontradable goods sector. The exchange rate was used as an inflationary anchor, but inertia eroded competitiveness enough to make the programs unsustainable. Specifically, the rate of the currency depreciation is set at a level below the previous level of inflation—zero in the extreme case of a fixed exchange rate. During the time it takes for inflation to come down, there is a severe currency misalignment, the current account deficit rises to unsustainable levels, and the experiment ends with an exchange rate collapse and a rise in inflation.[6]

The anchoring and dynamics of inflation in the region changed dramatically during the 1990s as a result of two key policy changes: central bank independence and the use of inflation targets.

Central banks were made legally independent in many Latin American countries, including Chile (1989), El Salvador (1991), Argentina (1992 and 2002), Colombia (1992), Nicaragua (1992 and 1999), Venezuela (1992 and 2001), Ecuador (1992 and 1998), Peru (1993), Mexico (1993), Bolivia (1995), Costa Rica (1995), Uruguay (1995), Paraguay (1995), Honduras (1996 and 2004), Guyana (1998), and more recently Guatemala (2001) and the Dominican Republic (2002). However, legal independence does not always equate to de facto independence. The process by which central bank board members are selected, approved, and removed can be key to a central bank's ability to act independently.[7]

In Argentina, for example, congress has failed to approve most board members for a full term, instead appointing them on an interim basis, which limits their ability to act independently. In addition, during 2010, the governor of the central bank was removed by use of a "presidential emergency decree" for refusing to allow the government to use central bank reserves to pay government debt. Finally, a 2012 change to the central bank law identified three objectives for the bank: monetary stability, financial stability, and the development of the economy with full employment of resources and social equity. While these are all fine public policy objectives, the third is completely inappropriate for a central bank. At the other extreme is Brazil, which has not yet passed a law granting independence to the central bank but did grant it de facto independence in a 1999 decree that established an inflation targeting regime. Brazil's central bank has enjoyed as much independence as many central banks

---

5. For the Mexican case see Dornbusch and Werner (1994) and for Chile Edwards and Cox-Edwards (1991).

6. One of the few examples of successful exchange-rate-based stabilization is Israel in the mid-1980s, which also pursued income policies to reduce the misalignment of the exchange rate. Inflation fell from about 400 percent in 1984 to 20 percent in 1986. But in Israel there was also a significant fiscal adjustment. See Bufman and Leiderman (1995).

7. For further discussion of central bank independence in Latin America, see Jácome and Vásquez (2008).

Table 2.1   Inflation targets in Latin America, 2012

Country	Target, 2012	Target horizon
Brazil	4.5 percent ± 2 percentage points	End of year
Chile	3 percent ± 1 percentage point	Two years
Colombia	2 to 4 percent	Medium term
Guatemala	4.5 percent ± 1.5 percentage points	End of year
Mexico	3 percent ± 1 percentage point	Medium term
Peru	2 percent ± 1 percentage point	At all times

Source: Hammond (2012).

that have been granted independence by law. However, by not being legally mandated, this independence is not assured since the government could exert undue influence on monetary policy.

Inflation Targeting

There are 26 inflation targeting countries, of which six are in Latin America (Hammond 2012), including five of the seven largest countries in the region (table 2.1).

Many countries in the region originally adopted inflation targets in the context of IMF programs in the wake of the debt crisis or as part of a set of policies to address broader issues such as fiscal imbalances. In general, inflation targeting was not considered a framework for monetary policy but part of a more consistent macroeconomic framework. As such, most countries initially set their inflation targets on an annual basis, and the targets served more as inflation forecasts than as policy targets, given that the ability to influence inflation during a one-year horizon is quite limited. Even so, the initial inflation targets were useful for building credibility and signaling the commitment and competence of central bankers. A number of countries later moved to set targets for multiple years and then for even longer terms.

Inflation targets have two key elements: the target itself, with its tolerance range, and the time horizon over which inflation deviations are expected to return to the target.[8] The method of defining the target horizon varies from country to country. Some countries seek to meet the target at all times (Peru), some at the end of each year (Brazil and Guatemala), but most seek to achieve the target most of the time. Moreover, some countries, including Peru, make note of deviations from the target and define in official monetary policy reports a forecast horizon over which any such deviation is expected to be corrected.

Conceptually, no country seeks to correct deviations over a very short period of time, which explains why they follow flexible inflation targeting regimes,

---

8. Given the autocorrelation process of inflation, there is a one-to-one relationship between the tolerance range and the time horizon (De Gregorio 2007).

rather than rigid ones. This is because it is costly in terms of employment to bring inflation back to target—there are output costs to disinflation. Flexible inflation targets implicitly take into account the implications for unemployment by virtue of the fact that shocks to inflation are expected to be absorbed gradually. The authorities minimize the losses resulting from deviations in inflation from the target and deviations of output from full employment by allowing inflation to adjust gradually. The target horizon and the tolerance range also reflect the lag with which monetary policy affects aggregate demand and inflation. The time horizon is generally the medium term, or two to three years.

The inflation target is expected to anchor inflation expectations over time, and for this reason it must remain highly credible. As long as the public expects inflation to be equal to the target, output and prices are less volatile and monetary policy can reach the target with low output costs. Overall, low inflation and low output volatility contribute to economic growth. In the past, the money supply or the exchange rate were used as nominal variables for anchoring monetary policy to achieve the inflation target. However, the demand for money can be highly unstable and therefore is not sufficiently correlated to inflation to provide a reliable anchor. The hazards of using the exchange rate as an anchor include the loss of monetary policy as a tool and the difficulties in absorbing shocks such as changes in the terms of trade or changes in the international financial conditions. As experience in the region also shows, inflation inertia generates relevant exchange rate misalignments.

Monetary Policy with an Inflation Target

As discussed above, inflation targeting is not a framework that cares only about inflation. However, since monetary policy has to do with inflation, the inflation target is an efficient framework to conduct monetary policy. The issue then is how to operationalize this framework: When should monetary policy be tightened or loosened?

The most traditional answer is to follow the Taylor rule, which defines the extent to which the central bank should change the nominal interest rate in response to changes in certain economic conditions, including inflation and output.[9]

Of course, the rule is an analytical simplification to explain central banks' behavior. Moreover, it contains two variables that are affected by the central bank—inflation and output—and that cannot be treated separately since they are related in the economy through the relationship between inflation and the output gap, the Phillips curve.

In practice, central banks do not use a mechanical rule to set interest rates. With monetary policy central banks want to make inflation reach the target in the policy horizon. Therefore, the optimal policy rule is to adjust the path

---

9. The Taylor rule was first introduced in Taylor (1993).

of interest rates in a way that the inflation forecast converges to the target in the policy horizon. This is actually how most central banks decide policy. The question in monetary policy committee meetings is what should be monetary policy, and its likely future course, in order for inflation to be at the target in the policy horizon? Here is where judgment and beliefs of committee members are key. Policy needs to be tightened (raise interest rates) when inflationary pressures indicate that inflation on the horizon could be above the target. But policy should be loosened when the target is likely to be missed from below, and hence a cut in rates should stimulate output and employment for inflation to rise to the target in the policy horizon.

Forecasting inflation rates can be quite complicated, and for this reason communication and transparency are particularly important in the context of inflation targeting. As in the rest of the world, in Latin America inflation targets are implemented with regular meetings, communiqués after the meetings, release of minutes, and regular quarterly or biannual inflation reports. It is essential that the markets have access to the views of the central bank and understand how the bank will use monetary policy to reach the inflation target over the policy horizon. Transparency also helps the private sector to smooth its expectations.

What variables should policymakers use to set interest rates: asset prices? exchange rates? commodity prices? unemployment? The simple answer is: whatever affects the inflation forecast. If asset prices reveal a boom in activity that will increase the output gap and put upward pressure on inflation, it may be appropriate to tighten. Unemployment is certainly related to price and wage pressure, and so it is clearly a relevant indicator. If the exchange rate has the potential to permanently affect inflation because its movements are large or persistent, it also must be taken into account when setting interest rates.

It is not just the level of a particular variable, for example, the exchange rate, but also its outlook over the policy horizon. Those types of forecast are difficult and are generally inaccurate, which means that the monetary policy stance must often be revised when actual developments differ from the forecasts.

This has been particularly true for commodity prices in recent years, which have risen sharply and fluctuated significantly. There are two issues involved in using commodity prices in setting interest rates. The first is whether the target should be based on headline or core inflation, and the second is whether monetary policy should be adjusted in reaction to commodity price developments.

There are sound reasons to focus on headline inflation instead of core inflation (De Gregorio 2012):

- Headline inflation is easier to understand. It is difficult to communicate why food and energy prices are excluded from general cost of living indices.

- The public is interested in the stability of prices for the entire consumer basket, including food and energy.

- Headline inflation is more consistent with price indices used for other policy purposes, such as the budget.

- When core inflation is targeted, expectations for headline inflation are more volatile, and this may in turn increase the volatility of headline inflation and possibly economic activity.

- The original idea behind inflation targeting was to exclude highly volatile prices that are subject to shocks of short duration. The problem is that commodities such as food and oil have been shown to have very persistent movements and may have significant second-round effects.

- The use of core inflation indicators may reduce the credibility of the central bank's anti-inflation commitment because proposals to use core inflation measures usually emerge when there are inflationary commodity price shocks.

- The use of headline inflation is also consistent with the fact that most inflation targeting countries that used to focus on core inflation have moved to target headline inflation, and their inflation targets are expressed in terms of headline inflation (Hammond 2012).

Regardless of how the target is defined, policymakers should pay close attention to commodity price developments since they directly affect inflation and can also have significant second-round effects on other prices.

The commodity price shock of the mid-2000s started with a dramatic increase in the price of oil. Between January 2004 and its peak in July 2006, the price of West Texas Intermediate crude increased by 125 percent, while food prices increased by only 14 percent (see figure 2.1). The surprising fact was that the severe oil price shock did not cause a global slowdown or a rise in inflation. Improved monetary policy was credited as one of the most important factors behind this unprecedented and unexpected performance (De Gregorio et al. 2007, Blanchard and Galí 2009). In addition, unlike previous oil shocks, this price spike was due to strong demand rather than a disruption of supply.

However, once food prices did start rising, the evolution of inflation changed dramatically, especially in emerging-market economies. Between July 2006 and the peak of food prices in June 2008, food and oil prices both rose by about 90 percent. This provoked a major rise in inflation in emerging markets (figure 2.5). The largest increase in inflation in Latin America occurred in Chile, which experienced a rise in the CPI of almost 17 percent. By October 2008 annual inflation in Chile was 9.9 percent, owing mainly to food price increases, but second-round effects were already under way as evidenced by the fact that, even excluding food and energy, inflation stood at 6.4 percent, more than double the 3 percent inflation target. More important, the increase occurred very quickly in mid-2008: The annual core rate of inflation was between 3 and 4 percent during the first four months of the year, very much in line with the inflation target. What accounts for the steep rise in inflation after May? Chile is a very open economy with few distortions in the price-

Figure 2.5 Accumulated increase in consumer price index, 2007–09

January 2007 to October 2008

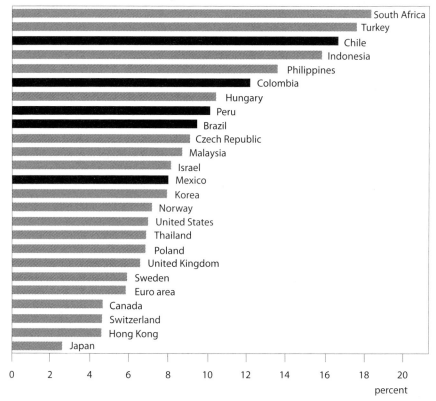

(continues on next page)

setting mechanism, and so changes in external prices are quickly reflected in the domestic market. Some idiosyncratic shocks also significantly increased the cost of energy. Mexico was at the other extreme of the sample, with only half the rise in consumer prices as Chile during those 22 months. In Mexico there are more controls on domestic prices, including some basic foodstuffs.

Once the global economic crisis hit in the fall of 2008, inflation declined and commodity prices retreated, and the countries that had the largest increases in inflation also had the largest declines, particularly Chile, Colombia, and Peru. Brazil and Mexico, which had the smallest increases in inflation also had the smallest declines. Within the region, relative prices eventually adjusted to the new external environment of higher relative prices of commodities. The second wave of commodity price increases, after 2009, had less effect on inflation because relative prices had already adjusted, and there was some room within these economies to absorb the higher international prices with limited

Figure 2.5 Accumulated increase in consumer price index, 2007–09
(continued)

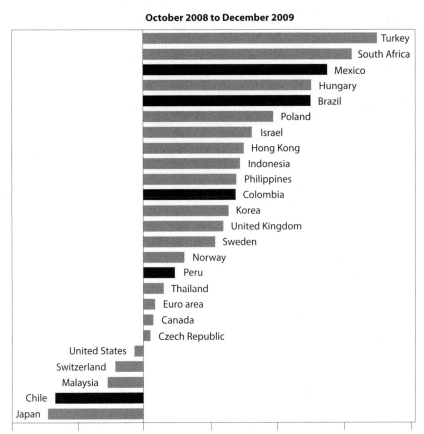

October 2008 to December 2009

Sources: National statistics bureaus; Bloomberg.

second-round effects. In fact, allowing prices to adjust without delay creates policy space, as there is no repressed inflation that may limit the ability to loosen monetary policy.

The recent experience also shows that food prices, much more than oil prices, can have pervasive effects on inflation, and prompt reaction to persistent increases in food prices may facilitate inflation control. The difficulty from a policy standpoint is assessing when food prices increase will be persistent. The overall lesson from this experience, however, is that despite the spikes in CPI inflation, it did not take long for prices to return to normal levels, compared with the past when indexation and other forms of inflation inertia were very pervasive. The empirical evidence, although not conclusive, indicates that inflation targeting has been generally effective in lowering inflation and reducing output volatility.[10] The experience in Latin America with inflation targets ratifies these findings.

Two countries have not reduced inflation as much as the others: Venezuela and Argentina (see figure 2.4). As we explore in more detail below, these are also the most fiscally vulnerable countries in the region because they have relied much more heavily on terms of trade windfalls.

Venezuela has had an average inflation rate of about 25 percent during the past 10 years with the rate very stable around that level. Unlike most other countries in the region, Venezuela has a fixed exchange rate regime with strong foreign exchange controls. When the currency is considered to be misaligned, the exchange rate is devalued; many times, devaluations come after the misalignment has been allowed to grow large, and they therefore do not correct the full disequilibrium, generating a cycle of devaluation and foreign exchange controls, reminiscent of the historical dynamics in most countries of the region before the 1990s.

In Argentina, the official inflation rate has averaged about 9 percent a year since 2007. However, independent analyses indicate that inflation has been much higher, on the order of about 25 percent a year.[11] The strongest indication that official inflation data are amiss is the behavior of other nominal variables, which are inconsistent with the lower officially reported inflation rates. For example, nominal aggregate wages have grown an average of 24 percent a year during the same period. Therefore, since 2007 real wages have grown 130 percent, while labor productivity has risen only 30 percent. It is extremely difficult to explain how real wages have almost doubled with respect to productivity. In addition, the problems with the consumer price estimates have translated into problems with GDP measures. According to some independent analysts GDP in 2012 was overvalued by as much 15 percent, due to the cumulative discrepancies starting in 2007.

Progress on the Fiscal Front

Establishing the independence of central banks with a focus on monetary stability and limiting, or forbidding, monetary financing of the budget was an important step toward conquering inflation. But it was also necessary to eliminate the deep roots of inflation, which in many countries were of fiscal origin.

---

10. Truman (2003), Hyvonen (2004), and Vega and Winkelried (2005), among others. Ball and Sheridan (2005) show that the available evidence does not support this conclusion for developed economies. Mishkin and Schmidt-Hebbel (2007) corroborate this differentiated benefit and conclude that the winners are emerging economies using inflation targets.

11. In an unparalleled move, in February 2013 the IMF issued a declaration of censure against Argentina and required remedial measures to be adopted to address the inaccuracy of consumer price and GDP data.

Figure 2.6   Public debt in Latin American countries and selected regions

percent of GDP

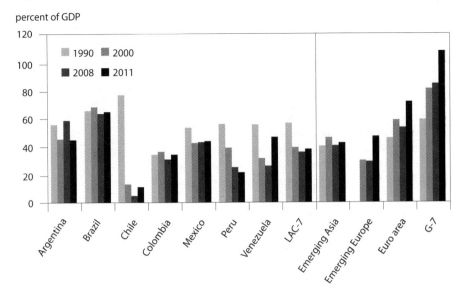

LAC = Latin America and the Caribbean; G-7 = Group of Seven

Source: Abbas et al. (2010), revised database at www.imf.org/external/pubs/ft/wp/2010/data/wp10245.zip.

Fundamental fiscal reforms and the adjustment of expectations, including by enhanced credibility, were central in reducing inflation in the region (Sargent, Williams, and Zha 2009). There were two important developments regarding fiscal policy. First, the beneficial international conditions before the crisis helped strengthen the fiscal position of the Latin American countries, which opened fiscal space for the expansionary policies launched to counteract the worst effects of the crisis once it hit. The second was that fiscal policies became countercyclical in several key countries.

The evolution of public gross debt in Latin American countries and in other regions since 1990 is presented in figure 2.6. Overall, public debt in the region declined before the crisis and has shown a small rise since then. The most significant declines have been in Chile, Peru, and Venezuela. Debt levels in the other countries in the region have been fairly stable. Latin American debt levels are not very different from those in emerging Asia and are below most advanced economies and emerging European economies. In Europe and the Group of Seven countries,[12] public debt levels mirror the difficulties these countries have faced since the crisis began and the implications for fiscal deficits.

Of particular interest is the evolution of public debt from 2000 to 2008, during the surge in commodity prices. Except for Argentina and Mexico, public

---

12. Canada, France, Germany, Italy, Japan, the United Kingdom, and the United States.

debt declined in Latin American countries. It is important to note that Brazil, Colombia, and Mexico are the countries that benefited least from the rise in commodity prices (see figure 2.2). However, even where debt was not reduced, creditworthiness improved, primarily because the value of these countries' natural resources at high commodity prices has increased. This should alleviate credit constraints (Caballero and Krishnamurthy 2001), allowing countries access to financial markets when needed to finance a fiscal expansion.

Since 1960, most developing economies have run procyclical fiscal policies, with spending increasing and taxes decreasing during booms, and spending decreasing and taxes increasing during recessions (Gavin et al. 1996, Gavin and Perotti 1997), while the opposite has been true of advanced economies, which follow either a more neoclassical or a Keynesian approach (Frenkel, Végh, and Vuletin 2013). The neoclassical approach to fiscal policy favors a smoothing of tax rates when the tax base fluctuates with the business cycle, and therefore a fall in revenues associated with a downturn is assumed to induce a fiscal expansion. In contrast, the Keynesian view suggests that, in order to smooth business cycle fluctuations, fiscal policy should be expansionary in recessions and contractionary during expansions.

Two main factors, which reinforce each other, account for the procyclical behavior of fiscal policy in emerging-market and developing economies. First, the history of debt defaults and a lack of fiscal responsibility constrained government borrowing. In the extreme case, if the government cannot borrow, it may be forced to completely spend its revenues at all times, and so during booms there will be a fiscal expansion and during busts there will be a contraction. The second factor is institutional weakness, mostly in the form of social conflict and political fragmentation.

Despite the overall trend for fiscal policy to be procyclical in most developing economies and countercyclical in most advanced economies, some emerging-market economies have escaped this pattern. Two studies in particular examine this issue in detail.

Céspedes and Velasco (2011) examine commodity price booms and the cyclical response of the fiscal balance for two episodes during the 1970s and the 2000s. The first period goes from 1965 to 1985 and the second from 1995 to 2008. Frenkel, Végh, and Vuletin (2013) study fiscal policy in emerging-market countries during two subperiods, from 1960 to 1999 and from 2000 to 2009, and show how several emerging-market economies have evolved to run procyclical fiscal policies.

The two studies look at the same issue from different perspectives. Frenkel, Végh, and Vuletin (2013) study the correlation between government expenditure and real GDP, and Céspedes and Velasco (2011) examine the elasticity of the fiscal balance with respect to the price of the relevant commodities for each country (a countercyclical fiscal policy would aim at a positive elasticity). Table 2.2 summarizes the findings of both studies.

According to Frenkel, Végh, and Vuletin (2013), all Latin American countries had procyclical government expenditures at the start of the period, except

Table 2.2   Cyclicality of fiscal policy in Latin America: A comparison of two studies

Country	Frenkel, Végh, and Vuletin (2013)		Céspedes and Velasco (2011)		
	1960–99 (1)	2000–2009 (2)	1965–85 (3)	1995–2008 (4)	Difference (5)
Argentina	+	0	−0.02	0.11	0.13
Bolivia	+	−	−0.02	0.09	0.11
Brazil	+	−	−0.09	0.08	0.17
Chile	+	−	0.10	0.21	0.11
Colombia	0	+	−0.03	0.06	0.09
Costa Rica	+	−	n.a.	n.a.	n.a.
Ecuador	+	+	−0.04	0.09	0.13
El Salvador	+	−	n.a.	n.a.	n.a.
Guatemala	+	+	0.02	0.04	0.02
Honduras	+	+	n.a.	n.a.	n.a.
Mexico	+	+	−0.04	0.06	0.10
Nicaragua	+	+	n.a.	n.a.	n.a.
Panama	+	+	n.a.	n.a.	n.a.
Paraguay	+	−	n.a.	n.a.	n.a.
Peru	+	+	0.09	0.07	−0.02
Uruguay	+	+	n.a.	n.a.	n.a.
Venezuela	+	+	0.05	−0.07	−0.12

n.a. = not available

Note: Columns (1) and (2) report the sign of the correlation between the cyclical component of government expenditure and the cyclical component of real GDP. Columns (3) and (4) correspond to the coefficient of a regression of the log of the fiscal balance on the log of the relevant commodity price for each country. Column (5) is the difference between the coefficients for the two periods.

Sources: Frenkel, Végh, and Vuletin (2013, figures 2 and 3); Céspedes and Velasco (2011, table 9).

Colombia, where it was acyclical. Bolivia, Brazil, Chile, Costa Rica, Ecuador, El Salvador, and Paraguay subsequently "graduated" from procyclicality. Céspedes and Velasco (2011) paint a somewhat better picture. All the Latin American countries in their sample, with the exception of Peru and Venezuela, increased the elasticity of the fiscal balance with respect to commodity prices in the most recent boom, i.e., increased the countercyclicality of their policies. For example, the improvement in the fiscal balance has increased for a given rise in commodity prices.

Both papers also explore the question of what explains the improved behavior of fiscal policy. They show that an improvement in the quality of institutions is central to this result. In addition, Céspedes and Velasco (2011) find that exchange rate flexibility increases countercyclicality to commodity price booms, and the presence of fiscal rules is marginally significant.

Like rules in monetary policy, fiscal rules, if they have enough flexibility to confront uncertainty, should help to improve the behavior of fiscal policy. Although causal evidence would corroborate this hypothesis, the statistical evidence is rather elusive. The reason is that, contrary to well-known monetary policy rules, not all fiscal rules are the same. They are not always designed to reduce procyclicality; they target different fiscal variables—the budget, debt, expenditure, or revenues; and, above all, they are not always enforceable because authorities have access to different mechanisms to limit and to sidestep the application of these rules.

In Latin America, Chile has been at the forefront of fiscal rules. In 2001 it implemented a rule that set a target for structural balance. This balance was adjusted by the cycle and by the long-term copper price, thereby building in countercyclical behavior. In addition, independent committees of experts determine the cyclical adjustment and the long-term copper price. The rule initially was set at 1 percent of GDP structural surplus, but it was then reduced to 0.5 percent in 2008 to take into account the improved fiscal position gained through high copper prices and, consequently, the need to generate surpluses. Later, it was reduced again to provide fiscal stimulus during the crisis. The current administration, which also faced exceptional expenditures from the 2010 earthquake, set as a target a 1 percent structural deficit in 2014.

The fiscal rule is the key to formalizing fiscal responsibility and accountability. In addition, it provides space for maneuverability of fiscal policy through the business cycle. But rather than stabilizing GDP, it has helped to stabilize fiscal expenditures.[13] However, fiscal responsibility has taken much longer. Chile's structural surplus was about 1 percent of GDP from 1991 to 1998, and the country entered a deficit situation only during the Asian crisis. Therefore, application of the fiscal rule does not account for all macroeconomic progress leading up to the global financial crisis; flexibility of the exchange rate and the inflation targeting regime also played a key role.

Policy Responses during the Global Financial Crisis

As noted, enhanced fiscal and monetary policy frameworks, as well as the policy space generated by good international conditions and steps taken to control inflation, were critical to allowing expansionary macroeconomic policies during the recent global financial crisis.

The fiscal policy actions during the crisis contrasted sharply with the traditional policy responses of Latin American countries to recessionary shocks from abroad. In the past, authorities relied on monetary and fiscal tightening. Fiscal policy usually had to be contractionary, not because of bad judgment but because there was no space to expand fiscal policy. Fiscal policy was procyclical as creditworthiness deteriorated during periods of bad external conditions, and governments' abilities to finance their budgets were severely impaired. During bad times, fiscal policy followed a very simple rule: Spend as much as you can finance.

---

13. For further discussion, see Marcel, Cabezas, and Piedrabuena (2012).

Figure 2.7 Monetary policy rates in Latin America, 2007–13

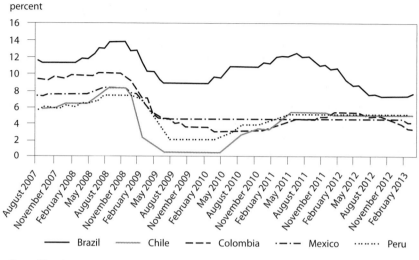

percent

Source: Bloomberg.

In earlier external crises, governments had usually tightened monetary policy because of fear of depreciation, an issue covered in greater detail in the next chapter. The potential inflationary and financial repercussions of a weakening currency were so pervasive that authorities were very reluctant to allow a full exchange rate adjustment, and they defended the parity with high interest rates.

A certain irony is associated with exchange rate management in the region and in many emerging markets. Such management has often begun with the intention of weakening the currency in order to improve competitiveness and then moved toward fiercely fighting depreciation in order to avoid inflation. It has then ended in severe overvaluation and loss of competitiveness.

According to de Carvalho Filho (2010), since August 2008, inflation targeting regimes have had a positive effect on postcrisis economic performance. As for monetary policy, during the global financial crisis countries that followed inflation targets—Brazil, Chile, Colombia, Mexico, and Peru—cut interest rates to historical lows. Although in most of these countries they have since been raised, they still have not returned to the precrisis levels (figure 2.7). The rate cuts began with 50 basis points in Colombia in December 2008, followed by 100 basis points in Brazil and Chile and 50 basis points in Mexico in January 2009, and then 25 basis points in Peru in February. By August 2009, all countries except Colombia were at their minimum levels.

The interest rate cycle was quite synchronized around the region, but the loosening occurred much later than in advanced economies, which were cutting rates by 2007–08. The scenarios were much different, however, in the emerging-market and advanced economies. The emerging markets were experiencing a positive shock from terms of trade, were growing, and also were facing serious challenges on the inflationary front because of the rise in commodity prices. In the context of inflation targets, the loosening in advanced economies did not imply that a cut had to be made in Latin America. Inflationary expectations were rising, and there was no need to use monetary policy to alleviate financial tensions.

Monetary policy actions, however, were under way during the crisis before the rate cuts. They started just after the collapse of the Wall Street financial services firm Lehman Brothers. Liquidity tensions grew as onshore-offshore spreads rose to unusual levels and interbank rates deviated from the central banks' target rates. Various instruments were used to alleviate liquidity tensions (Canales-Kriljenko et al. 2010). The range of collaterals accepted in liquidity facilities was broadened. The maturities of repo operations were lengthened. Swap lines were implemented to provide foreign exchange liquidity. Most of the liquidity measures were kept in place until mid-2009, but they worked quite effectively and quickly because tensions receded by November 2008. By then, the stage was set for the unprecedented interest rate cuts.

In Chile, in addition to the liquidity measures adopted in conjunction with the rate cuts, reaching the zero lower bound for interest rates, unconventional measures were used to stimulate the economy even further because it was deemed necessary to bring inflation back to the 3 percent target from the 0.3 percent annual rate reached in July 2009.[14] The central bank announced that the low interest rate would remain low for a long time, thus providing "forward guidance" in monetary policy. To reinforce this announcement, a term liquidity facility at the prevailing monetary policy interest rate and for terms of 90 and 180 days was implemented. Thus, if the central bank had changed the rate before six months, it would have incurred losses. Because it was expected to start increasing rates in mid-2010, the term liquidity facility was shortened monthly by 30 days beginning in late 2009.

Fiscal policy during 2009 was very expansionary. Figure 2.8 presents the adjusted cyclical primary budget balanced for the general government as a percentage of potential output. The result is a measure of the magnitude of the discretionary stimulus. The figure compares the two years pre- and postcrisis with 2009. The largest stimulus was in Chile, with about 4 percent of GDP, whereas for Peru and Mexico it was close to 2 percent of GDP and for the rest of the countries about 1 percent of GDP. Emerging-market economies had on average a stimulus of about 3 percent of GDP.[15]

---

14. The annual inflation rate in Chile declined from 9.9 percent in October 2008 to –2.3 percent in November 2009.

15. These expansions are based on the IMF measures of cyclically adjusted budget, and they are not necessarily the discretionary component announced by the governments because of measurement issues.

Figure 2.8 General government cyclically adjusted primary balance, 2006–12

percent of potential GDP

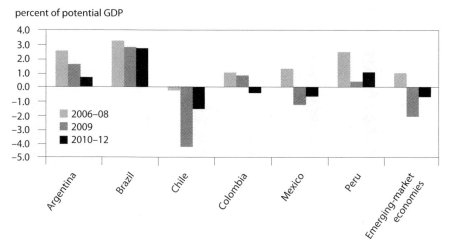

Source: IMF (2012b).

Even after the crisis, some countries—Argentina, Brazil, and Colombia—continued to increase their fiscal stimulus. The others, as expected in countercyclical behavior, withdrew the stimulus but not completely. Chile, Mexico, and Peru, following the same pattern as emerging markets, reversed only partially their fiscal expansion. This pattern revealed a problem with the flexibility of budgets in conducting countercyclical fiscal policy. The problem was the stickiness (resistance to change) of government expenditures (see figure 2.9). In no countries have government expenditures returned to their precrisis levels. This finding could be due to fiscal-stickiness or the timing of permanent increases in government expenditures. An example of the latter is Chile, where higher social protection expenditures were legislated before the crisis. However, the evidence on all emerging markets indicates that fiscal-stickiness along the cycle is a relevant issue.

One important lesson from the macroeconomic point of view is that more flexibility in government expenditure along the business cycle depends on having more automatic stabilizers on the expenditure side, which are basically nonexistent in emerging markets. The traditional automatic stabilizer on the expenditure side is unemployment insurance. The public provision of unemployment insurance is possible, but special care is needed in dealing with the effects on incentives. Otherwise, such programs can become a big fiscal drag and a big distortion of the labor market, such as those in southern Europe. A system that is carefully designed to avoid moral hazard can improve the process of matching in the labor market, raising productivity. In Chile, unemployment insurance is built into workers' savings, and when it is not used it goes into the pension plan. Chile also has a transfer component. Because of

Figure 2.9   General government expenditure, 2006–12

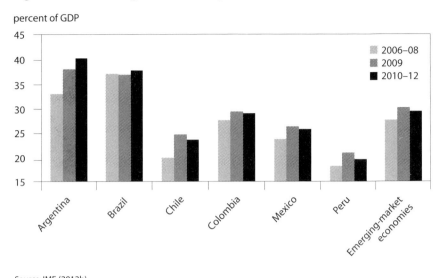

percent of GDP

Source: IMF (2012b).

its magnitude, it is not enough to be a relevant fiscal stabilizer, and because of the dynamism in employment creation in the last few years, there is no clear evidence of malfunctioning.[16]

From a comparative perspective, the monetary and fiscal expansions of Latin American as well as Asian countries were quite sizable. In figure 2.10, the numbers for fiscal expansion were taken directly from ministry of finance communications on the intended expansions and therefore are not the same as those in figure 2.8. However, they show basically the same orders of magnitude for the relative figures. Latin America had a significant and unprecedented reaction from its monetary and fiscal policy.

Final Remarks

As Latin American economies have enjoyed a good international environment for several years, evidenced most graphically by high terms of trade, the natural follow-up question is how vulnerable are they to a decline in terms of trade. In particular, if a slowdown in China and other major emerging markets occurs, how will the region react?

On the external front, a currency depreciation, in the context of flexible exchange rates, should operate as an adjustment mechanism if external conditions deteriorate. The current account deficits would widen, the currency

---

16. Fjanzylber and Repetto (2009) describe the unemployment insurance schemes in Latin America, several of which are based on individual accounts.

Figure 2.10   Fiscal and monetary stimulus, selected countries

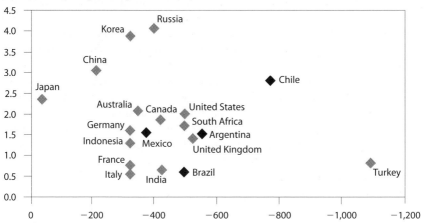

fiscal stimulus package, 2009 (percent of GDP)

December 2009 MPR versus maximum MPR during 2007–09 (basis points)

MPR = monetary policy interest rate

Sources: Central Bank of Chile; International Monetary Fund; Bloomberg; ministries of finance.

would depreciate, and, in the context of high reserves, financial repercussions could be mitigated. There could be some inflationary pressures, but low pass-through from the exchange rate to inflation, due largely to the credibility of the inflation objective, together with a slowdown of economic activity, should prevent this problem from becoming severe.[17] However, fear of inflation may induce authorities to fight a healthy depreciation of the currency.

The main risk Latin America faces is a potential deterioration in its terms of trade, resulting, for example, from a slowdown in China and in Asia in general. And some softening of commodity prices has recently being observed. A decline in terms of trade can be accommodated, from an external equilibrium point of view, by a depreciation of the currencies. However, from a fiscal point of view the challenges are more complex. Thus the issue is to what extent the fiscal position would deteriorate, forcing a fiscal adjustment and aggravating a potential slowdown of economic activity. A sensitivity analysis should be done of the fiscal position in the region to determine where there is glitter that is not gold.

Adler and Sosa (2013) have undertaken this task for South America, except Guyana, Suriname, and Mexico. They estimate the responses of the domestic economies to changes in external conditions and apply a public and external

---

17. For further discussion of the declining pass-through from exchange rate to inflation, see chapter 3.

debt sustainability framework to evaluate regional risks. In agreement with the earlier discussion, they find that the threats to external sustainability are not a major risk. In addition, on average, the region can fiscally accommodate a moderate deterioration of the external conditions, but a more protracted and deep external contraction may have very dissimilar effects across countries.

Not surprisingly, however, the authors conclude that Argentina and Venezuela are in a tighter spot and that their fiscal position could be severely impaired. A second set of countries—Brazil, Mexico, Uruguay, and, to a lesser extent, Ecuador—could have some space to undertake countercyclical fiscal policy. And finally, Bolivia, Chile, Paraguay, Peru, and, to a lesser extent, Colombia are well prepared to counteract even a sizable external shock with fiscal policy. The buildup of fiscal buffers during good times could pay off if the external scenario deteriorates sharply.

Avoiding fiscal complacency in good times is essential to being prepared for a change in international conditions. Moreover, even when countries can withstand a decline in terms of trade, relying on their high value is unsustainable. Fiscal needs grow along with the economy, whereas terms of trade, despite being high, will not have that upward trend. Sooner or later, countries that live at the fiscal limit will see their fiscal stance constrained. And yet a deterioration of the external environment can be handled with the policy frameworks already in place. Latin American economies are more stable today than in the past. But the maintenance of stability cannot be taken for granted.

The substantial decline in macroeconomic volatility in the United States and the world over the decades leading up to the global financial crisis has been widely documented by a large body of empirical research. Kim and Nelson (1999) and Blanchard and Simon (2001) were among the first to point to this phenomenon, which later became known as the Great Moderation.[18] The Great Moderation has been discredited, or at least ignored, in the discussions on macroeconomic stability since the global financial crisis. However, as argued in the next chapter, crises are much more related to bad financial regulation than bad macroeconomic policies.

Although it is clear that monetary policy was responsible for controlling inflation in the United States, the discussion about what caused the persistent decline in both output and inflation volatility is ongoing. In their review of the potential explanations of the Great Moderation, Galí and Gambetti (2009) conclude that the decline in the volatility of output stemmed from the smaller contribution of nontechnology shocks. It may be that the underlying shocks became smaller or that the transmission channels generated a more muted response. The authors interpret their results as smaller fiscal and monetary policy shocks and find they are inconsistent with the "good luck" hypothesis.

---

18. A predecessor was Taylor (1998), who called this period the "long boom." For further evidence on the timing and magnitude of the decline in volatility, see Smith and Summers (2002) and Stock and Watson (2003).

In particular, a stronger anti-inflationary stance led to the decline in output volatility.

Structural reforms, such as the increased openness, may also have helped economies become more stable. Cavallo (2007), for example, asserts that trade openness has reduced output volatility, and thus more open economies are also more stable economies. This evidence refutes the old view that more open economies are more exposed to volatility because they have more opportunities to adjust to international shocks. However, openness without the appropriate macroeconomic management risks forgoing the benefits for output volatility, as shown by the experience of Latin America during the Asian crisis.

Low and credible inflation targets bring significant benefits.[19] Indeed, a credibility bonus comes with a commitment to inflation stabilization. In a standard Phillips curve framework, inflation depends on the output gap (the reason for the output/inflation volatility tradeoff), inflation expectations, and a set of other variables, including inflationary shocks. Consider the case of low credibility in a low inflation objective. In such a case, an inflationary shock may feed back into price and wage formation, requiring a more aggressive monetary policy response and thus making it costlier to reduce inflation. This could happen when expectations not only are backward looking but also are affected by a high degree of inertia. By contrast, when expectations are well anchored to an inflation target, also becoming more forward looking, the monetary policy adjustment required to achieve stable and low inflation is milder and the sacrifice ratio declines, reducing the volatility of both inflation and output.

The unprecedented success of the emerging-market economies and the Latin American countries in particular is a demonstration that the Great Moderation is alive and well. However, these benefits also bring new risks. Higher stability, in particular in the context of low interest rates, induces financial intermediaries to search for yield, which ends up spurring investors to take more risk, as on display in industrial countries (Rajan 2005, King 2012). Indeed, a challenge for preserving stability is to monitor the health of financial markets in tranquil times; otherwise, stability may sow the seeds for the next financial crisis.

---

19. Gonçalves and Salles (2008) show that inflation targeting also reduces volatility in growth. Also see Corbo and Schmidt-Hebbel (2011) for empirical evidence on how the improved macroeconomic framework in Latin America led to better economic performance during the global financial crisis than during the Asian crisis.

3

Exchange Rates and International Reserves

The exchange rate is a crucial variable for any open economy, particularly emerging-market economies. It plays a key role in the transmission of external shocks to the domestic economy and the transmission of monetary policy actions. In recent decades, prolonged real exchange rate misalignments have been associated with many of the crises in emerging markets. Thus policymakers should pay special attention to the choice of the exchange rate regime and the evolution of the currency's value.

A central channel through which the exchange rate operates in an open economy is the expenditure-switching effect. By raising the price of foreign goods with respect to domestic goods, a real depreciation increases local and global expenditures on domestic products.

The exchange rate, then, directly affects inflation through its effects on the price of traded consumption goods and the cost of imported inputs. Beyond these effects, an exchange rate depreciation may directly affect the price of domestically produced goods because the monetary policy lacks credibility. If the main source of exchange rate movements is nominal disturbances, agents will likely increase the price of domestic goods in response to a nominal depreciation because a lack of credibility implies a lack of anchoring of inflation.

With respect to inflation, it is preferable for the exchange rate to have few effects on prices. However, for external adjustments it is preferable for the exchange rate to have significant effects on relative prices, which requires relevant effects on some fraction of traded goods prices. The issue of declining pass-through from exchange rates to inflation and the implications for external adjustment are discussed later in this chapter.

Inflation targeting regimes require a flexible exchange rate, but central banks do intervene in foreign exchange markets. In the past, fear of floating has caused massive defenses against currency movements. More recently, intervention has been done to stabilize or partially manage exchange rates, in particular from fear of appreciation. But international reserves, despite being in part the result of foreign exchange rate interventions, have been shown to help emerging markets to mitigate foreign financial shocks. Therefore, reserves are related to two policy objectives: (1) interventions to affect the value of the currency and (2) insurance to protect the economy from changes in the availability of international financial flows. The Latin American economies entered the global financial crisis with historically high levels of reserves, which implied strong financial positions, but these reserves were accumulated to a large extent to mitigate the appreciation of their exchange rates.

This chapter first reviews exchange rates, their transmission mechanism, their impact on inflation and external adjustments, and foreign exchange interventions. This review is followed by a discussion of reserves, the motives for accumulating them, and behavior during the crisis. The chapter closes with a brief overview of exchange rate developments after the global financial crisis.

Exchange Rates, Fear of Floating, and Evidence during Crises

Building credibility is a major goal when designing monetary policy, particularly in the context of inflation targeting and flexible exchange rates. Better monetary policy institutions are central to generating a virtuous circle. The more credible the central bank, the lower is the pass-through to the consumer price index (CPI) and the lower the volatility of inflation. These factors, in turn, reinforce credibility.

The optimal exchange rate regime can be analyzed in the context of the Mundell-Fleming model. When shocks to the economy arrive mostly from the monetary side, a fixed exchange rate is desirable. Such a regime insulates the economy from monetary shocks. When the exchange rate floats, monetary shocks are transmitted via changes in the interest rate and exchange rate, adding to business cycle fluctuations. Theory states that fiscal policy is the main instrument for stabilizing the economy under a fixed exchange rate regime. Therefore, when monetary policy cannot be used effectively and fiscal policy is powerful and flexible, a fixed exchange rate may be preferable.

Because of the inability of monetary policy to control inflation, many Latin American countries in the past adopted fixed exchange rate regimes to anchor inflation. These were the so-called exchange rate stabilizations—strategies to anchor inflation, which have been largely abandoned in recent years. The typical pattern was a fall in inflation, a boom in activity, a widening of the current account deficit, and a severe real exchange rate appreciation, as discussed in chapter 2. Most of the time, these experiments ended in a currency crisis.[1] For this reason, countries such as Ecuador and El Salvador

---

1. For the difficulties in fixing the exchange rate, see Obstfeld and Rogoff (1995) and Aizenman and Glick (2008). For exchange rate–based stabilizations and currency crises, see Calvo and Végh (1999).

have adopted a more extreme regime: They have dollarized completely and eliminated their currency.

By contrast, when shocks to an economy arrive mostly from the real side, the Mundell-Fleming model calls for adopting a flexible exchange rate. A shock to the terms of trade is the most common form of real shock in small, open economies, and it explains an important part of the business cycle. And a real shock that calls for depreciation is magnified in the presence of a fixed exchange rate. Flexibility makes a real adjustment easier because it can take place through the exchange rate rather than through prices. Developing countries have highly volatile real exchange rates compared with industrialized countries, which indicates the need for a high degree of nominal flexibility. Even though developing countries have usually managed their exchange rates in a way to avoid volatility, the variance in real exchange rates is higher in most developing than advanced economies.

In addition, a flexible exchange rate regime is consistent with an inflation targeting regime. An inflation targeting regime in which the policy instrument is the interest rate must operate within the context of a flexible exchange rate. This arrangement solves efficiently and unambiguously the well-known *impossible trinity* of financially open economies, and it allows the control of interest rates at a level consistent with the inflation objective. Adding an exchange rate objective weakens the capacity to control the interest rate, thereby affecting the ability to meet the inflation target. Another name for this situation is *trilemma of international finance,* which states that the following three things cannot be allowed to occur simultaneously: (1) controlling the exchange rate; (2) controlling the interest rate, which is the same as having an independent monetary policy; and (3) allowing for the free flow of international capital. In the context of an inflation targeting regime, which lets the exchange rate float and manages interest rates, an intermediate solution is to control capital flows, an issue discussed in chapter 4.

In an inflation targeting regime, everything that affects the inflation forecast should be taken into account when setting the interest rate (see chapter 2). Persistent movements in the exchange rate do affect inflation. In this case, the natural result is a *leaning against the wind.* When the exchange rate appreciates substantially, it prompts a fall in inflation, which results in a reduction in the interest rate. This reduction, in turn, induces pressures for depreciation. However, these are not very significant effects because, in a floating regime, the pass-through coefficient from the exchange rate to inflation is limited.

Many countries declare that they have a flexible exchange rate regime but in fact follow a system that is managed through a combination of exchange market intervention and movement of the interest rates. As Calvo and Reinhart (2002) have argued, there are strong reasons why countries may end up choosing to manage the exchange rate, despite claiming that they have a flexible system. Two explanations appear to account for a fear of floating. The first is the inflationary impact of exchange rate fluctuations. Authorities confronting a sharp depreciation of their currency may be tempted to intervene to avoid the pass-through to inflation. In turn, the pass-through may depend on the credibility of the inflation target and on the exchange rate system.

The other explanation of fear of floating and exchange rate fluctuations is balance sheet effects. If the corporate and banking sectors have assets in domestic currency and liabilities in foreign currency, exchange rate variation may be a cause of financial distress. A classic case is liability dollarization, a pervasive phenomenon in countries with a history of high inflation. This aspect of fear of floating is discussed in chapter 4 in the context of the financial systems in Latin America.

In recent years, countries such as Brazil, Chile, Colombia, and Mexico have been able to overcome their fear of floating. This development was evident during the global financial crisis. At the other extreme, Argentina and Venezuela follow strong management of their exchange rates through foreign exchange controls, and for this reason are the most macroeconomically vulnerable countries among the largest economies in the region.[2] Indeed, since 2003 Venezuela has fixed the exchange rate with adjustable parity and as of 2013 had undergone five devaluations. Both Argentina and Venezuela have had periods of dual exchange rates. As has been the tradition in countries that fix the exchange rate as the inflation anchor, with low financial integration in global financial markets, both countries have strong foreign exchange controls.

Peru is somewhat in between because it allows its currency to fluctuate. However, the central bank has put great effort into stabilizing the exchange rate—the country has a large degree of financial dollarization. With its relatively small base of domestic currency and less developed financial system, dollarization itself has made sterilized intervention more effective in reducing exchange rate fluctuations, but there is no evidence that this policy has been able to control the level of the exchange rate in the medium term, as shown in the last section of this chapter. The appreciation of the Peruvian nuevo sol in recent years has not been very different from that in countries that float. Important efforts are being made to reduce dollarization, which ultimately should reduce financial vulnerability.[3]

Figure 3.1 shows the evolution of exchange rates in countries that floated their currencies during the global financial crisis and compares it with their behavior during the Asian crisis. In both cases, a two-year window is considered and the exchange rate is normalized to 100 for the period average.[4] During the global financial crisis, shown in panel (a), exchange rate tensions were acute, and, except for some moderate intervention and provision of li-

---

2. In 2008 the International Monetary Fund classified Argentina and Venezuela as having fixed exchange rates, along with Honduras and several Caribbean countries. Bolivia and Costa Rica were defined as having a crawling peg system.

3. See García-Escribano and Sosa (2011) for an analysis of de-dollarization in Peru and also in Bolivia, Paraguay, and Uruguay.

4. The exchange rate is measured as the price of the foreign currency in terms of domestic currency, and so an index that increases in value is a depreciation.

Figure 3.1   Exchange rates in Latin American countries, 1998–99 and 2008–09

a. Global financial crisis

index (period average = 100)

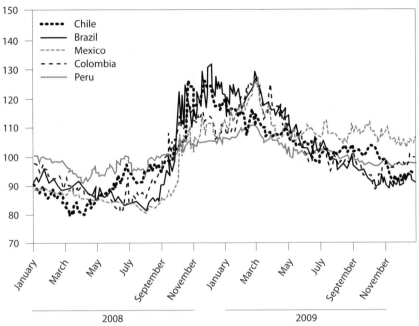

(continues on next page)

quidity in foreign exchange, currencies floated sharply and depreciations were severe. Indeed, Brazil, Chile, Colombia, and Mexico experienced depreciations of about 60 percent from their strongest levels before the Lehman Brothers collapse in a period of just a few months. Peru's exchange rate was more stable; it depreciated about 20 percent because it was also the country among the five that intervened the most. The inflationary consequences were muted because they were transitory and, as reviewed shortly, the pass-through coefficient from depreciation to inflation is small under a credible monetary policy regime. In the past, sharp depreciations like the ones in panel (a) would have caused serious financial distress. This time was different, and broadly financial systems remained strong.[5]

The movement of the exchange rate was consistent with the deterioration of the global outlook, which resulted in a decline in commodity prices. This was a fundamental reason to expect the currencies to weaken. In addition, the rapid depreciations helped deter speculation against Latin American currencies because the fact that the authorities allowed sharp depreciations signaled their

---

5. Indonesia and Korea also experienced large depreciations during the global financial crisis.

Figure 3.1   Exchange rates in Latin American countries, 1998–99 and 2008–09 *(continued)*

b. Asian crisis

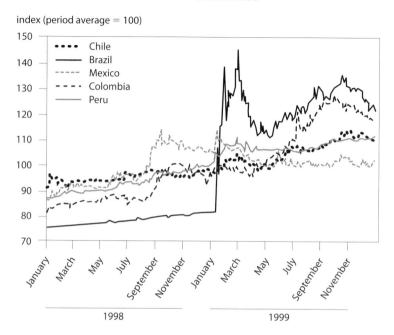

index (period average = 100)

Source: Bloomberg.

commitment to allowing the exchange rates to adjust significantly, thereby reducing the incentives to fight against incredible exchange rate defenses and obtain financial gains from central banks fighting market developments.

During the Asian crisis, shown in panel (b), countries were much more reluctant to let exchange rates adjust, thereby revealing their fear of floating. The evolution of exchange rates was more stable, but the gathering tensions about speculating against currencies made the adjustment more sluggish. Fear of inflation and financial instability led to efforts to defend currencies by hiking interest rates and using reserves. In the periods shown in figure 3.1, the behavior of reserves was much different. During the Asian crisis, Brazil spent about 50 percent of its reserves, and Chile and Colombia used about 20 percent each.[6] Also during the Asian crisis, Brazil experienced a currency crisis, while Colombia suffered its first serious financial crisis.

By contrast, during the global financial crisis, countries used limited levels of reserves, as discussed later in this chapter. Indeed, Brazil and Chile experi-

---

6. The data on reserves appear in table 3.2 and are discussed in more detail later in this chapter.

enced a decline of about 10 percent, whereas Colombia's decline was only 3 percent.

All these interventions, combined with other measures to provide international liquidity, were carried out to reduce tensions in the foreign exchange markets. Although they were successful in calming down markets, as figure 3.1 shows, their effects on the actual behavior of the exchange rate may have been very limited.

Defense of currencies, coupled with tightening of financial conditions, explains in part the poor performance of the Latin American countries during the Asian crisis. Expansionary macroeconomic policies in the context of a flexible exchange rate help explain the success during the global financial crisis.

Exchange Rate Pass-Through, Credibility, and Duration of Misalignments

Exchange rates directly influence inflation dynamics. A depreciation of the exchange rate affects the CPI through the prices of imported goods and the other prices considered in the index. The implications of a change in the pass-through to import prices go beyond its direct impact on inflation and involve potential changes in the expenditure-switching mechanism as well. This section focuses first on the effect of the exchange rate on total CPI and then on the import price effects and changes in resource allocation. The decline in the pass-through from exchange rate to inflation has been central to overcoming fear of floating.

Recent evidence indicates that the exchange rate pass-through to consumer prices (CPI) has declined in recent years in industrialized economies.[7] Indeed, Takhtamanova (2010) finds that there is a structural break among member countries of the Organization for Economic Cooperation and Development (OECD) and suggests that the reduction in the pass-through is due in part to the low-inflation environment of the 1990s.

The evidence on emerging-market economies also shows a significant decline in the pass-through from exchange rates to prices.[8] This decline allows exchange rate adjustments that have limited consequences for inflation and monetary policy. The reasons are related: An inflation target and low inflation, which have come together in Latin America, reduced the pass-through.

Credible monetary policy regimes are characterized by a clear objective and high degrees of central bank independence. All of these elements have reduced the sources of nominal shocks, and monetary policy has become more predictable and less volatile. This development implies that the sources of exchange rate variations are associated mainly with real disturbances. In this context,

---

7. See Campa and Goldberg (2005); Gagnon and Ihrig (2004); Bailliu and Fujii (2004); and Bouakez and Rebei (2008).

8. See Ca' Zorzi, Hahn, and Sánchez (2007); Coulibaly and Kempf (2010); Mihaljek and Klau (2008); and Nogueira (2006).

the effects of nominal depreciations on inflation are reduced because inflation expectations are well anchored.

It can be claimed that firms adjust their prices more often (i.e., a larger share of firms will optimally adjust prices each period) when what lies ahead for inflation is more uncertain and the central bank's commitment to its inflation target is perceived to be weak. Therefore, a more stable, low-inflation environment reduces the incentives for frequent price adjustments. Less frequent price adjustments reduce the pass-through from the exchange rate to the CPI.[9]

Other things being equal, a lower pass-through from exchange rates to CPI allows a larger degree of exchange rate flexibility. Higher flexibility allows the economy to deal with shocks more efficiently, as long as the relative prices between domestic and foreign goods change. The source of economic disturbances in monetary-stable economies is mainly real shocks. When dealing with real shocks, a credible monetary policy may respond in a more flexible way, reducing the impact of those disturbances on the economy. A more stable economy allows better anchoring of inflation expectations, which increases the credibility of monetary policy and reinforces the effectiveness of monetary policy when dealing with real disturbances, thereby producing a virtuous circle from low pass-through to low inflation to increased credibility and lower pass-through.

Contrary to expectations, more open economies have lower pass-through (Mihaljek and Klau 2008). Perhaps they have more flexibility to adjust the country origin of their imports when currencies fluctuate around the world.[10] This finding contrasts with the old notion that more open economies may be more vulnerable to external shocks. However, the evidence tends to show that openness results in flexibility and reductions in the inflationary impacts of exchange rates. Along the same lines, it is noted in chapter 2 that there is evidence that more open economies have more stable business cycles. Therefore, the usual perils of openness appear not to hold. However, this openness requires the appropriate support from macroeconomic and financial policies.

A flexible exchange rate is likely to be an important factor in reducing the pass-through. And because that flexibility is part of the inflation targeting regime, empirical identification becomes complex. The relative merits of maintaining flexibility of the exchange rate and applying an inflation targeting regime are not clear, but certainly both are relevant. Because managed or fixed exchange rate regimes tend to include infrequent and significant adjustments of parities, the changes in the exchange rate are persistent, inducing price-setters to adjust their prices when there is a devaluation. By contrast, flexible exchange rates are accompanied by less persistent adjustments of the curren-

---

9. See Fernandez-Villaverde and Rubio-Ramirez (2007) on the relationship between credibility and the frequency of price adjustments.

10. For evidence on the Chilean case, see De Gregorio and Tokman (2007).

Table 3.1   Duration of exchange rate misalignments in Chile, 1977–2007

Period	Error correction coefficient	Duration of real exchange rate misalignments (quarters)
1977–2007	−0.12	8.1
1977–99	−0.11	9.0
2000–2007	−0.31	3.1

Source: Caputo, Núñez, and Valdés (2008).

cies, and, as shown by Taylor (2000), lower persistence tends to reduce the frequency of price adjustments.

In the presence of low exchange rate pass-through to CPI, movements in the nominal exchange rate will translate into movements in the real exchange rate, as long as foreign prices in domestic currency rise with a depreciation while domestic prices move much less. Put differently, if foreign goods prices in local currency are the exchange rate, s, multiplied by foreign prices in foreign currency, P^*, and local prices are P, the real exchange rate, q, is $q = sP^*/P$, and moves more when s changes and the feedback from s to P (the pass-through) is low.[11] One potential consequence of this greater correlation between q and s is that the real exchange rate will converge faster to its equilibrium level when responding to a real shock. This faster convergence helps avoid "long-run" volatility of the real exchange rate.

Evidence on the Chilean economy, as reported in Caputo, Núñez, and Valdés (2008), supports this claim: Deviations of the exchange rate from its fundamental value tend to be of significantly shorter duration than they were before implementation of the flexible exchange rate regime. The coefficient associated with the error correction term (real exchange rate misalignment) in a vector error correction model for the real exchange rate has increased (in absolute value) since 1999 (table 3.1). For the period 1977–99, the error correction coefficient takes a value of –0.11, which means that the real exchange rate misalignments lasted an average of nine quarters. By contrast, after the adoption of a free floating regime (2000–2007), this coefficient declines to –0.31, which implies that misalignments now last on average only three quarters. As a result, when hit by real shocks, the real exchange rate adjusts much faster to its fundamental value in a flexible exchange rate regime, and thus misalignments are less persistent.

Conducting monetary policy in a more predictable, stable framework has been a key determinant of diminishing pass-through. But three other factors may also affect pass-through: exchange rate misalignment, current account deficit, and output gap.

---

11. There is an issue with adjustment if sP^* does not change, because exchange rate changes would not affect relative prices, impairing external adjustment. This issue is discussed in the next section.

A nominal depreciation when the exchange rate is far from equilibrium (or its fundamental value) should have a lower impact on inflation because the depreciation helps restore equilibrium. The real exchange rate misalignment may be associated with excess production in the nontraded sector, which is eliminated with a real depreciation.

The current account deficit and the output gap may reflect excessive aggregate demand growth. In periods of strong demand, retailers can increase prices rapidly when facing a nominal depreciation. If the economy is in a slowdown, with an improving current account balance and a negative output gap, retailers facing a nominal depreciation are more likely to not pass the depreciation through to domestic prices. By contrast, a depreciation in periods of high output gap increases the pass-through. There is also a relationship between the exchange rate and output, and as long as the exchange rate is not allowed to adjust, most of the relative price adjustments are achieved via changes in inflation and output.

Like the decline in the pass-through from commodity prices to inflation discussed in chapter 2, the decline in the pass-through from exchange rates to prices has much to do with the fact that countries such as Brazil, Chile, Colombia, Mexico, and Peru follow a credible monetary policy and have a flexible exchange rate.[12]

Does Low Pass-Through Impair Real Adjustment?

A key channel through which the exchange rate operates in an open economy is the expenditure-switching effect. If domestic import prices are sticky—set in the currency of the export—a nominal depreciation will increase the relative prices of imported goods. As imported goods become relatively more expensive, consumption will shift toward domestically produced goods.

The previous section referred to the exchange rate pass-through to CPI. The relevance of the expenditure-switching effect becomes clearer when taking a closer look at the exchange rate pass-through to import prices. An alternative way to see the strength of the expenditure-switching mechanism is to compare the pass-through from exchange rate to traded goods versus nontraded goods. This phenomenon is what Edwards (2007) calls the inflationary effect versus the shock absorber (or real adjustment) capacity of exchange rates. It shows that pass-through to the CPI is smaller than that to the producer price index (PPI), which is consistent with lower inflation but retaining the ability to induce real adjustment. However, some questions still surround the pass-through to import prices.

The evidence on the pass-through from exchange rate to import prices at the retail level indicates that the pass-through is almost zero in the United

---

12. Even in Peru, a country with limited flexibility, the pass-through has declined (Winkelried 2011). This would suggest that a prime factor reducing the pass-through is the commitment to low inflation through an inflation targeting regime.

States; it has declined over time. Moreover, the findings for many industrialized countries indicate that the exchange rate pass-through to import prices has fallen markedly in recent years (see Engel 1999, Marazzi and Sheets 2007).

The combination of pricing to market, as in Krugman (1987), and nominal rigidities in the price of final goods has become a solid theoretical explanation for the near-zero exchange rate pass-through to import prices.[13] In this situation, export prices are set in the buyer's currency and are rigid in nominal terms—so-called local currency pricing (LCP). The most significant policy implication of LCP is that it completely eliminates the expenditure-switching effect. In fact, because a nominal depreciation of the exchange rate would not alter the relative price between domestic and imported goods, it would not have effects on relative demands. In other words, the prices of imported goods in the local currency, sP^*, move little with changes in s, and thus the real exchange rate, sP^*/P, moves little with movements in the nominal exchange rate.

Despite the fact that the evidence on industrial countries shows near-zero pass-through from exchange rates to final consumer import prices, the evidence on wholesale import prices is less conclusive. Obstfeld and Rogoff (2000) present findings that are contradictory to the claim of zero pass-through at the wholesale level. In effect, if LCP dominates international trade, the correlation between nominal exchange rates and terms of trade should be negative.[14] However, the evidence indicates that this correlation is significantly positive for many industrialized countries. The implication, then, is that despite the fact that pass-through may be close to zero at the retail level, the expenditure-switching effect may still occur in trade between firms. This finding is consistent with those of Edwards (2007) on the different pass-through for CPI versus PPI.

The evidence on emerging markets is that the pass-through to import prices is somewhat larger, on average about 0.35 (Bussière and Peltonen 2008). For Latin American countries, Fuentes (2007) finds a coefficient of about 0.75, but this result applies to permanent shocks to the exchange rate. Overall, there is a somewhat higher pass-through in emerging markets to import prices but with limited effects on overall inflation.

The other factor that contributes to the exchange rate having effects on competitiveness is the price of exports. The assumption that export prices are denominated in terms of the exporter's currency may not be realistic for developing economies. In Latin America, international trade is usually set in foreign currency, in particular the prices of commodities. Moreover, the assumption that export firms have some degree of monopolistic competition in foreign

---

13. See Betts and Devereux (2000) and Engel (2003). Gopinath and Rigobon (2008) find that the prices of exports and imports in the United States are sticky in dollars, but this has implications for the party who bears the currency risk—that is, the US trading partner. In addition, they show that the currency denomination of trade is endogenous.

14. This is defining terms of trade as the relative price of home imports in terms of home exports. Under LCP, a depreciation of the exchange rate will generate a reduction in the terms of trade defined this way.

markets may also be unrealistic. Usually, the Latin American countries are price takers, and because their trade basket is composed of goods subject to little domestic consumption, the effects of those goods on the CPI are small. This is the typical case of commodities. These aspects, not thoughtfully discussed in the academic literature, are quite relevant in small, open economies. If one combines these assumptions, it can be argued that a nominal depreciation may have a significant expenditure-switching effect. The pass-through from exchange rates to CPI could be small but to export prices could be equal to one. A nominal depreciation increases the price in domestic currency that an exporter receives from abroad, thereby increasing the exporter's production.[15]

In summary, despite the fact that the pass-through from exchange rates to CPI inflation is small, the exchange rate still plays an important role in the allocation of resources between the traded and nontraded sectors, fostering external adjustment.

International Reserves and Exchange Rate Interventions

Why do countries hold international reserves? Even countries that float their currencies hold reserves, often in very large amounts. In theory, in flexible exchange rate regimes the value of the currency should adjust to fluctuations in capital flows and international business sentiments. However, maintaining reserves and floating would be an indication that exchange rate flexibility is not enough to accommodate drastic changes in global financial conditions.

Countries hoard reserves because they view them as a safety net for periods of financial stress. In practice, however, they seldom use them. As argued later, reserves play a stabilizing role simply because they are there but are not necessarily to be used. In that sense, reserves play a deterrent role. When it comes to insurance, however, there are cheaper ways to hedge against liquidity risk, such as the Flexible Credit Line (FCL) of the International Monetary Fund, the insurance pool proposed by Prasad (2012), or instruments available in financial markets.[16] But these options are hardly used, if ever. This begs the question, then, what is the role of reserves? Their role is twofold (Aizenman and Lee 2007): (1) to provide liquidity insurance and (2) to affect the exchange rate. This dual goal cannot be separated.

The first motive is the *precautionary motive*. Countries feel comfortable when they have liquidity in foreign currency, investing their reserves in liquid assets, because they may need them quickly in an emergency. Even if they have

---

15. Alternatively, a nominal depreciation reduces production costs expressed in foreign currency units, increasing production in view of the international price.

16. Alternatively, it is possible to establish a global swap agreement for times of distress. The agreement could be complementary to reserve accumulation because it is not a permanent credit facility (see, for example, Truman 2011).

no long-term financing problems, they may encounter liquidity constraints, so they need to have the funds readily available.

Similarly, accumulation of reserves seeks to minimize the risks of a balance of payments crisis. This reason was at the core of the research studies of the early 1980s. Although at that time the term *sudden stop* was not in use, the precautionary motive did surface as a reason to hold reserves should a country suddenly face a halt in external credit inflows. In any case, in general this has not happened. This is an interesting point because in the recent crisis there was no evidence of massive sudden stops or of any significant depletion of reserves because of the crisis.

Evidence also shows that having reserves reduces risk premiums because it is a sign that the country is hedged. This viewpoint prevails even when, in practice, the reserves will not be used and holding them is costly.

The second reason why countries hoard reserves is the so-called *mercantilist motive*. In general, small, open economies emphasize the importance of avoiding sharp deviations in their exchange rates from "reasonable values." In particular, a strategy to boost export-based growth consists of trying to achieve a depreciated real exchange rate. Therefore, even under a floating regime there are times when authorities decide to intervene in the foreign exchange market to prevent exchange rate deviations that might hurt growth and stability.

The accumulation of reserves must be understood as a policy in which the two underlying motives are tied together: buying insurance and protecting the exchange rate. Normally, reserves are accumulated when the local currency is relatively appreciated. This accumulation may respond to the two motives. When the currency is appreciated, buying foreign currency is cheaper and also can mitigate the appreciation of the currency. Whether implicitly or explicitly, the value of the exchange rate and its future outlook are inputs in the decision to determine whether to accumulate international reserves. In addition, in an inflation targeting regime, reserve accumulation and the resulting evolution of the exchange rate must be consistent with the target and the path of monetary policy.

Investigators have attempted to separate the precautionary motive from the mercantilist motive in the data—most recently, Ghosh, Ostry, and Tsangarides (2012). However, the mercantilist motive is proxied by currency undervaluation, which indicates that accumulation of reserves is effective in undervaluing the currency. Therefore, the estimation is carried out on the maintained hypothesis that the accumulation of reserves indeed produces undervaluation. However, many countries (and this has been the experience in Latin America) initiate interventions in the face of evidence that their currency may be overvalued. Intervention could ameliorate the overvaluation, but it is too extreme to suggest that it turns an overvaluation into an undervaluation. Finally, it is the magnitude of the intervention, not the level of reserves (i.e., the accumulated value of past interventions), that affects the exchange rate. Therefore, there is no convincing evidence of the relative importance of the two motives to accumulate reserves, and distinguishing the importance of each is a difficult task because both objectives are usually used together to justify interventions.

A foreign exchange intervention helps to improve insurance, and it affects the volatility, or transitorily the level, of the exchange rate. During periods of tension in the foreign exchange market or when authorities find that the exchange rate could be overvalued, central banks may decide to intervene. When the exchange rate is appreciated, it is an appropriate time to increase the international reserve holdings because of the lower cost of doing so. The next question therefore is, how do countries that follow an inflation targeting regime with a flexible exchange rate intervene?

Interventions must be sterilized. Otherwise, the control on monetary policy becomes subordinated to an exchange rate objective, which results in abandoning, de facto, the inflation target. However, sterilization is costly because the debt issue to purchase foreign exchange pays a higher interest rate than the return obtained by holding reserves. Under interest rate parity, the risk premium would be a first approximation of the cost incurred by accumulating reserves. For this reason, intervention has a limit because it involves quasi-fiscal costs.

Sterilized intervention is also less effective. Precisely because it does not affect the relative supply of monies, its effects on the exchange rate are more limited. In an interesting recent case, Switzerland imposed a floor on the value of the euro in Swiss francs through sterilized and nonsterilized interventions. A nonsterilized intervention is a nonconventional policy enacted at the zero lower bound of the interest rate. This policy certainly carries inflationary risks, but a nonconventional monetary policy that lowers the value of the Swiss franc is an option when interest rates cannot fall further. Many analysts and authorities in emerging markets find this an interesting experiment. However, the Swiss experience is closer to the US Federal Reserve's purchase of long-term assets to reduce long rates than to the attempts of emerging-market economies to affect the currency via intervention without losing monetary control.[17]

A foreign exchange rate intervention must attempt to fulfill two objectives, for which there are tradeoffs. First, it must be effective, which would tilt the balance toward massive and nonsterilized interventions. Second, it also must be consistent with the inflation target, which rules out the possibility of a nonsterilized intervention.

Another problem associated with intervention is "intervention addiction." Such a condition could lead to an ever-growing level of reserves with large quasi-fiscal impacts. In addition, the greatest political pressures to which independent central banks are subject are not interest rates but exchange rates.

---

17. For further discussion of recent experiences with intervention and their relationships to monetary policy, see Bordo, Humpage, and Schwartz (2012).

Thus to be effective and coherent with the inflation target, an intervention must meet some conditions:

- The intervention must be consistent with the inflation target so that it will not jeopardize the credibility of monetary policy. It must be sterilized, and it cannot pursue a specific value, or range, for the exchange rate.

- To safeguard the independence of monetary policy, the amount of the total intervention must be announced at the beginning of the period, in keeping with a rule-based approach. To be effective, the total amount must be significant.

- Because of the sterilization requisite, the cost of the intervention must be properly considered because it entails a quasi-fiscal component that could be significant.

The importance and effectiveness of a rule-based intervention depend on the particular characteristics of an economy. A rule-based intervention is more consistent with an inflation targeting regime that wants to ensure the autonomy of its monetary policy. Many countries perform small interventions based on rules—such as derivatives—to reduce volatility. Examples are Colombia and Mexico. The discussion that follows, however, focuses on the major process of reserve accumulation, which has also been directed at affecting the level of the exchange rate, not its short-term volatility.

During the global financial crisis, the Bank of Israel was the first to launch a significant rule-based intervention process. In March 2008, it announced it would purchase $25 million a day during a two-year period to increase its reserves by $10 billion. It later expanded its intervention to $100 million a day to accumulate between $40 billion and $44 billion in reserves. As a result, reserves at the central bank of Israel doubled from early 2008 to late 2009. The Central Bank of Chile followed in April 2008 by announcing the purchase of a maximum of $8 billion during a period of eight months at a rate of $50 million a day. In June 2008, the Bank of Colombia, which traditionally had intervened by selling options to stabilize the market, announced the purchase of $20 million a day. All of these interventions were intended to increase international reserves because of the deterioration of the global financial markets, and they all took advantage of the appreciation of the currencies. The interventions in Latin America stopped and even reversed during the collapse of Lehman Brothers. Chile achieved the most rapid accumulation, about $6 billion, which represented a rise of 35 percent but fell short of the $8 billion originally announced because of the sharp deterioration of the external environment. In other countries, the process of reserve accumulation was rather discretionary.

For interventions, countries have used direct purchases of foreign currency not only in the spot market but also the forward markets. Some have intervened through options. Colombia and Mexico used options as an instrument to stabilize exchange rate fluctuations rather than as a way to accumulate reserves. Moreover, several central banks in Latin America used swap lines to alleviate liquidity tensions, and they were credible because they were backed by massive amounts of reserves.

Are sterilized interventions effective? Yes, they are, but that is not enough. In fact, it is not even a very useful answer from a policy point of view. The relevant question is, how much and how long does an intervention have to be to affect the currency? This is the only way to evaluate the costs and benefits of intervention. Another question is, what modality of intervention is more effective on the exchange rate front?

Broadly, the literature has found that the effects of an intervention are transitory; they wane in a year, and a reasonable estimate is that a 1 to 2 percent of GDP intervention produces a 1 percent change in the value of the currency.

Understanding the channel through which interventions have effects is also useful in designing more effective and less costly interventions. Traditionally, the two most accepted channels are the signal effect, through which authorities indicate where monetary policy is heading, and the portfolio balance effect, which implies that exchange rate interventions affect the relative supplies of assets, domestic versus foreign bonds, and because they are assumed to be an imperfect substitute, the exchange rate—relative price of currencies—changes.

The empirical strategy to estimate the effects of intervention on the exchange rate has basically taken two routes. One is to estimate regressions, with a dummy or the size of the intervention as the explanatory variable. The other is to produce an exchange rate forecast, structural or nonstructural, and observe around periods of intervention the difference between the forecast and the actual value of the exchange rate.

For Israel, Sorezcky (2010) found that the actual exchange rate was about 10 percent above forecast during the intervention episode of 2008. This effect waned over time, but it appeared again after the new round of intervention, discretionary this time, in 2009. A similar strategy was followed by Adler and Tovar (2013), who produced a forecast of the exchange rate based on the exchange rates of other countries. They examined Chile, Colombia, Costa Rica, Israel, and Turkey. Using announcements of intervention as an identification device, they estimated the effects of the announcements and the evolution of the intervention over the next 45 days. According to their estimations, after the announcements the exchange rates depreciated by 5 percent, and the effects tended to diminish over time.

Other studies of interventions—such as Tapia and Tokman (2004) and Cowan, Rappoport, and Selaive (2007) for Chile; Kamil (2008) for Colombia; and Adler and Tovar (2011)—found that they had mixed and weak effects. They are at most transitory; they may slow the pace of appreciation, but most of the effect is felt when intervention is announced. Although not all studies report the orders of magnitude of the effects, they range from 0.5 to 1 percent depreciation for each percentage point of GDP of reserve accumulation. As for modality, Adler and Tovar (2011) show that it makes no difference whether it is a rule-based or a discretionary intervention. Meanwhile, the evidence on Asian countries is not that different from that on Latin America.[18]

As a policy conclusion, it is clear that sterilized intervention, which is consistent with inflation targeting and monetary autonomy, has limited effects, and so it cannot pretend to permanently change the exchange rate. For this reason, it is better to conduct interventions infrequently. In addition, despite the fact there is no clear winner between rule-based intervention and discretionary intervention, for infrequent and transparent interventions rules are better than discretion. First, they protect the authorities from political pressure to continue to intervene without limits. Second, this approach allows more coherence with the inflation target and more effective communications about the purposes of intervention and how it is consistent with meeting the inflationary goal.

The finding that intervention mostly affects the exchange rate when it is announced is interesting. This evidence would support the "signaling" channel of intervention. However, what is signaled is not changes in monetary policy but rather the view that authorities have of the exchange rate. Indeed, sometimes exchange rates may move transitorily beyond fundamentals, and this movement may persist for a while, generating domestic distortions and monetary policy complications. Such effects could be relevant in small, open economies with relatively shallow financial markets.

Chile experienced this sharp movement without clear fundamentals in the early 2000s when Argentina collapsed. Despite the minor trade and financial relations between Chile and Argentina, the exchange rate depreciated sharply and triggered an intervention. The same could happen in the other direction during a period of excessive optimism. If there is a bubble in the exchange rate or sharp speculative movements, an adjustment of monetary policy may aggravate the situation. For example, if during a boom domestic asset prices rise because of a sharp appreciation, tightening monetary policy—the appropriate solution in a closed economy—could exacerbate the appreciation as incentives for carry trade increase. In these cases, a temporary and massive intervention may help restore the health of markets. Such an intervention could also be used to alleviate tensions in the traded goods sector. But this policy cannot be adopted on a permanent basis or too frequently. Otherwise, its signaling capacity would vanish and authorities could become addicted to intervention.

International Reserves during the Global Financial Crisis

High levels of reserves played a role in the resilience displayed by emerging-market economies during the global financial crisis. Figure 3.2 shows how these economies significantly and steadily increased their holdings of interna-

---

18. For further references, see Disyatat and Galati (2007) and Adler and Tovar (2013).

Figure 3.2   International reserves in Latin American countries and selected emerging Asian and European countries

percent of GDP

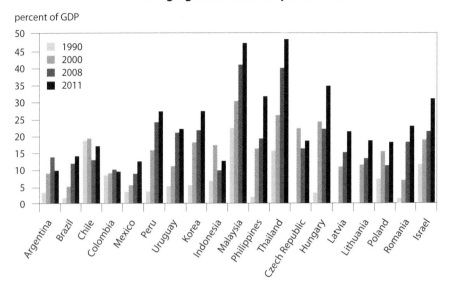

Sources: International Monetary Fund, *International Financial Statistics* and *World Economic Outlook* databases.

tional reserves as a fraction of GDP. Even the most recent data show that after the crisis the levels of reserves kept rising—the result of both the insurance motive and the mercantilist motive for reserve accumulation.

The emerging markets began the crisis with a strong position in international reserves. According to some econometric evidence, the economies that had high reserves were better prepared to weather the crisis. In fact, Frankel and Saravelos (2010), Gourinchas and Obstfeld (2012), and Dominguez, Hashimoto, and Ito (2012) find that countries with higher reserves suffered less during the global financial crisis and also had a lower probability of facing a national financial crisis. By contrast, Rose and Spiegel (2011) do not find significant effects. However, econometric evidence on the cross-country levels of reserves could be masked by high dispersion of reserves. However, figure 3.2 shows that most countries had higher levels of reserves on the eve of the global crisis than previously, regardless of the actual level they reached, and most countries did perform better than they did in response to previous similar events. This finding suggests that more robust results could be obtained using panel data such as those in Gourinchas and Obstfeld (2012).

The next relevant question is, were reserves actually used and to what extent? Figure 3.3 shows the evolution of reserves based on an index for the level of reserves in US dollars and normalizing it to 100 when Lehman Brothers collapsed in September 2008 and the crisis deepened substantially. Venezuela is not included because it was the only country that used about a third of its

Figure 3.3   Evolution of reserves in Latin American countries during the global financial crisis, 2007–09

index (September 2008 = 100)

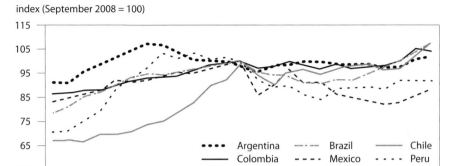

Source: International Monetary Fund, *International Financial Statistics* database.

reserves (as expected in a country that fixes its currency), thereby distorting the graph.

The data show that the Latin American countries used reserves to provide liquidity in foreign exchange as the crisis worsened. However, the magnitude of the deaccumulation of reserves was small and short-lived. It is notable that during the worst financial crisis since the Great Depression Latin American countries used so little of their reserves. They let their currencies fluctuate instead of fiercely fighting depreciation, which, as discussed earlier, was central to preventing speculation and letting the exchange rate handle part of the adjustment to tighter financial conditions and the sharp deterioration of the global outlook. Table 3.2 presents two alternatives to measuring maximum use of reserves during the global financial crisis and compares them with the use of reserves during the Asian crisis. The 12-month measure refers to the maximum yearly decline of reserves during the worst part of the crisis.[19] The other measure (pre-post) compares the maximum level of reserves reached within the six months before the crisis with the minimum level reached during the six months after the start of the crisis. The fact that for most countries the pre-post decline is greater than the 12-month decline is an indication that the use of reserves occurred mostly in the months surrounding the peak of the crisis.[20] Therefore, interventions were transitory and short.

---

19. See note to table 3.2 for the periods used.

20. Only Mexico and Venezuela continued to deaccumulate reserves six months after the peak of the crisis. The maximum drop for Mexico was 18 percent and for Venezuela 51 percent. See Prasad (2012) for evidence on the largest drop in reserves across emerging markets.

Table 3.2 Maximum decline in reserves of Latin American and selected emerging Asian countries (percent)

Country	Asian crisis		Global financial crisis	
	12 months (1)	Pre-Post (2)	12 months (3)	Pre-Post (4)
Latin American countries				
Argentina	−9.2	−2.4	−7.9	−10.9
Brazil	−53.5	−49.4	−3.1	−9.6
Chile	−17.4	−20.2	4.2	−9.8
Colombia	−16.2	−22.7	1.7	−3.3
Mexico	−0.1	−4.9	−14.1	−14.9
Peru	−17.9	−21.0	−13.9	−18.5
Venezuela	−32.3	−33.6	−34.4	−38.9
Average	−20.9	−22.0	−9.7	−15.1
Median	−17.6	−21.5	−8.8	−12.9
Emerging Asian countries				
China	3.8	2.8	8.5	−1.4
India	−7.6	−9.2	−20.4	−21.6
Indonesia	−18.4	−23.9	−11.9	−17.4
Korea	−40.2	−40.2	−23.5	−24.1
Malaysia	−28.5	−28.9	−29.6	−30.4
Philippines	−27.4	−31.6	3.0	−2.2
Thailand	−34.9	−32.0	−7.4	−5.8
Average	−21.9	−23.3	−11.6	−14.7
Median	−24.7	−26.4	−11.7	−16.1

Note: The decline in reserves is measured in columns (1) and (3) as the maximum decline in 12 months from January 1998 to January 2001 for the Asian crisis and from April 2008 to April 2010 for the global financial crisis. Columns (2) and (4) show the maximum decline from the maximum level reached before the crises—January 1997 to August 1998 for the Asian crisis and April 2008 to September 2008 for the global financial crisis—and the minimum postcrisis—September 1998 to January 2001 for the Asian crisis and October 2008 to April 2009 for the global financial crisis.

Source: International Monetary Fund, *International Financial Statistics* database.

There is a tricky issue in interpreting the evidence. Whether the use of reserves was massive or not depends to a large extent on what the analyst considers to be massive. Here, depleting 10 or 20 percent of reserves in the worst crisis since the Great Depression is thought to be rather small. Except for Venezuela, which used more than 30 percent of its reserves, intervention was limited. Brazil and Mexico intervened strongly to stabilize their currencies because of the very weak financial position of some large corporations.[21] Those firms were short in US dollars through the use of exotic derivatives, which caused large losses when the dollar depreciated in the aftermath of the crisis

---

21. The most well known in Latin America were Aracruz and Saida in Brazil and Comercial Mexicana in Mexico. For a review of experiences in emerging markets, see Dodd (2009).

(figure 3.1). Korea, Indonesia, and other emerging markets also faced big losses because of the large derivative exposures of corporations.

Derivatives serve to hedge currency risks, but, as these experiences show, they may pose serious risks to the financial health of companies. Because a moral hazard problem arises by inducing managers to take excessive risks to increase profits, most of the policy discussion has been around the appropriate disclosure of the currency exposure of companies. Derivatives allow companies to hedge against exchange rate risks, and yet they may also be used to speculate with company funds. Hedging is for insurance, not for making profits.

As noted earlier, early 2008 saw Chile and Colombia accumulating reserves in order to stem the appreciation of their currencies and to increase their holdings of international liquidity (mercantilism and insurance). In Chile, the accumulation was more intense (figure 3.3), but as the crisis grew worse both countries halted the intervention. Peru also made significant use of its reserves, and its currency fluctuated less. In Asia, reserves were used somewhat more during the global financial crisis, in particular in India, Indonesia, Korea, and Malaysia. As in Latin America, to both stabilize the currency market and ensure the appropriate liquidity in foreign currency, authorities sold, or provided via swaps and other instruments, foreign exchange. Interventions were limited, and currencies fluctuated sharply.

A comparison of the use of reserves (implicitly showing the strength of an intervention to prevent depreciation of a country's currency) during the Asian crisis and the global financial crisis is instructive. In Asia, the crisis epicenter in the 1990s, there was significant intervention. In Latin America, intervention, and thus fear of floating, was also very important. Then, exchange rate regimes were much more rigid. As tensions mounted and the inflow of capital suddenly stopped in several countries, Latin American countries used more reserves during the Asian crisis than in the global financial crisis. Brazil, which had a fixed crawling peg exchange rate, intervened massively, but that did not prevent the currency collapse at the end of 1999.

Overall, the limited use of reserves during the global financial crisis may have rendered credible the provision of liquidity in some cases and protected the exchange rate in others. Thus, the level of reserves and the significant depreciation of currencies may have helped mitigate the effects of the global financial crisis. What is interesting about these experiences is that the countries did not massively deplete their reserves, which may be an indication that, if unused, the benefits of reserves as insurance are limited. However, the evidence seems to confirm that a high level of reserves, even if unused, can be a strong deterrent to speculation when a country is facing sharp changes in capital flows. The evidence presented here is that the deterrent effects of reserves may be substantial, whether used or unused. The combination of overcoming fear of floating and having a substantial level of international liquidity allowed Latin American countries to navigate the financial storm of 2008–09 without the costs incurred in the past.

Emerging-market economies also accumulate reserves for mercantilist reasons, which may lead to levels above those necessary to protect the economy from fluctuations in international financial conditions. The majority of models seeking to determine the adequate level of reserves assume they are used.[22] However, as argued here, having reserves may act as a deterrent. If this deterrent effect is fully effective, in an equilibrium situation reserves would not be used, and the proper insurance would look like overinsurance. Excess reserves are useful, but how much is too much? Meanwhile, the precautionary and mercantilist motives are always present in the process of reserve accumulation, and so it is difficult to think that countries may be willing to replace international reserve holdings with a pure insurance mechanism.

Concluding Remarks: Exchange Rates and Global Adjustment

Exchange rates are an important issue in the Latin American region, and currencies strengthened after the global financial crisis. This should not come as a surprise in view of the strength of the Latin American economies and the high terms of trade. This strengthening is happening not only in Latin America but also in most emerging markets and commodity exporters.[23]

Figure 3.4 is similar to figure 2.2—it summarizes the behavior of broad real exchange rates since 1994 based on Bank for International Settlements (BIS) data covering maximum, minimum, and average in a given period. All real exchange rates are normalized to 100 for the average during the period. Real exchange rates are measured as units of domestic goods per unit of foreign goods.[24] The bars represent the maximum and minimum real exchange rates. The figure reveals that many emerging-market economies have had large and asymmetric fluctuations; for most of them, the maximum (most depreciated real exchange rate) is much farther from 100 than the minimum. This picture reflects the fact that many countries have experienced currency crises or sharp depreciations during the period, something that has not happened in terms of appreciation. The dot represents the average real effective exchange rate for 2012 (most data are through November).

---

22. See, for example, García and Soto (2006); Jeanne and Rancière (2006); Obstfeld, Shambaugh, and Taylor (2010); and Calvo, Izquierdo, and Loo-Kung (2012). Calvo et al. argue that emerging markets were close to their optimal reserves prior to the global financial crisis. However, the probability of sudden stops would be exaggerated if reserves were not used.

23. This situation started changing in May 2013 as commodity prices softened, activity in emerging markets started decelerating, and the Fed announced it would start tapering the program of long-term asset purchases.

24. This implies that an increasing value indicates a real depreciation, a gain in competitiveness, and cheaper domestic goods.

Figure 3.4 Real effective exchange rates in selected Latin American, Asian, and European countries, 1994–2012

index (period average = 100)

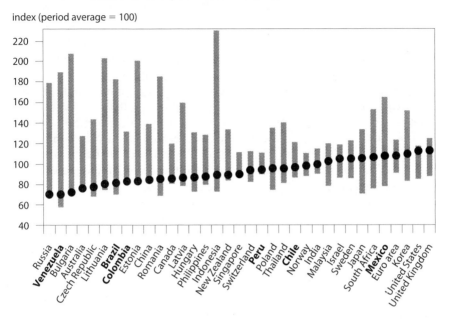

Note: The bars represent the maximum and minimum real exchange rates. The dot represents the average real effective exchange rate for 2012 (most data are through November).

Source: Bank for International Settlements.

Most of the emerging-market and commodity-exporting countries shown in figure 3.4 have real exchange rates that are below the period average, and most of those are close to their minimum—that is, the most appreciated real exchange rate. This is true of five of the six Latin American countries: Brazil, Chile, Colombia, Peru, and Venezuela. The only exception is Mexico, which is weak because its currency is highly correlated with the US exchange rate, which is also weak.

Intervention is an option, and some countries may try capital controls, but tensions will remain. Indeed, regardless of whether countries intervene or apply capital controls, the general trend has been clear: Strong countries have strong currencies, and this will last until advanced economies recover more fully or weaknesses arise in the emerging-market economies and commodity prices start falling, as partly has been happening since mid-2013. The strength of the currencies is in part the result of success. Assets in the emerging-market economies are more valuable because these economies are richer and less vulnerable. Whenever this situation changes, currencies should adjust accordingly to allow an efficient adjustment.

In fact, the appreciation of currencies in emerging-market economies is part of the global adjustment, and while advanced economies remain weak, it is difficult to believe that a significant realignment might take place. Countries can use policies to mitigate the cost of the adjustment, and many countries have done this though accumulation of reserves and capital controls. However, the broad global trends cannot be changed by small individual actions.[25]

In a scenario of weak advanced economies and high terms of trade, supported by the strong growth of China and other emerging-market economies, currencies will remain strong, and policymakers will have to live with the pressure to be creative and find ways to mitigate the appreciation. Some things can be done, but the strong forces in the global economy adjustment cannot be changed in a significant way. A global economy without a relative price adjustment will not move ahead and will retard a full recovery. However, the adjustment is taking place, and beyond the currency war and the beggar-thy-neighbor quantitative easing (QE) rhetoric, what is going on with exchange rates is what is needed for global adjustment and the resolution of global imbalances.

It is ironic that the discourse has completely changed from one of complaining that very loose monetary policy in advanced economies was provoking excessive appreciation in emerging-market currencies. With the important depreciation that has taken place in emerging markets since the tapering of QE was announced, now the complaints are that the withdrawal of stimulus in the United States should be gradual to avoid sharp fluctuations. This has a flavor of fear of floating. As recent experience shows, the recovery of advanced economies is the best scenario for a weakening of emerging-market currencies. The global economy should welcome all efforts by the advanced economies to recover and reduce their high levels of unemployment. This is the best that can happen to emerging markets and the continuation of their achievements.

---

25. In January 2011, the Central Bank of Chile decided to increase reserves during 2011 by about 5.5 percent of GDP. The argument was twofold. First, the intervention would strengthen Chile's international liquidity position. And, second, despite the fact that there was no clear evidence of a misalignment, the intervention would provide some transitory relief to the tradable sector, but on the understanding that the peso was likely to be strong for a relevant period ahead.

4

Financial Stability

Financial systems are essential to development, but they can also be a source of disaster and therefore a source of policy confusion and ambivalence.

A well-functioning financial system is key to prosperity. It promotes economic growth by channeling investment funds from savers to borrowers (Levine 2006), and it is central to promoting entrepreneurship and facilitating investment, including human capital accumulation. Meanwhile, it provides households with financing in order to smooth consumption, with insurance, and with safe and cheap means of payment. The difficulties faced by households and firms in many emerging-market economies because of underdeveloped financial institutions and markets should be a clear reminder of this positive role.

But financial deepness may also be a source of big problems. As in many situations, more is not always better, especially when more comes at the cost of excessive risk. When a recession or a currency crisis comes together with a financial crisis, its output costs increase significantly (Reinhart and Rogoff 2009). In the past in Latin America and Asia, currency crises had output costs of 7 percent of GDP over a five-year period, and when crises come with a banking crisis the costs double (De Gregorio and Lee 2004). Therefore, a strong financial system and a flexible exchange rate regime can be very effective in mitigating the cost of a crisis. Finally, unfettered financial markets are prone to deep crises, but regulation has its limitations and may even be a source of problems because of negligence, political capture, and other agency problems. Crises are not always avoidable, so it is also key to have appropriate resolution mechanisms to contain the costs of financial instability and quickly restore normalcy.

This chapter focuses on the policies that could prevent these problems and on the evidence of financial market resilience in Latin America. It discusses the role of financial stability in central banking and its interactions with monetary policy and the behavior of financial systems in Latin American countries on the eve of and during the financial crisis. It begins with a review of the origins of the financial crisis and whether they stem from monetary policy or financial distortions. A discussion of the role of asset prices in monetary policy follows, as well as the role of central banks in financial stability and the interactions between regulation and monetary policy.

As I discussed in the previous chapter, the inflationary consequences of exchange rate fluctuations has been a key factor in generating fear of floating. In this chapter I address the other cause of fear of floating, namely financial weakness. This chapter describes how Latin America has been able to overcome this difficulty and has provided a sound framework for allowing exchange rates to float. Finally, it presents evidence on the strength of the financial system in the region before the global financial crisis and discusses some current challenges.

Causes of the Crisis: Monetary Policy or Financial Fragility?

After the dot-com bubble burst in the United States during the early 2000s, US monetary policy was very loose. Interest rates fell to historically low levels, resulting at times in negative real interest rates. Some observers have pointed to this policy as one of the main causes of the global financial crisis. That argument has two components that are important to distinguish. The first is that loose monetary policy was responsible for the rising housing prices and the housing bubble. The second is that the bursting of the bubble ended in a financial collapse. As for the first argument, did loose monetary policy in fact induce an increase in asset prices? The answer is obviously yes, because that is a transmission mechanism of monetary policy. Indeed, monetary policy could be one of the reasons for the rise in housing prices, but it is unlikely to be the main cause of the housing bubble. Its direct effects on asset prices were limited; other factors were more important.

As for the second component of the argument, the bursting of a bubble does not necessarily bring on a financial and economic collapse—a collapse can be avoided. However, monetary policy can be responsible for a financial collapse, and, as argued here, it is not due to the way it deals with price stability, or whether it lags or goes ahead of the curve, but to the way in which it deals with the collapse of bubbles. The "benign neglect" approach followed in the Greenspan era[1] created massive moral hazard, which in the end was unable to cope with the aftermath.

As for the looseness of monetary policy, Taylor (2010) argues that monetary policy was loose compared with the policy suggested by application of the Taylor rule. Moreover, Ahrend (2010) shows that the larger the monetary policy excesses, as indicated by the Taylor rule, the larger the rise in housing

---

1. Alan Greenspan served as chairman of the US Federal Reserve from 1987 to 2006.

prices.[2] Bernanke (2010) opposes this view, maintaining that monetary policy accounts for only a small fraction of the increase in housing prices. As argued in chapter 2 of this book, rather than mechanically using the Taylor rule, those applying inflation targets should use a rule that calls for the inflation forecast to converge to the target on the policy horizon.

More recently, Hott and Jokipii (2012) show that when monetary policy interest rates are below the Taylor rule, especially for a prolonged period, the consequence may be a rise in housing prices beyond fundamentals—that is, a bubble. The static quantitative effects of interest rate deviations are not so large for the average country: A 1 percent deviation from the Taylor rule generates a 2 percent overvaluation. However, the longer the deviation, the more it reinforces the overvaluation effects from the interest rates. According to Hott and Jokipii, the duration and magnitude of the deviation explained 80 percent of the overvaluation in Ireland, 50 percent in Finland, and 20 percent in Norway. Even with this evidence, it is difficult to argue that the bubble was only the result of monetary policy, and certainly in Finland and Norway there was no financial collapse.

What does looseness mean? Indeed, a look at actual inflation performance rather than the Taylor rule, which is just a description, may allow for a better assessment of how expansionary monetary policy has been with respect to the inflation target.

On a more fundamental level, the question is whether the relevant variable from the point of view of asset bubbles is the level of the interest rate or its deviation from the Taylor rule. The Taylor rule controls for business cycle position, but the level of the interest rate is the relevant variable from the financial and asset price determination point of view. Fatás et al. (2009) show a correlation of virtually zero when looking at real interest and an increase in real housing prices.

Another, somewhat subtler and less discussed aspect of asset price bubbles is very relevant from an analytical point of view. The original theory of rational asset price bubbles predicts that bubbles grow at a rate equal to the interest rate. Therefore, raising rates would speed up, not slow down, a bubble. This result holds for even more general types of bubbles.[3] Indeed, one might expect a reduction in interest rates to lead to a jump in asset prices but the rate of growth of the bubble component to fall. This point has been formally included in a monetary policy model by Galí (2013), who questions the leaning against the wind policy on asset prices.

In general, it is not only reasonable but also important to expect high asset prices when interest rates are low, regardless of whether they keep rising faster

2. In contrast to Ahrend (2010), Fatás et al. (2009) argue that the relationship of monetary policy to housing prices is relatively weak.

3. For the original formulation of rational bubbles with all agents sharing the same information, see Blanchard (1979) and Tirole (1982). For a more recent discussion, and the implications of more complex informational environments, see Brunnermeier (2009).

Figure 4.1 Increase in housing prices in selected countries before the global financial crisis

index, 1996 peak precrisis

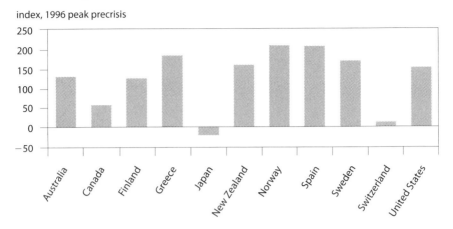

Source: Bank for International Settlements property price statistics.

or slower. The change in asset prices is one important transmission mechanism of monetary policy. The traditional view claims that investors shift their portfolios toward equity when their fixed income declines, while the financial view claims a step rise in asset prices is needed to reduce expected capital gains, reducing the return on equity. Nonetheless, soaring asset prices do not necessarily end up in a crisis like the global one in 2008–09. Closer attention must be paid to the financial fragility that accompanied this process, whose main culprit was the unrestrained financial innovation that generated deep distortions that neither markets nor regulators were able to predict. A large credit expansion fed itself into higher housing prices.

Many countries experienced rapid increases in housing prices and low interest rates, receiving clear signals that a bubble was being formed. However, their financial systems remained stable, and they avoided acute financial crises. Figure 4.1 shows the increase in housing prices from 1996 to the peak before the crisis for some countries in the property prices database of the Bank for International Settlements. Countries whose financial systems remained strong despite potential bubbles were Australia, New Zealand, Norway, and Sweden. All of them had periods of low interest rates.

Hott and Jokipii (2012) find that Australia, Norway, and Sweden did not have a large negative deviation from the Taylor rule.[4] However, as noted earlier, it is important for interpretation of the evidence to clarify whether one should look at the level of the interest rate or the deviation from a rule. The problem with the latter approach is that a stable country with large productivity gains,

---

4. New Zealand is not in the sample of Hott and Jokipii (2012).

anchored inflation, low interest rates, and a rapidly growing economy could experience a rise in housing prices, despite monetary policy being consistent with an inflation target. Monetary policy may lag the Taylor rule, because the increasing output could suggest a need for tightening, although inflation is well anchored. In this case there will be a spurious correlation between deviations of monetary policy from a rule and asset prices.

The key question, however, is, could the crisis have been avoided if monetary policy in the United States had held rates at, say, 200 basis points higher? Perhaps housing prices would have gone up somewhat less, despite the analytical caveat put forth earlier on speed versus step changes in asset prices. But the crisis could not have been avoided. The root of the problem was a heavily distorted financial system.

The argument that monetary policy played a leading role in the crisis is strengthened by the fact that low interest rates were combined with large current account surpluses in emerging economies, particularly the Asian and oil-exporting ones. These conditions created an abundance of liquidity that triggered excessive increases in asset prices (bubbles), particularly real estate. When the bubble burst, the crisis erupted. Caballero and Krishnamurthy (2009) add to this scenario the world economy's high demand for safe assets, which are mainly produced by the United States and which attract massive foreign capital inflows. Fatás et al. (2009) and Bernanke (2010) substantiate the positive correlation between housing prices and the current account deficit. However, here causality is not clear. Indeed, if investment and consumption in an economy are booming, for any domestic reason, housing prices will rise and the current account deficit will widen, but these phenomena were not the ones creating the boom in asset prices during the global financial crisis. All of them happened simultaneously and were due to the underlying causes of a booming, overheating economy. Bubbles, current account deficits, and credit expansions all happen in booms. It is important to uncover the fundamental causes of this correlation.

Many countries that did not suffer a deep financial crisis or recession have experienced rapid increases in housing prices in recent years. Examples in Latin America are Brazil, Chile, Colombia, and Peru. This is an important challenge for policymaking, but, as discussed shortly, monetary policy is not the most appropriate instrument for curbing asset prices when they seem to be misaligned and are threatening financial stability. In addition, the rise in housing prices in Latin America is not happening in the context of very low interest rates.

Recently, the argument about the perils of low interest rates in advanced economies has resurfaced but in the context of their impact on emerging-market economies. In this case, the current low interest rate environment, as a consequence of unconventional policy measures applied at the zero lower bound in advanced economies (quantitative and credit easing), has been blamed for the significant increase in asset prices in many emerging markets. In particular, low interest rates add pressure to strengthen the currencies of emerging markets. However, increases in asset prices do not imply that an economy is doomed to a financial crisis. These asset price fluctuations could exacerbate the business cycle, but with the appropriate financial regulations the final result need not be a financial collapse. The severity of a financial crisis cannot be explained by the conduct of monetary policy, in particular when geared to price stability.

When disproportionate increases in housing prices loom, both the level of borrowing and the building boom associated with it are symptoms that the downturn that comes with the cycle could be severe because of the deleveraging facing households and the contraction of the construction activity. Still, such conditions need not result in a systemic financial crisis.

In the United States, however, the conduct of monetary policy certainly played a significant role in feeding the bubble, but not because of how it dealt with price stability but how it dealt with bubbles. The strategy of benign neglect implemented during the Greenspan era may have encouraged the rise of asset prices with disregard for financial vulnerability. This was the so-called Greenspan put. The Federal Reserve was widely praised for following this rule: Do not react to the formation of a bubble but mop up its effects once it has burst (Blinder and Reis 2005). The mopping up approach consisted of providing unlimited amounts of liquidity and reducing interest rates sharply. Recent evidence presented by Hall (2011) confirms that including asset price deflation improved the fit of the Taylor rule. Moreover, the response of interest rates was more intense during the financial crisis. This finding demonstrates that markets were expecting an easing of monetary conditions when asset prices declined significantly.

This point was raised more than 10 years ago by Miller, Weller, and Zhang (2001, 18), who argued that eliminating the downside risk of asset prices fed a bubble, so bubbles were not so much the result of irrational exuberance but of "exaggerated faith in the stabilizing power of Mr. Greenspan and the Fed."

In the global financial crisis, the key assets were houses and structured credit products. The key vulnerabilities arose from the exposure of highly leveraged institutions—many of which had a substantial maturity mismatch—to these assets. Indeed, the toxic combination is bubble plus leverage, which can explain the different responses of the US economy to the bursting of the dot-com bubble, mostly financed by low-leverage investment funds, and the housing bubble. The bursting of the dot-com bubble had much fewer effects on the economy than the bursting of the housing bubble. The key difference was leverage and financial contagion.

Asset Prices, Inflation Targets, and Bubbles in Emerging Markets

Those who blame monetary policy for the creation of bubbles argue that monetary policy should consider asset prices when setting interest rates beyond their direct impact on forecast inflation.

Under an inflation targeting regime, rising lending and asset prices can have repercussions for the inflation outlook through their impact on the output gap. Such a situation requires an adjustment in monetary policy to prevent a persistent rise in inflation. Thus in an inflation targeting regime, asset prices and the level of credit aggregates affect the monetary policy decision to the extent that they affect the inflation perspectives (Bernanke and Gertler 1999). Central banks, then, have to react to developments in the credit and financial markets. If these developments spurred output to grow beyond full capacity, the inflation forecast would rise above the target, and monetary policy would be tightened. However, if financial developments were consistent with price stability, no action would be necessary.

Some observers will argue, though, that monetary policy should react directly to asset prices—for example, by including them in the Taylor rule. Cecchetti et al. (2000) are perhaps the best representatives of this position, claiming that any central bank targeting inflation should react to asset price misalignments *beyond* their implications for inflation expected over the policy horizon. Therefore, according to this view, monetary policy may have to be tightened when asset prices go up significantly, despite the fact that the inflation forecast may be well aligned with the inflation target.

The view here is that monetary policy in general should not react to asset prices beyond their impact on projected inflation for the following reasons:

- It is not clear that an increase in interest rates will stop an increase in asset prices. The required adjustments might be so large that they could end up unnecessarily generating high unemployment and an undesired drop in inflation. The interest rate is a blunt instrument that should not be used as the main tool to control asset prices.

- What matters is safeguarding the stability of the financial system. An excessive interest rate aimed at controlling asset prices and maintaining financial stability could trigger financial instability, especially if the increase in asset prices is accompanied by higher financial fragility.

- Under inflation targeting, any interest rate movements that are inconsistent with inflation converging to the target may undermine the credibility of monetary policy, thereby destabilizing inflationary expectations and weakening the effectiveness of monetary policy. This is particularly important for emerging economies with shorter records of monetary stability.

- Finally, in small, open economies, raising interest rates may be self-defeating in trying to stem the rise of asset prices, because such a measure induces an appreciation of the main asset price—the domestic currency. Raising interest rates will increase the incentives for carry trade, bolstering the currency and raising asset prices in terms of foreign currency.

Another reason put forward for avoiding attempts to affect asset prices through monetary policy is simply that it is impossible to determine when prices are significantly misaligned with their fundamentals. Indeed, it can be argued that bubbles are difficult to identify. But that is not a strong reason to follow a benign neglect policy. Indeed, even though it is difficult to determine when prices are fundamentally misaligned, policymakers should worry about rapid increases in asset prices regardless of whether they are based on fundamentals, because those fundamentals may change and prices may collapse.

Acting through monetary policy may not be the best option, however, and it is better to look more closely at financial regulation and how to limit the procyclicality of the banking system and build enough cushions for the downturn. Such an approach should also reduce fragilities generated during the upturn.

Often, empirical analyses of asset price bubbles are based on a number of variables presumed to be fundamentals and then examine whether asset prices can be explained by these fundamentals. As usual, the evidence tends to be inconclusive. For example, Gürkaynak (2005) finds that, for every study identifying a bubble, another study finds the opposite. Just few weeks before the collapse of the housing bubble in the United States, there was a heated debate on whether there was a bubble. Although it is important to determine whether an asset price has a bubble, it is more important to determine the resilience of the financial system to abrupt changes in asset prices and economic conditions. Central banks play a key role in such an assessment. They conduct a careful analysis of the balance sheets of financial intermediaries to determine their exposure and financial strength. Stress testing, simulating sharp drops in asset prices, may provide a first indication of financial stability.

Bubbles may be a serious problem in emerging-market economies. If a country, viewed as an asset, has a bubble, it will appear in the relative valuation with other countries: the exchange rate. Contrary to housing, a bubble in the exchange rate cannot last a long time. The current account will soon reach unsustainable levels, the tradable sector will be severely affected, and economic activity will suffer. This will lead to a depreciation and adjustment. However, letting this adjustment happen automatically may be too costly; containing a potential bubble in advance may be worthwhile.

If a country is attracting foreign capital flows, raising interest rates, the appropriate policy response to an overheating in a closed economy may be damaging in an open economy. The increase in domestic returns may, in turn, generate more incentives for capital to move in. This problem may worsen if authorities fight against the appreciation with transitory defenses. In this case, it may be advisable to conduct a sterilized exchange rate intervention: If there is a bubble, a massive intervention may burst it. If there is no bubble or the intervention is ineffective, accumulating reserves for precautionary motives may be a good idea.

Because a bubble can come with leverage, particular attention must be paid to vulnerabilities in the banking sector. For this, macroprudential tools may help.

Figure 4.2 Daily foreign exchange market turnover in selected Latin American countries

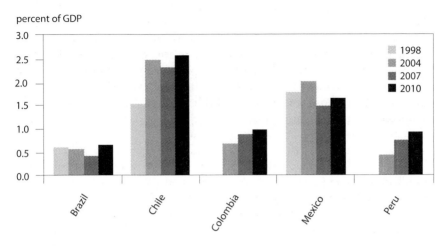

percent of GDP

Source: BIS (2010).

Exchange Rate Volatility and Financial Stability

Policymakers dealing with exchange rate flexibility may be concerned about the excessive volatility that can arise from classical overshooting (Dornbusch 1976) and other types of shocks. The introduction of a flexible exchange rate regime has indeed been associated with more volatility. In the short run, a more volatile exchange rate could be associated with greater exchange rate uncertainty, which, in turn, could affect investment decisions. This volatility may generate financial fragilities that could prompt fear of floating.

Short-term volatility does not imply longer-term uncertainty. In addition, volatility, in the context of a well-functioning financial market, leads to development of the foreign exchange derivatives market. This market makes it possible to hedge against short-term fluctuations in the exchange rate, reducing the costs of volatility. Thus exchange rate flexibility shifts risk management and the provision of hedging from the central bank to corporations and the derivatives market.

Figure 4.2 shows the daily turnover of foreign exchange in Latin American countries that float their currencies. These data, for the period 1998 to 2010, include spot and derivatives transactions. The figure conveys a general sense of the development of the derivatives market because spot transactions make up about one-third of all foreign exchange transactions in the region. There are two trends. Chile, Colombia, and Peru have seen an increase in the size of their foreign exchange markets. In Chile, the only one of the three countries with data from the 1990s, there was a break after the Asian crisis when the exchange rate was allowed to float, which suggests that indeed causality runs from flexibility to development of derivatives.[5] The other countries, Brazil and Mexico, have had a stable level of foreign exchange activity since the late 1990s. These two countries, as explained in chapter 2, experienced serious problems with the exposure of some corporations to exotic derivatives, which may have discouraged further developments of the derivatives market after the crisis. However, their troubles with derivatives did not launch an upward trend in the size of foreign exchange rate transactions. Therefore, expansions of derivatives markets—such as those of Chile, Colombia, and Peru—did not necessarily lead to problems in the derivatives markets like those in Brazil and Mexico, where the exchange rate market size was relatively stable.[6]

Volatility may increase financial vulnerability because of currency mismatches. In the past, many financial crises have arisen from the accumulation of unhedged foreign currency debt in banks and nonfinancial corporations. This was one of the main amplifiers of the Chilean banking crisis of the early 1980s, in which firms in the domestic sector built up substantial amounts of US dollar–denominated debt during a period of fixed exchange rates and capital account opening. It was also an important factor in the Mexican crisis of 1995, in the Asian crisis of the 1990s, and more recently in the financial problems in some Eastern European countries. On the other hand, during the global financial crisis low currency mismatches allowed the central banks of many emerging markets to lower interest rates aggressively in response to falling demand without fear that depreciations would cause a financial crisis.

Exchange rate flexibility is a key component of any policy mix to reduce currency mismatches. It sends a signal to the private sector to manage exchange rate risk appropriately. But flexibility must be complemented with regulation. Indeed, bank regulation should incorporate currency risks not only explicitly but also indirectly by dealing with the credit risks that arise from currency mismatches in the corporate sector. In Latin America in the 1990s, currency mismatches dropped after currencies were allowed to float following the Asian crisis, as agents and regulators adjusted to increased exchange rate volatility.

Figure 4.3 shows that for the period 1992–2009, after exchange rates were allowed to float, the exposure of the nonfinancial corporate sector to foreign exchange rates declined significantly. Some increase in liability dollarization was observed in 2009, but it was much more related to the depreciation of the currencies and some small accounting changes.[7] The private sector has the incentive to hedge against currency risks when the central bank is not doing it

---

5. For further evidence comparing the depth of derivatives markets in floaters and nonfloaters, see De Gregorio and Tokman (2007).

6. Another country that suffered seriously from the excessive exposure of corporations to exotic derivatives was Korea, which had a rising trend in the foreign exchange market.

7. For econometric evidence showing that in Latin America corporations reduce their exposure to exchange rate shocks through liability management, see Kamil (2012).

Figure 4.3 Dollarization of liabilities of the corporate sector in Latin America, 1992–2009 (annual average across firms)

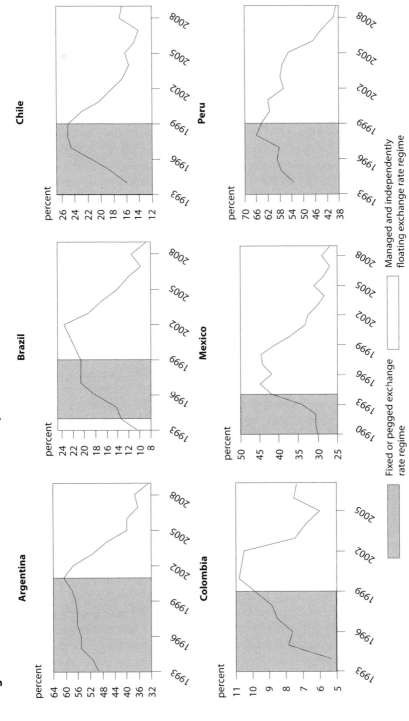

Source: Kamil (2012).

via exchange rate management, which is a positive development that reduces financial vulnerability when the exchange rate floats.

Central Banks and Financial Stability

The onset of the global financial crisis spurred a renewed discussion of the role of central banks in securing financial stability. This is not new. The first central banks (in Sweden and the United Kingdom) were created in the 17th century, but no proper role for central banks was established until the 19th century when the Bank of England was given the monopoly to issue banknotes and was assigned the role of lender of last resort.[8] Therefore, the original role of the central bank was to secure the functioning of the payment system. Financial stability was thus not a new issue, but it became a secondary issue compared with the conduct of monetary policy, which gradually turned from monetary stability to the ultimate goal of price stability. Indeed, financial stability was mostly ignored.

In emerging-market economies, which have a history of financial crises, the role of financial stability has always been central to policymaking. Indeed, the most relevant aspect of financial stability has been in the area of international financial transactions. For this purpose, central banks generally manage exchange rate policies, hold international reserves, and dictate norms to avoid currency mismatches and external payment crises. Indeed, in times of managed exchange rates a main concern of central banks was avoiding external crises, which often led to financial crises.

In Chile, for example, the central bank's objectives are price and financial stability. The Constitutional Law explicitly establishes that "the Bank shall have as its purposes to look after the stability of the currency and the normal functioning of internal and external payments." Indeed, the resilience of financial systems in emerging markets during the global financial crisis owed much to the fact that financial stability was already an important piece of the policy framework. The recurrence of a financial crisis in emerging-market economies, the last one just 10 years before the global financial crisis, may have led policymakers and financial institutions to take a cautious approach to financial innovation and globalization.

Price stability is usually the main mandate of central banks, and it is widely understood as maintaining low, stable inflation, which also reduces the deviations of output from its potential. However, the central bank's mandate for preserving financial stability is less explicitly defined, probably in part because there is less agreement on what financial stability is and how it is measured. Broadly understood, financial stability encompasses stable and fundamentals-driven credit and asset price growth as well as the absence of large mismatches in the financial sector. It includes efficient intermediate financial flows in

---

8. The Bank of England was actually founded to finance the war with France in the late 17th century (Davies and Green 2010).

normal times and resilience in times of turbulence. Here the term is used in a broad sense. A distinction also must be made between micro- and macrofinancial stability. Speaking of terms, Borio and Drehmann (2009, 2) provide some useful definitions:

> We define financial distress as an event in which substantial losses at financial institutions and/or their failure cause, or threaten to cause, serious dislocations to the real economy. We define financial instability as a situation in which normal-sized shocks to the financial system are sufficient to produce financial distress, i.e., in which the financial system is "fragile." Financial stability is then the converse of financial instability.

Because of the many dimensions of financial stability, many institutions are involved in attempts to achieve that stability. Central banks are usually in charge of the stability of the whole financial system. Thus they focus on interactions between different segments of the market. Financial supervisors, such as superintendents of supervisory agencies, look after the soundness of specific financial institutions. Some countries combine in the central bank the roles of banking supervisor and purveyor of monetary policy. The effectiveness of this institutional arrangement depends on the specific characteristics of a country. However, conflicts of interest may arise from vesting all tasks to preserve financial stability and monetary policy in a single institution. It is better to resolve those conflicts with institutional coordination and a clear delegation of responsibilities than to centralize control and monitoring in a single body.

Central banks are the guardians of price stability. They should also be independent institutions. By creating money and setting the interest rate, they can control inflation. In addition (and there are some differences across countries), central banks should have control over the exchange rate regime because the ability to conduct monetary policy depends on this regime. However, the issue is not so straightforward regarding financial stability, which depends on several institutions. Both central banks and financial regulators have a say in financial markets. However, as lenders of last resort, central banks should have a say in which institutions have access to central bank liquidity by having a role in the definition of the perimeter as well as the conditions that institutions must fulfill to have access to the central bank window. Therefore, its role in safeguarding overall financial stability is central.

As for the instruments of financial stability, they have been termed *macroprudential tools*, as opposed to microprudential regulation, which targets the health of specific financial institutions. One of the first tools used for financial stability was the dynamic provisioning of housing loans implemented in Spain in 2000. It is still too early to know how well this instrument performed because it is not known how much worse the Spanish crisis might have been had dynamic provisioning not been in place. Spain was not able, in fact, to avoid a housing bubble or a financial crisis in many of the small and medium institutions dedicated to housing finance, the *cajas*, which went bust during the crisis. The Spanish problems were, however, also related to corporate governance, because many *cajas* were instruments of political parties rather than of sound financial institutions.

Along the time dimension, the idea of macroprudential tools is to avoid the buildup of financial vulnerabilities in the upturn of the business cycle and to have a cushion for the downturn. Financial systems tend to be procyclical, and thus some braking system should be implemented to avoid excessive risk taking. This notion underlies the new rules in Basel III,[9] especially in the definition of the countercyclical buffer in the new capital requirements.

Along the cross-section dimension, it has been proposed that systemic institutions have extra capital in order to make them more resilient to financial turbulence. But the definition of a systemic institution is still blurred, and because of the evolution of financial innovations, what today may be a nonsystemic institution may eventually become systemic. Indeed, a nonsystemic institution on a worldwide basis might be considered systemic by particular economies.

Again, these issues are not new in emerging-market economies, which in general have better-capitalized banks. In Latin America, most of the industry already satisfies the requirements that are supposed to be in place by 2019. This has been achieved by the internal decisions of banks or regulatory requirements. For example, in Chile there are larger capital requirements for banks that have high market shares, which could be interpreted as a forerunner to too-big-to-fail charges.

Latin America has made significant progress in other areas as well, such as restrictions on currency mismatches, liquidity management, and the use of derivatives. In most of these areas, central banks in the region have the authority to set prudential regulation. For banks, these relate to authorizing the use of derivatives and regulations on market and liquidity risk, among other things.

In other systemic areas, central banks also have a say. For example, in Chile and Peru the central bank can impose constraints on the investments of pension funds, such as limits on investment abroad or limits on the type of instruments funds can hold. This scheme accommodates recent policy concerns because it avoids the conflicts of interest that arise from mixing the microsupervisor with the monetary authority, while preserving an institution that looks broadly at the stability of the financial system.

What can central banks do to further improve financial stability? For one thing, they could continue to strengthen coordination with other regulators. The creation of financial stability committees that bring together political authorities, regulators, and central banks goes in that direction. From a systemic point of view, it is important for central banks to evaluate financial vulnerabilities and strengths. Between 2002 and 2006, the central banks of Argentina, Brazil, Chile, Colombia, Mexico, and Peru began to issue financial

---

9. The Third Basel Accord (Basel III) is a voluntary global regulatory standard on the adequacy of bank capital, stress testing, and market liquidity risks.

stability reports (on an annual basis in Mexico and semiannual basis in the rest of the countries). The empirical evidence on financial stability reports suggests that in their current form they have not reduced the incidence of financial crisis (Čihák et al. 2012). However, overall, financial stability reports are the main instruments through which central banks can communicate financial vulnerabilities and discuss corrective actions.

Interactions between Financial Stability and Price Stability

The traditional view of the interactions between macroprudential policies and monetary policy has been influenced by the Tinbergen principle, which states that for each policy target there should be at least one policy instrument.[10] This view is reinforced by the fact that, as argued earlier, the interest rate is too blunt an instrument to deal with asset price bubbles and financial dislocations. Therefore, the interest rate—the monetary policy instrument to achieve the inflation target—and the macroprudential tools to deal with financial stability should be thought of separately.

The global financial crisis, however, has called into question the view that macroeconomic stability and financial stability are separate objectives. In the end, though, both are related, directly and through the instruments used to achieve each of them. The direct linkages are natural: It is difficult to imagine a stable financial system operating in a volatile macroeconomic environment. Financial systems are good at dealing with idiosyncratic risks, but their ability to deal with aggregate risk is more limited, especially in emerging markets. Vice versa, financial instability typically ends up adding to macroeconomic fluctuations. Faced with the uncertainty that accompanies periods of financial instability, investors and consumers tend to postpone investment plans and the purchase of durable goods, with foreseeable consequences for output and inflation. Moreover, extreme episodes of financial instability that lead to financial crises almost always end up in a sharp and costly recession.

There are also indirect linkages between macroeconomic stability and financial stability through the instruments used to achieve them. The main tool used by most central banks to achieve macroeconomic stability is management of the short-term interest rate. Movements of this benchmark rate not only directly affect the consumption and saving decisions of firms and households but also have consequences for all assets, the cost and availability of credit, and the willingness of investors to take risks. For example, in a stable context persistently low interest rates may generate incentives for investors whose incomes depend on absolute returns (such as hedge fund managers and insurance companies) to invest in riskier assets. They also may make it more profitable to engage in carry trades and create currency or maturity mismatches. On the unintended side, success in achieving macroeconomic stability may change the perception of agents about the riskiness of the environment and convince

---

10. See Bernanke (2011) for discussion of these issues.

them to pursue riskier bets in the expectation that good times will continue indefinitely (or at least until the bets pay off). Meanwhile, on the one hand, the monetary policies adopted to deal with bubbles, such as the Greenspan put, may increase the chance of bubbles. On the other hand, micro- and macroprudential regulatory tools, such as caps on credit growth or capital requirements, have direct consequences for the cost and availability of credit, with the corresponding impact on investment, consumption, employment, output, and the transmission channels of monetary policy.

The links between macroeconomic stability and financial stability as goals, as well as the cross effects of their main tools, do not mean, however, that they can be managed using a single type of instrument. For example, interest rate movements affect credit and asset prices, but they are not the most appropriate tool for addressing financial stability concerns. To illustrate, raising the interest rate could in principle tame the growth of stock or housing prices in a closed economy, helping to prevent the formation of bubbles or bursting them at an early stage before they threaten financial stability. But even if it were possible to identify a bubble from a fundamentals-driven increase in an asset price, controlling the rise in an asset price may require substantial increases in the interest rate, which will reduce the credit supply and the prices of other assets that may or may not be part of the bubble, with the attendant negative effects on output and inflation. In other words, the impact of such a policy would be felt across the board in financial markets on top of the detrimental impacts it would have on the real economy by unnecessarily depressing output, employment, and real investment. In an open economy, such a policy may be ineffective in controlling the growth of asset prices and may even worsen the prospects for financial stability.

That said, monetary policy should not ignore asset prices. As long as those prices relay information on inflation perspectives, they should be considered in interest rate decisions. Indeed, soaring asset prices tend to produce increases in credit and rapidly growing economies—the ingredients of rising inflation as excess capacity falls.

The use of regulation to achieve macroeconomic stability draws the same criticism as the use of interest rates to achieve financial stability. It might be possible to use bank capital requirements to control inflation through the supply of credit and real activity, but it would raise the cost of capital and would hit bank-dependent firms and consumers especially hard; other borrowers would turn to other sources of financing. Furthermore, the relatively frequent changes that managing macroeconomic conditions may require could create policy-driven volatility in financial markets. All this indicates that it is more appropriate to tackle each goal with its own type of tool. However, separating the instruments does not necessarily mean that achievement of the goals can be separated operationally. Because of the dual causality of price and financial stability, monetary and financial policies should be explicitly coordinated, with clear allocation of responsibilities, as noted earlier.

Another issue is whether macroprudential tools could be used to complement monetary policy. For example, adjusting capital requirements over the business cycle or introducing dynamic provisioning may have effects on the output gap, inflation, and interest rates. Likewise, the automatic stabilizers of fiscal policy have implications for monetary policy. Therefore, there should be no conflicts between financial stability and price stability tools, as long as financial regulation reduces the procyclicality of the banking system. As for the inflation target, this is just part of the environment in which decisions have to be made.

Another type of complementarity is that in which a particular tool serves both macroeconomic stability and financial stability. One example is the unconventional monetary policies followed in advanced economies. With interest rates at the zero lower bound, these economies are intervening in financial markets to affect the long part of the yield curve. This intervention involves buying treasury securities, as well as some private securities. Intervention in private markets consists of choosing segments of the market that are not working properly. For example, the US Federal Reserve bought structured securities to alleviate financial distress in some markets and helped to revive the economy. Many issues are involved in these types of policies, such as their fiscal implications or exit strategies, but from a central banking point of view, unconventional policies are tools that can serve both central bank objectives.

Perhaps a more controversial issue is the use of macroprudential tools as a substitute for monetary policy. Recently, some emerging markets have used banks' reserve requirements to tighten credit. This is used as a substitute to raising interest rates in order to avoid the collateral effects on asset prices, especially the exchange rate. There is no evidence and no reason to believe that macroprudential tools can replace macroeconomic policies. Acting through standard fiscal and monetary policy to stabilize the business cycle is more efficient than the use of indirect tools. Macroprudential tools are a good complement to standard macroeconomic policy, using direct measures to protect financial stability along the business cycle.

The advantage of using the interest rate for monetary policy is that the transmission channels are well known. Changes in monetary policy interest rates affect the cost of financing, asset prices, and the availability of credit. The macroeconomic consequences of changing regulation are less well understood. Tightening restrictions on banks may create disintermediation and move credit to unregulated segments of the market. In addition, the latitude of changes in regulation is much more limited than that of interest rates. A more constructive approach may be to design rules-based countercyclical regulation clearly aimed at minimizing the risk of financial crisis. Nonetheless, there is still much more to learn about the interactions between monetary and financial policy.

Figure 4.4   Regulatory capital and leverage ratios in 2008 (times and percent)

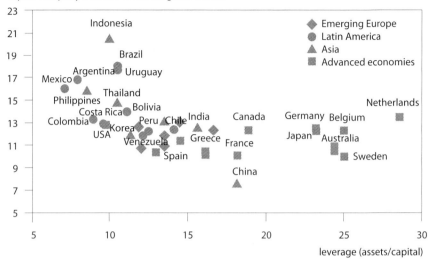

capital adequacy ratio (tier 2/risk-weighted assets)

Note: Only commercial data are used for the United States.

Source: IMF (2008, statistical appendix tables 22 and 23).

Latin American Banks and the Financial Crisis

Latin American countries were applying macroprudential tools long before the global financial crisis, even if they did not call them that. This section discusses some features of Latin American banking systems that help to explain their resilience to the global financial crisis.[11]

One characteristic of Latin American banking systems is their relatively high levels of capital and low levels of leverage (figure 4.4). Before the crisis, all countries had levels of regulatory capital above the 8 percent required by Basel II[12]—the result of higher regulatory capital requirements and limits on leverage, as well as the internal strategies of local banks willing to hold higher levels of capital. Asian banks also had a relatively strong capital base. Banks in

---

11. For recent examinations of the use of macroprudential tools and the institutional arrangements of financial regulation in Latin America, see Céspedes and Rebucci (2011); Cifuentes et al. (2011); Jácome, Nier, and Imam (2012); and Tovar, Garcia-Escribano, and Martin (2012). Because of the complexities of a full comparative analysis, the reviews are in general partial and focus on country experiences.

12. Chile appears to have the largest leverage ratio in the region. However, it is one of the countries that had the lowest volatility of output, and evidence shows that the lower the volatility, the higher the leverage (see figure 4.4).

emerging Europe, within emerging markets, were the weakest; the Asian and Latin American banks were more capitalized.

The figure clearly shows the high levels of leverage in advanced economies before the crisis. They all met the Basel II requirements, but leverage was very high. This finding reveals the problems of not regulating leverage directly, as intended in Basel III. Regulatory arbitrage expands leverage to very risky levels while maintaining regulatory capital requirement within limits. Bruno and Shin (2012) find that leverage fluctuates widely over the business cycle, whereas regulatory capital remains stable, exacerbating the business cycle and financial fragility.

The global financial crisis itself revealed that leverage could have been larger through arbitraging the risk weights of assets, but also through off-balance-sheet investment operations that reduced leverage artificially. This behavior is at the center of the issue of leveraging in the trading book. Proposals along the lines of the Volcker rule separating investment banks from commercial banks head in the direction of reducing financial risks. The route followed in emerging markets and that avoids complicated regulation is to set limits on the instruments that can be held by banks. For example, in Chile banks can only hold corporate and Chilean sovereign bonds. In terms of derivatives, only interest rate and exchange rate derivatives are allowed. All other operations must be carried out through other financial institutions, which are also subject to financial regulation and can be subsidiaries of banks. Brazil and Mexico have also been limiting the use of derivatives in the banking systems because their financial markets were affected during the crisis by corporate exposure to exotic options.

Strong financial systems were not able to avoid a sharp contraction of credit during the peak of the crisis. However, credit expansion resumed as the economies recovered. It is difficult to determine how much of this was due to a decline in the demand for credit or restrictions from the supply side. Certainly, both factors may have played a role, because the increase in uncertainty tightened financial conditions and reduced demand, as the surveys on financial conditions showed.

It is not correct, however, to assume that all credit contraction stemmed from a supply shock external or internal in origin. At least from an external point of view, foreign credit to Latin America apparently remained fairly fluid during the crisis, with the exception of several weeks in which financial markets worldwide were paralyzed.

Evidence on the actual interest rates and spread at which Latin American economies borrowed do not show signs of severe credit constraints. On the contrary, the cost of foreign credit declined in conjunction with global interest rates (see figure 4.5 for Chile). Although spreads above the London interbank offered rate (Libor) increased after the crisis and interest rates spiked in October 2008, the cost of external financing for domestic banks declined after the crisis. But credit also declined. Despite this indication of a fall in demand, interpretation of the data as a contraction in demand is not straightforward.

Figure 4.5 Cost of short-term external financing for resident banks in Chile, 2003–10

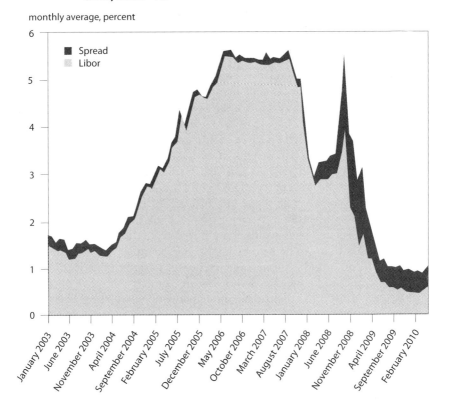

monthly average, percent

■ Spread
▒ Libor

Libor = London interbank offered rate

Note: Data correspond to the floating rate of bank loans.

Sources: Central Bank of Chile; Bloomberg.

Because many firms wanted to preserve their credit lines fearing that they would be more costly to renew, credit demand contracted. But this contraction was the response to a fear of supply contraction.

The degree of financial deepness from the point of view of the banking system is usually measured by the ratio of private banking credit to GDP. Latin America ranks relatively low, as do many other emerging markets. Therefore, periods of financial deepening may be associated with credit booms, not only because average household debts are increasing, but also because of the entry of new households to the banking system (bancarization).

Figure 4.6 shows the degree of deepness of the banking system for Latin America and other regions for 2000 and 2008. Except for Chile, the level of private credit as a share of GDP is quite low. During the 2000s, however, most

Figure 4.6   Private credit as share of GDP in Latin American countries and selected regions, 2000 and 2008

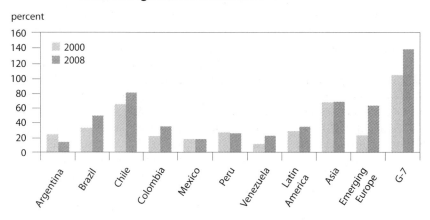

Source: International Monetary Fund, *International Financial Statistics* database.

countries of the region exhibit an increase. This increase is much gentler than that of emerging Europe or advanced economies.

In emerging Europe, it is possible to think about financial deepening as the arrival of new households in the financial system. However, it is not possible to explain such a large increase in credit, as a share of GDP, without recognizing that there was a large credit boom. The advanced economies also underwent a credit boom.

The recent evidence on Latin America contrasts sharply with that on liberalization of the 1980s. It featured significant credit booms, which were followed by the debt crisis and the lost decade. During that period, there was a rapid increase in domestic credit, largely fueled by capital inflows in the form of external debt. Countries that experienced greater expansion were also the ones that suffered greater output losses from the crisis (De Gregorio and Guidotti 1995). Prudential regulation, together with macroeconomic policies that did not pursue unsustainable expansions, may have been behind this fact, although more empirical research is needed to contrast both experiences.

The debt crisis did end the myth that when the private sector is the one borrowing, it is not a problem. Moral hazard and incentive problems were massive. Beyond the belief that the Greenspan put would save the world, the defects of the compensation scheme in the finance industry, the serious problems with rating agencies, and the practice of offering nonrecourse loans to people who would not qualify under normal conditions to receive credit were among the many failures in the financial market.

Many of these problems were evident in Latin America, where the debt crisis and the ideology of unfettered financial markets were very costly. Indeed, it was Carlos Díaz-Alejandro who eloquently said in the mid-1980s, "Good-bye financial repression, hello financial crash" (Díaz-Alejandro 1985). Some recent research also points in the same direction—that is, beyond a certain level, financial deepness contributes marginally to growth (Arcand, Berkes, and Panizza 2012; Cecchetti and Kharroubi 2012)—which is consistent with the evidence from the early 1980s reported in De Gregorio and Guidotti (1995).

In recent years, the macroprudential tool most used in Latin America to reduce credit expansion has been reserve requirements, by which banks are required to hold some fraction of their deposits as liquid reserves. Raising reserve requirements increases the costs of borrowing. All countries have reserve requirements, but as a macroprudential instrument they must be changed during the business cycle. In recent years, Brazil, Colombia, Peru, and Uruguay have used changes in reserve requirements to stem credit booms. According to Tovar, García-Escribano, and Martin (2012), the effects of this policy are moderate and transitory. Although changing reserve requirements may be effective, the practice also has some side effects because banks look for new forms of funding to avoid raising requirements, which may end up generating vulnerabilities. They may also move credit to unregulated credit providers, thereby encouraging continuation of the shadow banking system.

The Achilles heel of financial systems in emerging markets has been currency mismatches, not only in the banking system, which is easy to regulate, but also in the exposure of corporations that borrow in foreign currency and mostly conduct their business in the nontraded goods sector. Moreover, in emerging Europe even mortgages are in foreign currency. This practice exposes the financial system to weaknesses stemming from the currency mismatches of its borrowers. All Latin American countries surveyed by the Inter-American Development Bank have regulations on currency mismatches in the banking system (IDB 2005). Those regulations range from quantitative limits to currency exposure, which includes exchange rate exposure in quantifying credit risk, with its consequences for capital requirements. Regarding corporate risk, banking regulations require internalizing the risk of currency exposure of their borrowers. For example, in Chile, such regulations result in higher provisions on foreign currency lending when the borrowers have most of their income in domestic currency. Of course, this requires more forward-looking provisions, something that is currently being studied and implemented in several Latin American countries (Cifuentes et al. 2011). In Peru, a dollarized economy, as well as Uruguay, additional capital requirements are applied to foreign currency lending to unhedged borrowers.

From a factual point of view, as shown in this chapter, during the global financial crisis the balance sheets of banks were resilient to the large, unprecedented fluctuations in exchange rates. Only in Brazil and Mexico in Latin America, and several other emerging markets, were some large corporations exposed to exotic exchange rate derivatives. These derivatives were highly complex, and there was concern about financial stability. The lesson to be learned from this situation is that markets require more disclosure in the financial

Figure 4.7   Foreign claims of BIS reporting banks, Europe, Asia, and Latin America, 2011Q2

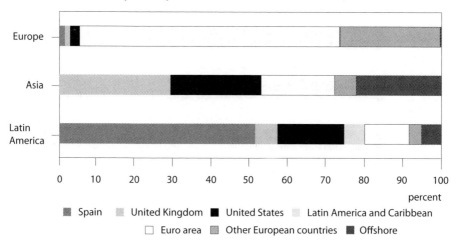

Source: Bank for International Settlements (BIS), consolidated banking statistics (immediate borrower basis).

statements of corporations about their effective currency exposure, especially when dealing with complex instruments. Banks should take this need into account when making provisions and extending credit.

Another important source of financial risk is the exposure of the domestic banking system to foreign banks. Cross-border flows are highly volatile (see chapter 5). The composition of foreign claims by source country is presented in figure 4.7 for emerging Europe, Asia, and Latin America. Emerging Europe is more exposed to European banks, whereas Asia is more evenly exposed across regions. Latin America is exposed to Spanish banks, mainly Santander and BBVA. In dealing with Latin America, Spanish banks have adopted an arm's-length strategy. But the main feature, which may have resulted in Latin American countries' being less affected by their exposure to foreign banks, is that the affiliates of most foreign banks operating as commercial banks are constituted as subsidiaries. Thus the subsidiary operates like a domestic bank, with its own capital, its own board of directors, and strict rules for deposits of the subsidiary in the parent bank.

Many countries such as Chile adopt the same regulations for branches and subsidiaries. The most relevant difference is that branches do not have a local board, whereas subsidiaries do, thereby limiting the foreign bank's responsibility. Subsidiaries also can have local or other partners. There are thus strong incentives for banks to use the subsidiary model to expand across regions.

Another incentive is that subsidiarization induces more local funding. Among the three regions shown in figure 4.8, Latin America is the one in

Figure 4.8   Composition of foreign claims in Europe, Asia, and Latin America, 2011Q2

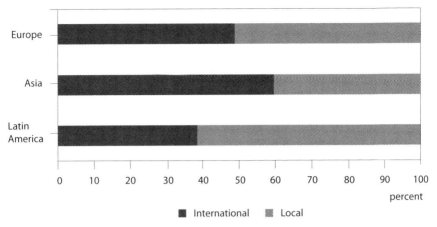

Source: Bank for International Settlements, consolidated banking statistics (immediate borrower basis).

which funding comes more heavily from local sources.[13] Indeed, Kamil and Rai (2010) find that Latin American financial systems were resilient in the global financial crisis because global banks' credit is mostly channeled in domestic currency and foreign banks operate as local subsidiaries, funded mostly with domestic deposits. Therefore, subsidiarization, strong regulation of currency mismatches, a broad base of deposit funding, low reliance on short-term wholesale funding, and a simple trading book may help to explain the strength and resilience of the banking system in the region.

Concluding Remarks

Latin America has enjoyed the benefits of having overcome the global financial crisis successfully. However, in times of success and stability financial vulnerabilities build up. In addition, misperceptions that an economy is stronger than it really is may lead to complacency and risks may be overlooked. Financial markets in the region thus continue to face challenges.

The first challenge is financial innovation. Despite considerable public debate and criticism, financial innovation is essentially welfare enhancing. However, it also can become a form of circumventing regulation. Financial innovation was at the center of the global financial crisis. The ways in which

---

13. For further discussion on cross-border banking, see CIEPR (2012), and for an analysis of the vulnerabilities of the Latin American economies in their exposure to Spanish banks, see IDB (2012). Montoro and Rojas-Suárez (2012) also analyze the resilience of Latin American banks. Subsidiarization does not necessarily produce full "ring-fencing," as the cases of Central and Eastern European countries show, where foreign banks also operated as subsidiaries.

Figure 4.9 Leverage and GDP volatility in Latin America, 1997–2007
(times and percent)

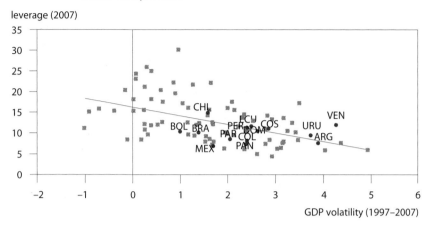

Note: The dots denote Latin American countries: ARG = Argentina; BOL = Bolivia; BRA = Brazil; CHL = Chile; COL = Colombia; COS = Costa Rica; DOM = Dominican Republic; ECU = Ecuador; MEX = Mexico; PAN = Panama; PAR = Paraguay; PER = Peru; URU = Uruguay; VEN = Venezuela

Source: Central Bank of Chile (2009).

some securitized assets were used was the clearest illustration of this abuse. They were structured in a way in which only secure tranches remained on the balance sheets of banks, and the others were sold, many times to off-balance-sheet vehicles, allowing credit to expand with a weak capital base. The result was excess demand for certain securitized assets and excess exposure of highly leveraged intermediaries to these assets. Going forward, financial innovation needs to move in step with regulation to ensure that it adds value and is not just a route to evading regulation and aggravating financial fragility.

The second challenge is dealing with the effects of stability on risk taking. The interactions between stability and fragility cannot be ignored. As the business cycle becomes more stable, investors search for yield by increasing risk taking. Indeed, one of the risks of the Great Moderation, as discussed in chapter 2, was risk taking and financial fragility.[14] In countries with more volatile GDPs, bank leverage is lower, and banks (either by choice or by regulation) put more capital aside to deal with uncertainty (see figure 4.9). Most Latin American countries are not far from the line indicating that as GDP volatility rises leverage falls, and many are below it, which indicates that leverage is still within reasonable levels. As a result, it is not hard to imagine that a period of declining volatility in prices and output leads to increased risk taking across several economies. However, the countries with high levels of leverage had a different fate during the global financial crisis, and the differences can be

---

14. For a recent discussion on the search for yield, see Stein (2013).

found in the role of regulators and the incentives of the financial sector to manage risk. Stability has a lot of benefits in terms of welfare, but it requires close monitoring of financial risks.

The third challenge, at the current juncture, is that Latin American countries have to deal with rising asset prices, particularly when expressed in foreign currency. One area of concern is housing. The region is not accustomed to rising housing prices, but in recent years that has changed, and memories of the global crisis are generating concerns. Indeed, recently stock markets have not been performing strongly, but housing and real estate investment are doing much better, which is an indication of a portfolio reallocation. Continuation of this trend will maintain the upward pressure on housing prices.

Part of what has been happening in the region can be explained by the dynamics of recovery. Because there has been a strong monetary impulse with very low interest rates, the construction sector has grown more rapidly than the rest of the economy, and housing prices have risen. Cubeddu, Tovar, and Tsounta (2012) show that, comparatively, housing prices do not appear to be misaligned and the postcrisis development has not been unusual from an international perspective. In addition, there is no evidence of a credit boom in the mortgage markets. Perhaps the only exception is Brazil, where prices in some metropolitan areas such as São Paulo began to rise much before the rest of the region, reaching very high levels. However, in recent months, the slowdown of growth momentum in the region has come together with some stabilization of housing prices, although the situation has some heterogeneity across countries.

Certainly, housing is doing unusually well, but it is too early to confirm that there is a bubble. However, that is not the most important issue; recall that on the eve of the financial crisis in the United States, experts were still debating whether there was in fact a housing bubble. If prices keep rising, sooner or later there could be a bubble. But, as argued in this chapter, the problem is not necessarily the bubble itself but an asset price boom financed with the debt. As prices fall, the health of the banking system may be in danger. Moreover, housing prices can fall for reasons other than a bubble, although a bubble is the more likely reason and the fall in prices is more likely to be deeper. Thus the authorities have to take great care in evaluating the resilience of the banking sector to a fall in housing prices.

Increases in housing prices often occur in periods of strong economic performance. Under these circumstances output can grow beyond full capacity, inducing inflationary pressures. The natural response to such pressures would be to tighten monetary policy. Growth, however, can also bring a sanguine inflationary outlook—if, for example, there are productivity gains. If this is the case, and authorities are concerned about housing prices, they can employ macroprudential measures. The most important, and apparently the most effective, measures are to reduce loan-to-value (LTV) ratios for lenders and caps on debt-to-income ratios for borrowers.[15] A combination of these two policies

---

15. For further discussion on macroprudential tools in real estate, see Crowe et al. (2011), Cubbedu,

is desirable because individually they can be circumvented. For example, LTV can be accompanied by other forms of credit. In addition, reporting income in Latin American countries is not easy to verify, although improvements in the reporting would bring an additional benefit of strengthening tax information. Regulators can also require higher capital levels to limit the amounts of loans by banks. Such steps must be carried out with good evaluations of the vulnerabilities and potential side effects in the banking system, however. The risk when regulation tightens is that credit could move from regulated to unregulated, more expensive, and riskier segments of credit markets (i.e., shadow banking), weakening the goal of safeguarding financial stability.

Finally, in view of their experience during the global financial crisis, Latin American countries should review their regulatory and supervisory frameworks.[16] Efforts to coordinate all the domestic institutions responsible for financial stability are essential. Particularly relevant is the inclusion of consumer protection in the financial stability architecture, so that all decisions and policies are consistent with preserving stability. Revisiting regulatory parameters, information requirements, regulatory perimeters, and so forth in light of the crisis is important. It has become clear that basing capital requirements on risk-weighted assets is not enough and introduces distortions in banks' investment decisions. As Basel III recognizes, capital adequacy ratios must be complemented with limits on leverage. However, the current limits, allowing more than 30 times leverage ratios, seem too weak. This is not a serious concern in the region because banks are better capitalized and leverage is smaller. Nonetheless, regulation must be simpler and stronger and recognize the vulnerabilities that emerge during the upturn. The resilience of the financial system in the region must be preserved and reinforced if the financial system is to be a key factor in promoting growth.

Tovar, and Tsounta (2012), and Central Bank of Chile (2012).

16. For more on regulatory guidelines with a macro perspective, see Brunnermeier et al. (2009).

5

Capital Flows

Policymakers and researchers have a keen interest in capital inflows and how to manage them. However, the ways in which the data are viewed in popular discussions are often incomplete and sometimes misleading. Capital flows affect the economy from many angles. And, like many economic issues, they have a nontrivial ideological content. In the economic sphere, capital flows are relevant to financial stability, macroeconomic fluctuations, and exchange rates.

An important distinction should be made, however, between gross and net capital inflows, which have different implications for macroeconomic management and financial stability. Exchange rate pressures are associated with net rather than gross capital flows. By contrast, financial stability is much more associated with gross flows because the volume of flows—as well as their composition—is relevant to the vulnerabilities of the financial system, in particular the banking industry.

Indeed, in distinguishing between price stability and financial stability in central banking, in general, price stability has to do with low and stable inflation and a smooth business cycle (in short, macroeconomic stability) and financial stability with low vulnerabilities in the financial system. Therefore, in the area of capital flows macroeconomic stability has to do with net flows, whereas financial stability has to do with gross flows.[1]

But first an obvious clarification: Capital account opening is welfare enhancing, but it has risks that, when not appropriately managed, may end up incurring costs that outweigh the benefits. Just like trade in goods and services, intertemporal trade is beneficial. Capital-scarce countries can finance valuable

---

1. For further discussion, see CIEPR (2012).

investment and anticipate consumption, just as young households do in the domestic economy. In addition, once idiosyncratic shocks are added to the mix, financial flows allow economies to trade financial assets, providing insurance and worldwide risk sharing. Consumption can then be smoothed across different states of nature and over time. Capital account opening may also serve as a vehicle for spreading governance practices and managerial expertise worldwide, just as foreign direct investment is supposed to do.

Although the vast literature on growth and trade openness suggests that opening to trade is good for growth and welfare (but with some caveats), the evidence on capital account opening is more elusive. Most surveys and recent research have found small or no significant effects, and the policy conclusion is generally that to reap the benefits from financial integration, capital account opening must be done within a healthy regulatory and supervisory framework. Certainly, unfettered financial integration has proven to be risky, and most of the time has had very negative consequences. However, the evidence does not support financial autarky. Indeed, the evidence shows that as countries grow, their level of financial integration also increases (Obstfeld 2009). Causality does not go from financial integration to development, but from high levels of income to more financial integration; therefore, countries must prepare to be more financially integrated as they grow.[2]

There is, however, some evidence on the benefits of integration, given some threshold effects. Prasad et al. (2003) find in a broad sample of countries no clear correlation between capital account opening and economic growth. However, their evidence suggests that once a minimum threshold of institutional quality is crossed, capital account opening fosters growth. Cline (2013) reviews the evidence and claims that no one study finds a negative effect, although the statistical significance of the positive effects is rather small. At least the evidence shows that financial integration is not harmful per se, and, as shown shortly, Latin America is more financially integrated and, as its performance proved during the global financial crisis and in the aftermath, less vulnerable. Causality does not imply that Latin America has been more resilient because of financial integration, but clearly financial integration does not result in greater vulnerability if it is appropriately managed.

This point leads to a first policy implication: Capital account opening should take place once proper institutions have been set up, in particular those dealing with the rules and regulations of the financial system. The issue is not whether the intermediaries are local or foreign or whether countries are big enough and capable enough to support their own financial institutions. Rather, the issue is whether, regardless of nationality, there is an appropriate regulatory system, especially one that limits financial excesses, as discussed in chapter 3.

---

2. For further discussion of the evidence on financial integration and development, see De Gregorio (2013).

This chapter seeks to shed some light on the issues of capital flows, beginning with a discussion of some of the analytical issues. The next section discusses the role of reserve accumulation in understanding capital inflows and then looks at some recent empirical evidence on capital inflows. At that point, the discussion shifts from a focus on net capital flows to one on gross capital flows and their implications for financial stability and how to manage capital inflows from the perspective of an inflation targeting regime and through the use of capital controls.

Capital Flows, Current Account, and Exchange Rate: The Basics

Positive net capital inflows are the counterpart of a current account deficit. Therefore, a surge in net capital inflows may simply reflect a widening current account deficit. At the same time, capital inflows may be the flip side of reserve accumulation. Indeed, many large inflows have occurred with a limited current account deficit but large reserve accumulation.

Since the issue of capital inflows was raised by Calvo, Leiderman, and Reinhart (1996), empirical work has distinguished between the *pull* and *push* factors underlying surges of capital inflows.[3] Pull factors are developments in the domestic economy that attract foreign capital, such as productivity growth, new investment opportunities, financial deepening, and institutional strength. Push factors originate outside the country, such as a surge of global liquidity, higher savings in the rest of the world, low foreign interest rates, and global uncertainty. A special pull factor that should be treated separately is the reserves factor; it is discussed in the next section.

Consider balance of payment accounting in which

$$CA + FA = \Delta R \tag{5.1}$$

where *CA* and *FA* are the current account and financial account balances, respectively, and ΔR is the change in international reserves. In the discussion that follows, it is assumed that *FA* consists only of net private capital inflows. Thus some less important items are ignored such as errors and omissions, derivatives, official flows, and the capital account.[4]

---

3. Also see Fernandez-Arias (1996) and, more recently, Fratzscher (2011).

4. Until recently, the financial account was called the capital account. However, the IMF definition has changed. Currently, the capital account is a minor component of the financial account, which includes mainly transfers. The "new" capital account is ignored here because many countries have not yet computed it, and it is a very small component of the financial account. Finally, that part of net inflows is not considered to be official (e.g., from multilaterals). Here it is assumed that there are no official flows in *FA*—a reasonable assumption for the economies being analyzed here. The most significant official flow is changes in reserves. The terms *capital account* and *financial account* are used interchangeably in this chapter.

Therefore, net capital inflows may be the result of both a current account deficit ($-CA$) and international reserve accumulation (ΔR). Or, with causality running the other way around, accumulation of reserves may be the result of large capital inflows. In this section, it is assumed that no reserves are accumulated—that is, $\Delta R = 0$.

The basic, frictionless theory of capital flows and exchange rates begins by recognizing that net capital inflows are just the result of the current account deficit. Indeed, the current account is the change in the international net asset position of an economy resulting from discrepancies between income and expenditure. It is the outcome of the saving-investment decisions in the domestic economy. Therefore, *net* capital inflows are simply the financing of the current account deficit. The variable to look at when observing massive net inflows is the current account.

An increase in investment or a decline in domestic savings widens the current account deficit and generates an increase in net inflows. The widening of the current account may be the result of internal (pull) or external (push) factors.

A current account deficit that brings capital inflows is not necessarily a sustainable or a good thing. It is possible, as has happened many times in emerging-market economies and more recently in southern Europe, that distortions in the domestic economy or in the global financial system lead to unsustainable current account deficits. Chile during the early 1980s, Mexico in 1994, and some countries during the Asian crisis of the late 1990s were running unsustainable current account deficits largely because of rigidities in their exchange rates. The counterpart of these unsustainable current account deficits was excessive net capital inflows.

Whether the current account is leading the capital account or the other way around is difficult to separate conceptually and empirically, even when the driver is the private sector. Indeed, many experiences show that large current account deficits in the absence of fiscal imbalances are not always sustainable, contrary to the Lawson doctrine.[5] Policymakers should worry about potential misalignments and unsustainability, even when the source is the private sector. The recent European crisis reveals the importance of looking not only at public imbalances but also at private ones.

Indeed, policymakers should worry about persistent current account deficits because they may be signaling a buildup in vulnerabilities. In this case, net capital inflows being driven by external factors (push), or, in other words, the current account being driven by the financial account, may generate overheating and economic booms that end up in costly and severe adjustments. In addition, the boom may be associated with excessive exchange rate appreciation.

---

5. Named after Nigel Lawson, Britain's chancellor of the exchequer in the late 1980s, this doctrine says that current account deficits produced by a shift in private sector behavior should not be a public policy concern.

The equilibrium real exchange rate is the relative price of domestic goods in terms of foreign goods that makes the current account consistent with the saving-investment balance. In other words, the equilibrium real exchange rate generates an allocation of resources between tradable and nontradable goods consistent with the current account resulting from the gap between savings and investment. The larger the deficit, the more the real exchange rate needs to appreciate. Appreciation ensures that more resources are allocated to the production of nontradable goods while the expenditure on tradable and nontradable goods rises, leading to a deterioration of the current account balance.

Interpreting the "problem of capital inflows" in this context requires considering the notion that an increase in the supply of foreign credit will appreciate the exchange rate and widen the current account deficit. This result is expected in traditional theories. A drop in foreign interest rates or a relaxation of liquidity constraints on foreign financing resulting, for example, from a liberalization of the capital account reduces domestic savings and also stimulates investment.[6] Consumption and investment increase, resulting in a larger current account deficit and an appreciation of the exchange rate. Meanwhile, domestic activity undergoes a boom, most intensely in the nontradable sector. Whether this is desirable will depend on the distortions that this process causes. The one most frequently mentioned is a threat to export-led growth that may have permanent consequences for the ability of the economy to maintain high, sustainable rates of growth. This distortion is very relevant, but it is inconsistent at the global level if all countries want to depreciate their currencies.

Because the current accounts and financial accounts are jointly determined, there is a simultaneity problem in interpreting the data. Consider, for example, a widening of the current account deficit because of expectations of higher future productivity. Higher productivity could stem from the implementation of progrowth reforms, which take time to improve productivity. In this example, a rise in consumption and investment will induce a net capital inflow because of pull factors. The real exchange rate will appreciate.

By contrast, consider a scenario in which global financial conditions improve because, for example, the world interest rate falls, producing more global liquidity or a bigger appetite for risk. Alternatively, a capital-scarce country could open its capital account. The results will be expanded investment and consumption, a widening of the current account deficit, greater net capital inflows, and exchange rate appreciation. In both cases, a country's currency will appreciate, and it will experience a widening of the deficit in the current account and more net inflows.

Perhaps it would be better to look at current account–driven net capital inflows vis-à-vis financial (or capital) account–driven net capital inflows. This would make sense from an accounting point of view when referring to reserves-

---

6. The reduction of savings would come from a fall in the interest rate and a relaxation of liquidity constraints.

driven capital inflows. Of course, it is much easier to count domestic (pull) and external (push) factors than to separate the ultimate causes of the flows.

In summary, whether capital flows drive the current account or the current account drives capital flows is not always obvious. For capital flows to drive the current account, relative prices have to change—that is, they must have effects on the real exchange rate.

Capital Inflows and Accumulation of Reserves

Analysis and interpretation of the data on capital inflows are complicated somewhat when a country accumulates reserves. In principle, in the frictionless model reserves do not play a role in the real side of the economy. However, the accumulation of international reserves has an effect on the exchange rate, and through that effect it may alter the current account, and consequently net inflows, as discussed in chapter 3. For most of the discussion, and consistent with the situation in recent years, reserve accumulation is considered to be fully sterilized, which is also consistent with an inflation targeting regime that sets short-term interest rates.

When reserve accumulation has no effect on the exchange rate, and therefore no effect on the current account as in the frictionless model, *FA* in equation (5.1) will change one to one with ΔR. In terms of the net international asset position of the economy, there will be just a portfolio change, in which the purchase of reserves (i.e., more domestic agents will be holding foreign assets), a capital outflow, will cause an equal increase in capital inflows (i.e., more foreign agents will be holding domestic assets). In other words, foreigners, through capital inflows, will be financing the accumulation of reserves. If this were to happen, the appropriate metric to evaluate capital inflows would still be the current account.

However, to avoid a situation in which the accumulation of reserves fully translates into capital inflows, it must affect the real exchange rate and through that effect affect the current account. A process of reserve accumulation that depreciates the exchange rate should cause a reduction in the current account deficit, and therefore net capital flows should increase less than one to one with reserve accumulation. Differentiating the previous equation (accounting identity) and denoting the real exchange rate as q produces[7]

$$\frac{\partial CA}{\partial q}\frac{dq}{d\Delta R} + \frac{dFA}{d\Delta R} = 1. \qquad (5.2)$$

---

7. This is comparative statics with equilibrium relations because *CA* and *q* are endogenous and simultaneously determined. In addition, it is assumed that the accumulation of reserves may have effects on the "real" exchange rate. The real exchange rate is the relative price of foreign goods in terms of domestic goods. Thus an increase in *q* is a real depreciation.

Therefore, if $dq/dR = 0$—that is, the accumulation of reserves has no effect on the exchange rate as in the frictionless case—net capital inflows will increase by the same magnitude as the increase in international reserves. In this case, $dFA/dR = 1$. By contrast, when reserve accumulation affects the exchange rate, the impact will be less than one to one because $dq/dR > 0$ and thus $dFA/dR < 1$.

The magnitude of the effect will depend on how large the effects of reserve accumulation are on the exchange rate, combined with the current account elasticity to the real exchange rate. At the other extreme is when the first term of the sum on the left-hand side is one, and thus the increase in reserves will not have effects on private flows and the current account deficit will decline at the same magnitude as reserve accumulation. This would be a case of maximum effectiveness of reserve accumulation. The evidence, discussed in chapter 3, suggests that the effects of sterilized intervention are relatively small and temporary, and because of lags in the effects of exchange rates on the current account as well as the magnitudes of trade elasticities, dFA/dR is not likely to be too far from one.

Some recent work looks at the effects of reserves on the current account ($dCA/dR = 1 - dFA/dR$); it focuses on analyzing "currency manipulation." The International Monetary Fund, in estimating the effects of reserve accumulation on the current account, finds a coefficient of 0.4 for accumulation when interacting with capital controls (IMF 2012a). This means that a \$1 increase in reserves results in an improvement of \$.40 in a current account balance with the highest level of capital controls and zero for economies without capital controls.

According to this result, one of the most successful countries in managing its exchange rate, Switzerland, would have a zero coefficient ($dFA/dR = 1$) because it has no capital controls. However, Switzerland has been able to place a floor on the Swiss franc (euro rate)—that is, it has been effective in managing its exchange rate. The reason for the success on the exchange rate front is that intervention has not been sterilized, and money supply has adjusted to achieve the exchange rate target. Unless the exchange rate has no effect on exports and imports, dFA/dR cannot be one, because the current account would also adjust.[8] This situation clearly reveals a problem with the existing evidence: It does not control for whether interventions are sterilized, which should yield important differences in the response of the economy to international reserve accumulation.

By contrast, Bergsten and Gagnon (2012) find that in the long run an increase in reserves of \$1 results in a much larger improvement in the current account, about \$.70 to \$.90. This result is large for the evidence on the effects

---

8. Switzerland has been successful because it pursues nonsterilized intervention, a form of quantitative easing not in the treasury market but in the foreign exchange market. In addition, intervention does not have the typical quasifiscal cost as in emerging-market economies, because Switzerland's borrowing costs are lower than the return on its reserves. Therefore, Switzerland actually benefits financially by intervening.

of sterilized intervention, and current account and trade elasticities, as well as the country evidence presented shortly. These results are based on IMF regressions (IMF 2012a), but without controlling for capital controls and without distinguishing whether or not the accumulation of reserves is sterilized.

Central banks may decide to undertake sterilized intervention to weaken the currency regardless of the presence of capital inflows or as a response to these inflows. It is important to differentiate the cases. In the first case, the central bank decides to intervene for mercantilist or insurance reasons, as discussed in chapter 3. Causality runs from reserves to capital inflows. The application of equation (5.2) is direct, and the effect of reserves on capital inflows will depend on the magnitude of dFA/dR. In the second case, there is a shock to capital inflows, and the response is to accumulate reserves to absorb the inflows without affecting the domestic economy. For example, foreign investors may decide to increase their exposure to a country because of an increased appetite for risk or because they just want to hold a share of the country in their portfolios. This movement, completely exogenous to the country, would not affect the current account directly.

When there is a capital inflow shock, what are its effects on the exchange rate and the current account? In the frictionless world where savings and investment do not change, the capital inflow shock would be offset by an equal adjustment in capital outflows by other private agents. The shock would only result in a portfolio change. If the central bank decides to buy the foreign exchange from those inflows, it, instead of private investors, would undertake the portfolio adjustment. The final impact would depend on how strong the effect of capital inflows is on the exchange rate and, through that mechanism, on the current account. In other words, what would happen to the current account if a shock to capital inflows were not mitigated by the accumulation of reserves? Empirically, the effects of a capital flow shock should not differ from the effects of reserve accumulation. In both cases, the effects on the exchange rate must stem from the imperfect substitutability of foreign and domestic assets.

The effects of reserve accumulation on capital flows are not known precisely, and, more important, these effects may differ from country to country—for example, depending on the degree of openness of the capital account and the degree of development of financial markets. Thus one should look at the balances of both the current and the financial accounts. A large surplus in the financial account, large net capital inflows, may, however, be the result of an explicit policy of reserve accumulation rather than a capital inflow push, or an excessive expansion of domestic expenditure that leads to a current account deficit. Alternatively, a large accumulation of reserves may be the policy response to massive capital inflows.

Figure 5.1 Current account balances in Latin America, developing Asia, and emerging-market economies, 1985–2012

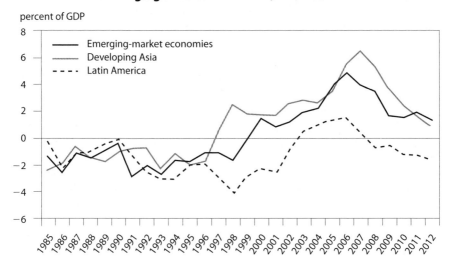

percent of GDP

Source: IMF (2012d).

Surges of Capital Inflows

Net capital inflows should surge with a widening of the deficit in the current account, unless an effective process of reserve accumulation offsets all surges of inflows. However, this effect is likely to be small. As emphasized earlier, the effects of intervention depend on whether the policy is sterilized and can vary from country to country, especially with the degree of financial integration. In less integrated economies, these effects could be more important.

Figure 5.1 shows the current account from 1985 to 2012 for three groups of countries. Calvo, Leiderman, and Reinhart (1996) raised the "problem" of capital inflows in the early 1990s, when there were relatively large current account deficits, which, as discussed earlier, accompanied an exchange rate appreciation and overheating. In Latin America, this was the end of the debt crisis and the renewed access to international capital markets. The widening of the current account ended with the Asian crisis, but deficits remained somewhat longer in Latin America than elsewhere because of the sharp decline in terms of trade, which lasted until commodity prices began to rise in the mid-2000s.

During the 2000s, current account deficits have been more moderate, and some countries have even enjoyed surpluses. Only recently has the current account deficit begun to widen, but the cause should be associated with strong growth, not capital inflows. However, net foreign capital can increase deficits.

The experience of the 1990s resulted from several factors. Latin American economies were coming out of the debt crisis with much better macroeconomic policies, and there was abundant liquidity in global markets and thus a relaxation of foreign liquidity constraints. These are conditions that do not last forever, and they may induce vulnerabilities when a reversal occurs. In addition, policies frequently leaned with the wind, as discussed in previous chapters. This procyclicality induced a sharp boom in economic activity, which, more often than not, comes to an end with a sharp reversal of flows. For this reason, it is important to implement policies that are coherent and able to adjust smoothly to changes in international conditions.

An important difference between now and then is the evolution in terms of trade. The recent low current account deficits have largely stemmed from strong terms of trade. The increase in terms of trade, other things being equal, results in an appreciation of the exchange rate. For given levels of domestic output and expenditure, the real exchange rate must appreciate. In addition, the increased value of domestic production vis-à-vis foreign production and saving of part of the terms of trade shock lead to an improvement in the current account. When countries have a surplus, they become exporters of capital, not importers. It is still possible that improvements in international financial conditions lead to a declining surplus, putting additional pressure on the exchange rate, but currently the exchange rate evolution is primarily dominated by terms of trade rather than capital inflows.

Country Examples

The current account balance and net capital inflows for Chile for the period 2006 to 2012 are presented in figure 5.2. During this period, the current account deficit moved close to the evolution of the terms of trade. The deficit of late 2008 into 2009 was largely due to the sharp decline in the price of copper. In 2008 and 2011, net capital inflows were significantly larger than the current account deficit, which, in turn, was relatively small. In these two periods, the central bank of Chile decided to accumulate reserves to strengthen the international liquidity position and support the exchange rate.[9] There was certainly no problem with capital inflows. Moreover, despite the intervention, the current account deteriorated, but mostly because of the decline in terms of trade.

By late 2011, the current account was almost in balance, and capital inflows reached a peak of about 6 percent of GDP. By contrast, in 2006–07 and 2010, there were net outflows because the current account was in surplus. There was no inflows problem, and during the years of international reserve accumulation net inflows were more related to the increase in the level of reserves than to large current account deficits. Indeed, the year 2008 in Chile was a year of surge in net capital inflows, but this surge was mostly induced by a policy decision to accumulate reserves.

---

9. The first intervention was from March 2008 until October 2008. The second intervention was the entire year of 2011. The figure presents accumulated yearly data, and so intervention periods appear approximately two quarters ahead.

Figure 5.2 Current account balance and net capital inflows in Chile (accumulated annual flows), 2006–12

percent of GDP

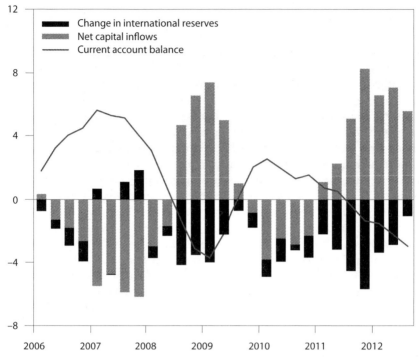

Note: An increase in international reserves appears with a negative sign since it is an outflow. So negative numbers for changes in reserves are periods of accumulation (intervention).

Source: Central Bank of Chile.

Based on the idea presented by Blanchard and Leigh (2012) of looking at forecast errors to identify the effects of policies, the following calculation may provide further evidence of the role of accumulation of reserves in inducing capital inflows. In the Central Bank of Chile's *Monetary Policy Report* of September 2007 (issued before the bank decided to intervene in March 2008), the current account was forecast to be a surplus of 2.6 percent of GDP (Central Bank of Chile 2007). However, it turned out to be a deficit of 1.5 percent, despite reserve accumulation of about 4 percent of GDP. Therefore, the accumulation of reserves has no distinguishable effect on the current account and hence should have resulted in increased private capital inflows.

Similarly, in the September 2010 issue of *Monetary Policy Report*, before any decision on intervention was made, the current account forecast was a deficit of 2.5 percent of GDP. After the intervention of about 6 percent of GDP during 2011, the current account ended up with a deficit of 1.3 percent of GDP. One could attribute this fall in the current account deficit to reserve accumulation, but it was mostly due to the price of copper: the initial forecast was $2.90 per pound, but it turned out to be $4 per pound. The private sector forecasts were not very different from the official ones.

These two episodes show that capital inflows to the Chilean economy increased mostly due to the accumulation of reserves rather than an exogenous increase in the appetite of foreigners to take positions in Chile.

Figure 5.3 shows the current account balance and net capital inflows of four other countries: Brazil, Colombia, and Peru in Latin America, as well as Israel, a country that has accumulated important levels of reserves and sterilized its monetary effects. The movements in the current accounts coincide more with terms of trade and economic activity than with reserve accumulation. Only in Israel does the accumulation of reserves co-move with an improvement in the current account balance. However, the orders of magnitude are quite different: Reserves move much more than current account balances. Therefore, the increase in reserves holdings seems to have a small effect on the current account, and therefore its effects are primarily on capital inflows. This finding supports the claim of the previous section that dFA/dR is probably much closer to one than zero, and conversely dCA/dR is closer to zero than one in the countries shown in figures 5.2 and 5.3. The only exception is perhaps Israel, which could be more in between. Additional research is needed, however, to estimate the effects of intervention on the current account and capital flows, and especially to understand what could explain differences across countries.

Explaining Capital Inflow Surges

Many emerging-market economies have accumulated massive amounts of reserves, and thus the data reveal a large number of capital inflow surges, when it is more appropriate to think of international reserve surges. This surge of reserves is an outflow that could be offset by private inflows.

As noted earlier in this chapter, pull factors originate in the growing domestic demand for foreign financing, and push factors originate in the increased foreign demand for domestic assets stemming from external developments. This analysis suggests a third factor—the reserves (or policy-pull) factor.

Using a large sample of emerging-market countries, Ghosh et al. (2012) have analyzed surges of capital inflows. They look at significant changes in net private capital inflows from 1980 to 2009. The more recent surges are therefore not included, but their work is broad enough to use their results to interpret the sources of recent capital inflows. Table 5.1 shows some aggregate groups of countries (see appendix table 5A.1 at the end of this chapter for details). Ghosh et al. (2012) use two methodologies to determine whether in a single year there is a surge of capital inflows. The first is the traditional definition using thresholds—that is, a surge is when net capital inflows are larger than

Figure 5.3   Current account balance and net capital inflows in Brazil, Peru, Colombia, and Israel (accumulated annual flows), 2006–11

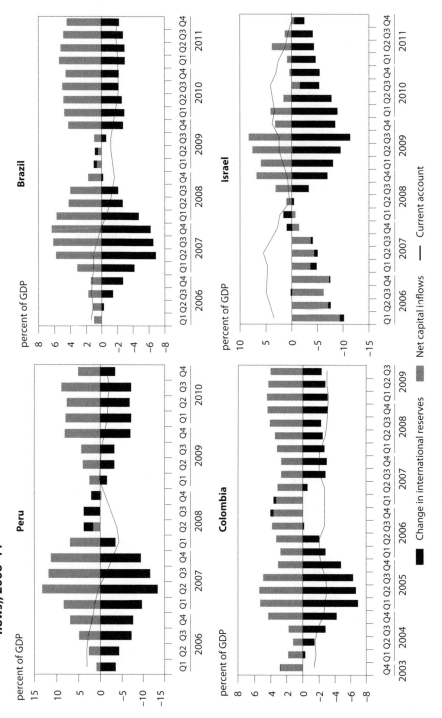

Note: A negative number for change in reserves (outflow) is accumulation.

Source: International Monetary Fund, *International Financial Statistics* database.

Table 5.1   Surges of capital inflows, 1990s and 2000s (percent of GDP)

Region/period	Net capital inflows	Current account	Change in reserves
Latin America			
1990s	7.5	−4.6	2.5
2000s	6.7	−1.7	4.2
Asia			
1990s	7.6	−4.8	2.8
2000s	3.7	3.2	5.6
Europe			
1990s	11.0	−6.4	4.4
2000s	17.3	−10.5	3.1

Sources: Ghosh et al. (2012) for net capital inflows; International Monetary Fund, *International Financial Statistics,* for current account and reserve accumulation.

a given threshold. The second approach is based on statistical clustering in which countries are classified as having a surge of inflows, normal flows, or outflows. Both techniques yield similar results. Here, surge episodes are considered regardless of the method, and when both methodologies coincide defining a surge, the common period is used.

In the 1990s, capital inflows to Asia and Latin America were more significant than in the 2000s. In Asia, the average surge was 7.6 percent of GDP, and the current account deficit was 4.8 percent of GDP. Similarly, in Asia, several countries ran significant current account imbalances before the crisis. By contrast, during the 2000s only Korea had surge episodes, but, as the tables show, they were mostly associated with a large accumulation of reserves, while running current account surpluses, i.e., exporting capital.

In Latin America, net capital inflows during the 2000s were slightly less than in the 1990s, although the breakdown between current account deficit and accumulation of reserves was quite different. During the 1990s, there was much less reserve accumulation, and consistent with figure 5.1, net capital inflows were indeed the counterpart of significant current account deficits.[10]

The situation in emerging Europe was the opposite. Surges of capital inflows were much more frequent and larger than those in Latin America and Asia. In addition, during the 2000s capital flows responded much more to the very large current account deficits—that is, they were more than double those experienced in the other regions. In hindsight, emerging Europe really suffered from capital inflows–unsustainable current account problem.

---

10. The current account deficit plus reserve accumulation does not add up to equal net capital inflows for several reasons. First, there are errors and omissions. Second, Gosh et al. (2012) consider only private capital inflows and exclude official lending and exceptional financing. Finally, there may be discrepancies in the data used. However, the broad trends discussed in the text are not affected by these discrepancies.

According to the evidence, then, the interpretation of surges in capital inflows is not unique, and therefore the policy implications are not straightforward. Indeed, recent research estimating the determinants of capital inflows does not include reserve accumulation as an explanatory factor.[11] On the one hand, Ghosh et al. (2012) include variables that may be triggers of intervention, such as deviation of exchange rates and a definition of the optimal current account, among others. On the other hand, Fratzscher (2011) includes in a factor model the current account and the stock of reserves, but not the relevant one, the flow of reserves. Therefore, the literature does not help to gauge the magnitude of the effects of reserve accumulation on capital inflows and the current account, which is a key parameter from the point of view of policy.

Another relevant issue is whether capital inflows are the result of reserve accumulation with a limited, or nonexistent, current account deficit. This appears to be the case in most Latin American and Asian countries during the 2000s. During the 1990s, large capital inflows were financing relatively larger current account deficits, although not in the magnitudes found in the emerging European countries. In most recent years, net capital inflows to Latin America and Asia have been accompanied by an increased demand for international reserves. But what would have happened to the current account and net inflows had international reserves not increased? The country evidence shown earlier suggests that the current account would not have been significantly different, but inflows would have been lower since there would not have been additional demand to accumulate reserves (figures 5.2 and 5.3).

From a policy perspective, this discussion raises the issue of capital controls. The evidence, as well as practice, indicates that capital controls, and accumulation of reserves, have been used to mitigate the exchange rate effects of capital flows. In this regard, a successful strategy would call for reducing the current account deficit. However, it is not clear why this may be welfare enhancing, in particular in capital-scarce economies running sustainable levels of current account balances. A capital control that cannot reduce the current account deficit will not have persistent effects on the exchange rate.

Gross Flows and Financial Stability

International financial integration may be welfare enhancing, but it also may be the source of wide boom-bust cycles, accompanied by exchange rate pressures. This is the macroeconomic stability dimension of net capital flows. But gross financial flows are central to financial stability. The composition of capital flows, and thus the nature and volume of gross flows, is an important determinant of the vulnerabilities of emerging-market economies.

---

11. There is a serious endogeneity problem with using reserve accumulation as a regressor. The same problem applies to using the current account. Adequate instruments are not easy to find.

Figure 5.4 Capital flows to emerging-market economies, 2007–12

billions of US dollars (12-month accumulation)

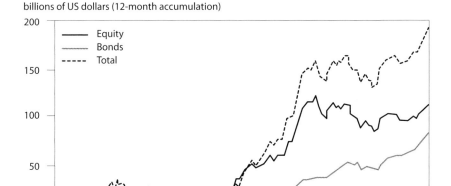

Source: Emerging Portfolio Fund Research.

Figure 5.4 shows a sharp rise in the lead-up to 2011 in gross capital inflows to emerging-market economies. But those data are just a fraction of the total gross inflows. They are a sample of portfolio flows to Africa, Asia, emerging Europe, Latin America, and the Middle East and of global investments in emerging economies from a variety of investment funds. They include only bonds and equity, and thus they exclude foreign direct investment and cross-border credit flows. These figures, then, do not give a clear picture of the net inflows to emerging-market economies. However, they are a good approximation of the risk appetite for emerging-market assets.

The concern about gross capital inflows is that they are highly procyclical, exacerbating business cycle fluctuations, overshooting in the upturn and reverting rapidly in the downturn. These characteristics suggest common push factors at work that could magnify the business cycle.

The concern about financial stability requires looking beyond net flows to gross flows, their volume, and their composition. Particularly relevant to emerging-market economies are sudden stops. Capital tends to flow massively and gradually in the upturn, but in times of crisis those flows may suddenly be interrupted. The probability of a sudden stop depends on the weakness of the economy. An economy well prepared to face sudden stops—for example, by allowing exchange rate flexibility and having an adequate level of international reserves—may be able to prevent them.

Sudden stops of capital inflows occur as often in advanced economies as in emerging markets (Cowan et al. 2008), but they do not always coincide with a reversal in the financial account. The difference between advanced and developing economies is that in the former domestic residents tend to compensate for the sudden stop of inflows with a reversal of outflows. Therefore, sudden stops of inflows coincide with reversals in the capital account when the interruption of inflows is not compensated for by offsetting changes in outflows. This scenario occurs more frequently in emerging-market economies with low holdings of international assets and few policy tools. But the resilience of emerging markets to the global financial crisis shows that these conditions have improved.

Volatility

Foreign direct investment (FDI) is an important component of foreign financing, and it is also the more stable one. Figure 5.5 shows that for Latin America FDI is the most important and also the more stable component of gross flows. By contrast, cross-border credit flows, which are mostly the "other investment" component, and portfolio flows are quite volatile. Cross-border credit flows, which were the main source of capital flows, have become a small proportion of total flows, which may explain the resilience of financial flows to the region. From a growth point of view, composition matters. As the evidence presented in Kose, Prasad, and Terrones (2009) suggests, portfolio inflows and FDI are more growth promoting than cross-border banking.[12]

Although portfolio inflows are volatile, changes in asset prices may reduce the incentives for sharp swings in the equity component of these flows. However, significant changes in asset prices may affect the health of the financial system and, through the value of collateral, the financial conditions of the economy.

Furthermore, as reported in the detailed review of Jeanne, Subramanian, and Williamson (2012), there is evidence that countries that have grown to rely less, not more, on foreign savings. Countries that have grown quickly, especially in East Asia, have relied more strongly on a very high saving rate and capital accumulation, and so their needs for net foreign capital are relatively small.

Figure 5.5 shows another relevant development in Latin America that mirrors conditions in most emerging markets and advanced economies: Gross financial flows have increased. Although net flows may be stable, gross flows have increased substantially. Indeed, between 2005 and 2010–11 gross inflows, especially portfolio inflows and debt, almost tripled while FDI was much

---

12. See also Borensztein, De Gregorio, and Lee (1998) for the growth-promoting effects of FDI.

Figure 5.5 Gross capital inflows to Latin America, 1985–2011

billions of US dollars

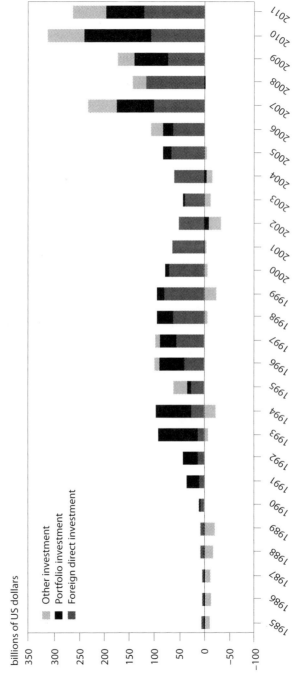

Source: International Monetary Fund, International Financial Statistics database.

more stable. As for outflows, the significant increase in financial integration and portfolio diversification creates opportunities but also entails risks. This is consistent with the evidence on increased integration as income grows (see Obstfeld 2009).

Behavior of International Banks

An important characteristic of Latin American banking systems has been the behavior of international banks. There is abundant literature on the role and impact of foreign banks (e.g., Claessens and van Horen 2012), and chapter 4 presents some characteristics of foreign banks in Latin America. This section looks at the behavior of these banks during the global financial crisis.

Figure 5.6 shows the evolution of cross-border credit flows for Latin America, Asia, and emerging Europe from 2005 to 2011. The peak of the crisis saw outflows of cross-border credit in Latin America and Asia, which were sharper in Asia. The recovery in mid-2009 was also strong in both regions. The dashed line in figure 5.6 shows the evolution of cross-border credit flows in emerging Europe.

The decline of credit flows in Latin America and Asia in 2008 can be interpreted in two ways. First—and this has been the most common interpretation—it could have been the result of a sudden stop in credit flows, which is a supply contraction. A sudden stop and its contagion of emerging markets were a critical factor during the Asian crisis (Calvo 1998). For this reason, the risks of financial integration have raised concerns on the policy front because economies may be exposed to a sudden stop. A second interpretation of the decline in credit is a fall in demand. Indeed, aggregate demand collapsed worldwide in late 2008 and early 2009. The consumption of durable goods and investment were interrupted by the escalation of uncertainty. And yet the data on the interest rates paid on foreign loans and debt by domestic investors did not reveal the increase suggested by a supply shock. Indeed, in Chile the cost of foreign borrowing declined (see figure 4.5, chapter 4). In the end, then, the rapid recovery of credit and activity—evidence that there was not much financial stress—as well as evidence showing that interest rates were low during this period appear to support the second interpretation.

Associating the decline in cross-border lending to a demand shock is not so straightforward and some caveats are required. As discussed in chapter 4 many corporations in emerging markets had access to credit lines during the crisis, and the fall in demand was also triggered by a fear of losing access to new credit. They chose not to use available credit and keep it for unforeseen future needs. Therefore, the decline in demand could have been due in part to the desire to preserve credit lines in case of a supply disruption.

Meanwhile, there were also some supply frictions because many banks in advanced economies had serious problems to intermediate. Nevertheless, these frictions were for the most part resolved in large emerging markets by using the swap lines with the US Federal Reserve and the several forms in

Figure 5.6　Quarterly change in cross-border banking claims, 2005Q1–2011Q4

billions of US dollars

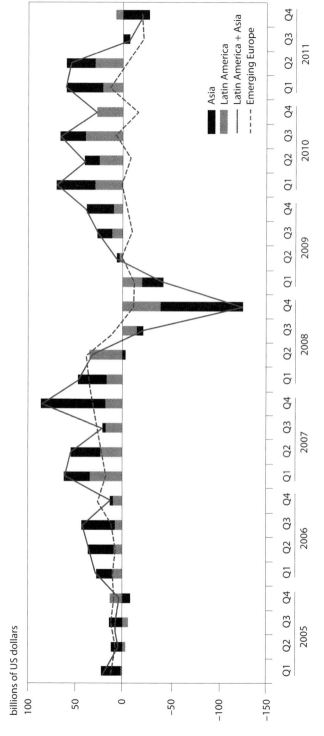

Legend:
- Asia
- Latin America
- Latin America + Asia
- Emerging Europe

Source: Bank for International Settlements, consolidated banking statistics (immediate borrower basis).

Figure 5.7   International financial integration in Latin America, 1980–2010

international assets plus liabilities as a percent of GDP

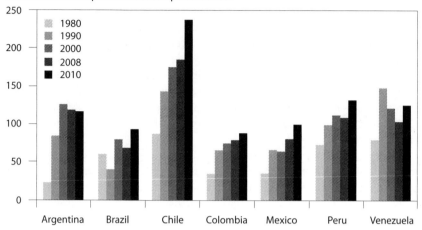

Source: Lane and Milesi-Ferretti's revised and updated External Wealth of Nations (EWN) II database (based on Lane and Milesi-Ferretti 2007).

which emerging economies provided liquidity in foreign currency during the height of the crisis.

In summary, international financial integration has increased in Latin America (figure 5.7). The larger volume of gross flows has resulted in emerging-market economies possessing larger international assets and liabilities. Except for Argentina and Venezuela, the Latin American countries under study here were financially more open on the eve of the global financial crisis than in 1990 and 2000. And most of them have increased their openness since the crisis. What is remarkable is that despite the fact that financial integration has increased, and thus these countries have more exposed balance sheets, their resilience was much greater during the crisis than in previous global crises. Therefore, it can be concluded that being more open to trade as well as to cross-border flows does not necessarily lead to crisis and sudden stops. The appropriate policy frameworks and policy spaces may mitigate the risks of greater integration in the global economy, and the experience of Latin America is noteworthy.

Managing Capital Inflows in an Inflation Targeting Regime

The first line of defense against massive capital inflows is exchange rate flexibility. Frequently, exchange rate rigidities and unsustainable defenses of parities that are far from their fundamental values give way to speculation against the foreign exchange regime.

The literature on speculative attacks shows how an exchange rate that is inconsistent with the rest of policy actions can trigger massive capital outflows that end up forcing its abandonment. The same rationale applies to inflows. If the exchange rate level to be defended is inconsistent with economic fundamentals, massive inflows may speed up because sooner or later there will be an appreciation. Investors take advantage of a relatively cheap currency to invest in the country before appreciation, so they can have a significant capital gain once the appreciation takes place. Thus within a framework of capital mobility, foreign exchange flexibility avoids one-sided bets on the exchange rate and eliminates a perverse dynamic when facing an appreciation: defense to avoid appreciation→capital inflows→capitulation on the exchange rate→defense at a new level and so on.

Monetary policy in the context of an inflation targeting regime also contributes to stability by leaning against the wind. Capital inflows lead, other things equal, to an appreciation of the currency, which reduces inflationary pressures, allowing easing of monetary policy. This easing, in turn, reduces incentives for capital inflows and reduces the pressure on the currency. Furthermore, an inflation targeting regime with a floating exchange rate acts as a good buffer for smoothing the impact of changes in capital flow cycles. Meanwhile, the same monetary policy reaction to a currency appreciation that reduces inflationary pressures allows limiting the currency appreciation process by narrowing interest rate differentials. As pointed out in the next section, shielding monetary policy via capital controls may lead to excessively high interest rates.

A floating exchange rate and an inflation targeting regime may, however, be insufficient for stabilizing large amounts of capital inflows. The appreciation that results from massive capital inflows and a credit boom cycle may require other instruments to stabilize the economy and ensure the smooth functioning of the financial system. Under such circumstances, fiscal policy plays a key role. Countercyclical fiscal policy should relieve pressure on the currency and stem the boom. Unfortunately, the space to use it actively, and in a relevant magnitude, is limited.

Another capital inflow problem in emerging markets is bubble formation. Because capital is being driven by the financial accounts, with a boom in domestic activity and a widening of the current account, domestic asset prices may rise beyond fundamentals. The problem in emerging markets is that the bubble may be in the exchange rate. In this way, all assets become overpriced, not necessarily by higher prices in domestic currency (which may also be happening) but by the increasing value of the currency.

A much debated issue in industrial countries, as discussed in chapter 4, has been whether tightening monetary policy can help burst a bubble in asset prices. This problem is even more acute for capital inflows. If capital inflows fuel a bubble in the exchange rate, tightening monetary policy will actually induce more capital inflows.

For this reason, other tools cannot be ruled out, in particular exchange rate intervention. It acts directly to solve the problem, and it will be most effective if transitory and massive. It is difficult, though, to detect significant deviations of the currency from fundamentals, which happen infrequently. Therefore, intervention to burst a potential bubble must be exceptional. Capital controls are unlikely to serve this purpose, as discussed in what follows. Indeed, it is important to distinguish—although it is not always possible—between the use of controls for net capital inflows and for gross inflows. Gloss inflows are related to financial stability, and capital controls are part of the toolkit of macroprudential policies.

Capital Controls

Capital controls are used for a variety of purposes, which frequently are not clearly spelled out. They are used

1. to reduce the volume of capital inflows,
2. to avoid an appreciation of the currency,
3. to achieve monetary policy independence, and
4. to change the composition of inflows.

Rationales 1, 2, and 3 are related to macroeconomic stability and rationales 1 and 4 are related to financial stability. When applied to rationales 1 and 4, capital controls belong in the macroprudential toolkit. Avoiding an appreciation of the currency may be justified in terms of financial stability, but there are more efficient ways to deal with the risk of currency mismatches in the financial system, as discussed in chapter 4.

Among the rationales indicated above, the most important have been 1 and 2: limit capital inflows and avoid an appreciation of the currency.[13] Broadly, significant effects on the exchange rate have not been detected, but some small effects have been found on the volume of inflows. The most frequent finding is that capital controls affect the composition of inflows, increasing maturity.[14] This effect stems from the fact that market-based controls act like a Tobin tax, making short-term flows more expensive by acting as an upfront fee proportional to the volume of inflows. By making the short-term inflows more expensive, the controls tilt the maturity of external flows to the long term.

Much of the evidence was provided by Chile's use of an unremunerated reserve requirement (URR) for capital inflows. It is ironic that in Chile, the poster child for capital controls during the 1990s, skepticism remains about their usefulness, and they have not been used for almost 15 years. The reason

---

13. Extensive research has been devoted to evaluating the effectiveness of capital controls in many dimensions, most recently by Magud, Reinhart, and Rogoff (2011); Ostry et al. (2011); and Habermeier, Kokenyne, and Baba (2011). For an early review, see Edwards (1999).

14. During the 1970s, Japan used market-based capital controls to reduce short-term inflows. Using propensity score matching to handle endogeneity problems, Esaka and Takagi (2012) find that the controls were fairly ineffective. They conclude, "market-based controls must be nearly prohibitive, perhaps combined with administrative measures, to be effective in a meaningful way."

is that they have not been needed in the current macroeconomic framework. Indeed, progress in macroeconomic and financial management can dispense with the need for capital controls. However, they are a valid tool, and for this reason Chile's central bank and the government have intentionally maintained the bank's legal authority to impose controls in free trade agreements (FTAs).[15]

The URR required that a fraction of the capital inflow be deposited in a non-interest-bearing account in Chile's central bank. The URR was introduced in June 1991 at a rate of 20 percent of the inflow for a period of 3 to 12 months, depending on the maturity and the nature of the credit. Trade credit was excluded. Later, in 1992 and then in 1995, the base was broadened to include foreign currency deposits and the proceeds from the issuance of ADRs (American depositary receipts). The rate was increased to 30 percent and the period set at 12 months, regardless of the term of the credit. The tax equivalent was between 100 and 200 basis points.[16] The URR was discontinued in 1998.

According to the empirical evidence, the effects of the URR on the volume of inflows and on the exchange rate were insignificant. Only Gallego, Hernández, and Schmidt-Hebbel (1999) found significant effects on total flows: for the whole period, a total impact on net inflows of about 2 percent of GDP, with total capital inflows that amounted to nearly 27 percent of GDP in the same period. Clearly, it is a very small effect and is not robust across studies.

Some small, short-run effects of the URR have been found on the real exchange rate. Edwards and Rigobon (2009) estimate some statistically significant effects on the extent of the appreciation of the peso. However, the magnitude of such effects is also economically small. According to their estimates, the elimination of the URR, from its maximum, would have appreciated the exchange rate between 2 and 2.5 percent. In any case, it is useful to recall that in Chile the most appreciated real exchange rate in the last 25 years was in 1997, a year that featured capital controls, massive reserve accumulation, an exchange rate band, and high interest rates.

The most robust finding across different studies is that the URR affected the composition of flows, increasing long-term flows and reducing short-term flows. That is, the resulting composition of external debt tilted to longer maturities. However, when the effects of the URR on composition are quantitatively evaluated, the conclusion is that the effects are small. Cowan and De Gregorio (2007) have found that short-term debt would have declined by 0.5 to 1 percent of GDP as a result of the URR, which at that time represented less than 2 percent of external debt.

---

15. For example, the FTA between Chile and the United States imposes some constraints on the use of controls, although it does not rule them out. For further discussion, see Cowan and De Gregorio (2007, section 7).

16. This review of the findings is based mostly on De Gregorio, Edwards, and Valdés (2000). Cowan and De Gregorio (2007) revise the evidence and calculate the magnitude of the effects when they appear statistically significant. For an early assessment of exchange rates, see Valdés-Prieto and Soto (1996).

Colombia used the URR from 1993 to 1998 and again from 2007 to 2008. The first episode was constrained to external borrowing and the second to portfolio inflows. Researchers have found no effects on the exchange rate and limited effects on the volume of inflows.[17] The only significant effect was a shift in the composition of inflows toward longer-term maturities.[18]

The other important case of capital controls in the region has been the financial transaction tax (IOF) in Brazil. The formal argument for introducing controls was to protect competitiveness, and thus in March 2008 the government levied a 1.5 percent tax on fixed-income foreign investment. This tax was reduced to zero at the peak of the currency crisis and then reintroduced in late 2009 based on the rhetorical argument of a "currency war." The tax has undergone some modifications over time. The IOF was zeroed again in June 2013 in response to a stronger US dollar. The main finding from recent research is that the effect of the tax on the magnitude of the inflows is muted, although some small short-run effects when controls are relaxed have been found (Jinjarak, Noy, and Zheng 2012). This effect could be related to signals about the course of future controls. As for the effects on exchange rates, Chamon and Garcia (2013) find no significant effects, concluding the IOF tax did not prevent appreciation of the real. They argue that the "real game changer" of the appreciating trend of the real during most of 2011 was a surprise interest rate cut in September 2011.

The finding that capital controls can change the composition of inflows has been adopted to justify their use as a macroprudential tool to reduce financial vulnerability by lengthening the maturity of external liabilities. The simple calculation made by Cowan and De Gregorio (2007) for the Chilean case reveals that the magnitude of this effect could be small. Surveys of the existing evidence and proposals should move beyond checking statistical significance and evaluate the size of the effects.

In late 2010, Korea implemented a more direct and cleaner way of changing the maturity of external liabilities. Because authorities believed banks' external funding was reaching dangerous proportions, they decided to apply a capital levy on noncore liabilities denominated in foreign currency.

Earlier, in June 2010, Korean authorities began to introduce measures to limit the impact of foreign finance disruptions because of the high reliance of domestic banks on foreign borrowing. The levy, enacted in December 2010, consisted of an annualized tax of 20 basis points on the wholesale foreign exchange–denominated liabilities of banks, with maturities up to 12 months. Lower rates were applied to maturities of over a year. In an assessment of this macroprudential policy, Bruno and Shin (2013) demonstrate that the authori-

---

17. For recent estimations of the effects of capital controls during the 2000s, see Baba and Kokenyne (2011).

18. See Cardenas and Barrera (1997) for more on Colombia's experience with capital controls in the 1990s. There is no quantitative evaluation of the magnitude of these effects.

ties were successful in reducing the sensitivity of banking capital inflows to global financial conditions.

One very relevant topic not covered by the literature on the effects of capital controls is the sensitivity of flows to global liquidity conditions. Capital controls can foster financial stability but that applies only to banking liabilities, and thus the macro effect is more limited. In Korea, the increase in noncore liabilities has been a serious concern because of their impact on financial stability. During the 2000s, noncore liabilities as a share of M2 increased from about 15 to 50 percent (Hahm, Shin, and Shin 2012). Moreover, the volatility of cross-border banking flows in Korea and Asia in general has been much more pronounced than in Latin America (figure 5.6).

The excessive vulnerability stemming from cross-border credit is not a new concern; in the Latin American region it dates back to the debt crisis. Excessive foreign borrowing caused the debt crisis of the early 1980s. Foreign credit was suddenly interrupted as Mexico declared that it could not pay its obligations. The crisis spread over Latin America, kicking off the lost decade. It led to a major revision of regulations to prevent such an event from happening again, and so cross-border banking claims were clearly not a problem in the region during the global financial crisis, despite the fluctuations shown in figure 5.6. Strengthening financial regulation and applying macroprudential rules are a good route to follow. However, the objectives must be clear, and the tools used must be the most efficient ones for the kind of financial stability being sought. Controls may be efficient or distorting, and this is an important factor to take into account when choosing instruments (Jeanne, Subramanian, and Williamson 2012).

Another important and common finding is that monetary policy has gained independence with capital controls. In other words, interest rate differentials have gone up in the presence of capital controls. However, it is not clear whether having wider interest rate differentials is good or bad, so it is also not clear, as discussed below, that this finding represents a beneficial effect of capital controls.

It is well known that in a flexible exchange rate regime monetary policy is independent of foreign monetary conditions. Central banks can set interest rates, and a key transmission mechanism is the effect on the exchange rate. In contrast, capital controls are intended to eliminate the impossible trinity: set interest rate without repercussions for the exchange rate. However, that means that the main channel of monetary policy will be to affect the financial conditions. It is not clear that a balance between exchange rate appreciation and tighter financial conditions calls for eliminating the exchange rate channel. Moreover, the presence of capital controls that allow for greater interest rate differentials with the rest of the world may increase the burden on small firms that have access mainly to short-term financing.[19]

---

19. This issue has been raised and documented for Chile by Forbes (2007).

The monetary policy independence argument is one of the main perils of capital controls. If capital controls do not affect the exchange rate significantly, they may create a false sense of security on the exchange rate front. Indeed, according to the evidence, the wedge in the covered interest rate parity condition increases,[20] but the orders of magnitude are relatively small. In addition, it is not clear why covered interest rate differentials increase, but, as indicated by the evidence discussed here, this has no significant effects on the exchange rate.[21] It may be possible that this is a result of a very short-lived effect on the exchange rate, as some evidence indicates, or other signaling effects, such as fear of appreciation and lack of additional instruments, may be offsetting the effects of interest rate differentials on the exchange rate.

The use of capital controls may give central bankers the impression that they can raise interest rates significantly without affecting the exchange rate. But if controls have small effects on the exchange rate, more severe monetary policy steps that lead to higher differentials will cause an appreciation of the currency. The reason for this appreciation would be the misperception that the currency is immune to monetary policy.

Therefore, the finding that capital controls increase monetary independence coupled with no effects on the exchange rate could simply be interpreted as follows: In the presence of capital controls central banks raise interest rates higher than they might otherwise. The fact that the most appreciated real exchange rates in Chile and Brazil occurred in the mid-1990s and the late 2000s, respectively, in the presence of capital controls and large interest rate differentials lends support to this interpretation. In Chile, during the URR period ex post interest rate differentials in the same currency fluctuated between 5 and 16 percent (De Gregorio, Edwards, and Valdés 2000). In Brazil, what made a difference in the weakening of the exchange rate has been the sharp decline in the Selic rate (monetary policy rate in Brazil). In Chile, during the 1990s the capital inflow surge peaked, and by late 1996 the monetary policy rate had reached about 14 percent.[22] The monetary policy rate in the United States, the federal funds rate, was at 5.25 percent. Brazil had a similar experience. By mid-2008, when the real reached its maximum, the Selic rate was at 12 percent, and it continued to rise to 13.75 percent. The fed funds rate was at 2 percent. Later, the real suffered again from strong pressures, reaching a historical maximum, about 1.6 reals per dollar. The interest rate reached a postcrisis maximum of 12 percent, whereas the fed funds rate was at the zero lower bound. It was not capital controls but the reduction in interest rates from 12 to 7 percent in the context of a weak economy that sent the real back to levels closer to 2 reals per

---

20. Eduardo Levy-Yeyati, "Are Capital Controls Effective?" VoxEu.org, January 20, 2011.

21. It is not entirely clear whether this is caused by deviations between forward and realized exchange rates or it is simply a matter of policymakers exhausting the wedge.

22. By that time, monetary policy was set in UF, an indexed unit of account, so to have the nominal equivalent, which is the one used in the text, I use the yearly inflation rate at that time.

dollar. Of course, at those interest rate levels whoever can take a position in domestic assets will do so.[23]

Capital controls cannot be discarded from the macrofinancial toolkit, but the perils are associated with their use: excessive interest rate differentials, fostering capital inflows, and strengthening the currency. In this case, the perverse dynamics mentioned earlier—defense to avoid appreciation→capital inflows→capitulation on the exchange rate→defense at a new level, and so on—would have a new stage: defense to avoid appreciation→capital inflows→capital controls→capitulation on the exchange rate→defense at a new level, and so on.

Concluding Remarks

The problem of capital inflows is not easy to detect, and therefore the appropriate policy responses are not obvious. Net capital flows may just be the result of large current account deficits, or the causality may go in reverse.

The analysis is complicated by international reserve accumulation. Inflows may just be a way of accommodating the central bank's greater demand for foreign currency for its reserves. It is possible to argue that reserve accumulation could "absorb" a shock to capital inflows, thereby preventing a widening of the current account and an appreciation of the currency. However, the causal evidence presented here, together with the limited, transitory effects that intervention has on the exchange rate, makes it likely that this absorption effect is small. More research is needed to evaluate these mechanisms.

Contrary to the experience of the 1990s, when capital inflows financed current account deficits, the most recent experience has been characterized by very limited deficits (and surpluses in many cases), which suggests that surges in net capital inflows are very much related to exchange rate interventions. Capital flows may be the response of foreign investors to some underlying domestic distortion—for example, a temporary defense of an undervalued currency and high domestic interest rates. This may have been the situation in Chile during the 1990s and in Brazil more recently. Indeed, during the recent crisis the Chilean economy performed much better than during the Asian crisis, and capital controls were not used at all during the 2000s.

In adopting capital controls, policymakers cannot afford to wait until all the analytical questions have been answered. However, it is important to have a good sense of the distortions as well as the purposes of different policy tools. Transparency in this area reinforces the effectiveness of policies. In many instances, policymakers express concern about the vulnerabilities stemming

---

23. Of course, the evidence is also consistent with a very strong economy, high neutral interest rates, strong inflows, and capital controls as a mitigating measure. This was indeed the narrative during the 1990s in Chile, and some of the recent one in Brazil. However, it is difficult to sustain this argument for long taking into account the experience of Chile after 1997 and Brazil after 2010.

from capital inflows, when the real concern is competitiveness and the level of the exchange rate. This issue is at the core of discussions on capital controls.

If the problem is massive capital flows that widen the current account deficit and generate an appreciation of the exchange rate, broad-based capital controls could be applied. However, their effectiveness on this front is questionable, and perhaps to be effective they must really be broad-based. This policy could affect the gross volume of flows, but it is a regular capital control, not a macroprudential tool. If the concern is about financial stability, targeting particular flows, or more properly targeting particular components of the balance sheets of different agents in the economy, may be the right response, and these policies would be undertaken for macroprudential reasons.

A control intended to affect specific components of capital flows may end up shifting the composition of capital flows toward noncontrolled segments of financial markets without affecting their overall volume. For this reason, policies to reduce net capital flows should be broad-based. Regardless of their effectiveness, some broad-based policies, much disputed, have the effect of a general tax on capital flows. Measures applied to particular components could be helpful in terms of financial stability, but they are unlikely to change net capital flows significantly.

There is a serious lack of research pinning down the magnitudes of the effects of different policies. The experience with sterilized intervention indicates that its effects are nonzero, small, and short-lived. It appears that capital controls in many countries have had at most small effects on exchange rates and capital flows. But the aggregate evidence shows that the effects of reserve accumulation on the current account could be larger than one would conclude from adding the evidence for specific effects, especially in countries with capital controls (Bergsten and Gagnon 2012). The massive evidence on particular policies seems to be inconsistent with the aggregate evidence. An effort is needed to integrate the knowledge available and develop more effective policy advice.

Here a conceptual caveat is in order on the issue of capital controls and capital account opening. An economy closed to financial flows will have a balanced current account. If it is a capital-scarce economy, like a typical developing country, it will have a higher interest rate, higher savings, lower investment, and a more depreciated real exchange rate than if it were financially open. However, not allowing flows has welfare costs. The issue in the real world is economies that are actually open to financial flows. The fact that the controls in many emerging markets have shown limited effectiveness stems from the fact that they can be circumvented, or that limiting some flows may generate other types of flows to meet their international financial needs, or that the magnitude of the controls must be high in order to have relevant effects. It will always be possible to introduce controls large enough to affect the total volume of flows and the exchange rate. However, that may not be true in emerging-market economies. Indeed, the levels of capital controls required to be effective may be prohibitive, or they may harm domestic financial conditions. Thus the political equilibrium leads to some capital controls that, even though they have limited effectiveness, at least demonstrate the concern and activism of policymakers.

Finally, it is interesting to note that even as financial integration has increased in Latin America, resilience has increased as well.[24] Experience has shown that countries more open to trade are not necessarily more vulnerable to the global business cycle. Along the same lines, countries more integrated financially are not condemned to financial crisis, macroeconomic imbalances, or recurrences of sudden stops. Indeed, and contrary to the debt crisis, the decline in credit during the global financial crisis was not the result of a generalized sudden stop but of an important decline in demand.[25] Good macroeconomic policies and financial regulation can mitigate shocks from the global economy, while taking advantage of the trade in goods and services and intertemporal trade. However, when the institutional requirements, in particular the quality of policies, are not in place, financial integration can be a source of trouble.

---

24. Adler and Tovar (2012) find that the Latin American and Asian economies are less vulnerable to financial shocks, despite being more financially integrated, when the exchange rate regime is flexible.

25. Unfortunately, little research has been done to determine the relative importance of sudden stops vis-à-vis declines in demand during credit contractions in emerging markets. Most analysis treats declines in capital inflows as sudden stops.

Appendix 5A

Table 5A.1 Episodes of surges in capital inflows (percent of GDP)

Country	Period	Net capital inflows	Current account	Change in reserves
Argentina	1993–94 *	8.6	−3.8	2.2
	1997–99 *	5.4	−4.0	1.1
Brazil	1994 *	7.3	−0.2	1.6
	2007 *	6.5	−0.1	5.8
	2009	4.4	−1.3	2.6
Chile	1990 *	8.4	−1.7	8.5
	1992–94 *	7.7	−3.5	4.1
	1996–97 *	9.7	−4.4	3.9
	2008 *	5.1	−2.3	4.6
Colombia	1996–97 *	5.9	−5.3	1.0
	2007 *	4.8	−2.7	2.2
Mexico	1991–93 *	7.7	−5.8	1.6
	1997 *	5.2	−2.0	4.9
Peru	1994–97 *	7.9	−7.2	1.9
	2002	4.9	−2.0	1.8
	2007–08 *	10.5	−1.6	6.1
Latin America	1990s	7.5	−4.6	2.5
	2000s	6.7	−1.7	4.2
Indonesia	1990–93	3.2	−2.4	1.3
	1995–96 *	4.6	−3.4	1.4
Korea	1995–96	3.8	−2.9	0.8
	2003	3.2	2.4	9.2
	2009	4.2	3.9	2.0
Malaysia	1991–93 *	7.7	−5.6	7.0
	1995–96 *	9.3	−7.2	0.3
Philippines	1991 *	5.6	−2.2	3.8
	1994–97 *	9.9	−4.7	1.3
	1999 *	5.2	−3.6	4.7
Thailand	1989–96 *	10.5	−6.5	3.7
Asia	1990s	7.6	−4.8	2.8
	2000s	3.7	3.2	5.6
Bulgaria	1993 *	18.0	−11.3	1.0
	2002 *	22.8	−1.8	0.0
	2005–08 *	33.7	−19.6	0.2
Czech Republic	1995 *	11.9	−2.5	13.5
	2002 *	14.2	−5.2	8.1
Hungary	1993–95 *	14.9	−8.8	6.4
	1998–2000 *	11.1	−8.1	3.2
	2004–06 *	11.5	−7.5	2.5
	2008 *	8.8	−7.8	3.0
Latvia	2005–07 *	23.6	−18.7	5.4
Lithuania	1998 *	11.7	−11.5	3.8
	2006–07 *	21.3	−11.9	3.8
Poland	1995–96 *	7.4	−0.8	4.9
	1998–2000 *	6.8	−5.9	1.3
	2005 *	7.1	−2.4	2.7
	2007–09 *	8.3	−5.8	1.8

(continues on next page)

Table 5A.1 Episodes of surges in capital inflows (percent of GDP)
 (continued)

Country	Period	Net capital inflows	Current account	Change in reserves
Romania	2002 *	7.9	−3.4	4.0
	2004–08 *	14.3	−10.6	4.7
Europe	1990s	11.0	−6.4	4.4
	2000s	17.3	−10.5	3.1

* = Both methods to define surges, described in the text, coincide, and the period that contains both episodes is reported.

Sources: Ghosh et al. (2012) for net capital inflows; International Monetary Fund, *International Financial Statistics,* for current account and reserve accumulation.

6

From Macroeconomic
Policies to Long-Term
Growth

Latin America has made important progress in both macroeconomic and financial policies. It was able to weather the global financial crisis, but the road ahead is not risk-free.

In this chapter I discuss some important challenges that need to be addressed in order to take advantage of good macroeconomic policies to go from resilience to sustained economic growth. I also delve into some current trends produced by a deceleration in emerging markets, the downward pressures on commodity prices, and the prospects of an end to quantitative easing in the United States.

Today, countries are recognizing the need for policies that increase productivity and growth. The first phase of growth is the easier one and usually goes as follows: An economy is stabilized; a strong macroeconomic framework is put in place, perhaps opening up the economy; and then strong growth follows for several years. These well-known growth accelerations flow from the removal of basic, first-order distortions and achievement of macroeconomic stability. Acceleration concludes once the economy reaches its potential level of output. Increasing this potential growth is more difficult. It is not obvious which reforms are the most important to undertake. Also not obvious are the characteristics of those reforms. The devil is in the details.

Two sources of constraints limit the implementation and effectiveness of reforms. The first is populism. Dornbusch and Edwards (1991) define *economic populism* as "an approach to economics that emphasizes growth and income distribution and deemphasizes the risks of inflation, external constraints, and the reaction of economic agents to aggressive nonmarket policies." The emphasis is sound; the deemphasis is the tragedy. Because of inequality, populism is always a temptation, but it is an ineffective shortcut to social progress.

During the current period of cyclical deceleration, the chances of taking populism in the wrong direction are higher.

The other source of constraint in the implementation of reforms in conflict with vested interests. Many institutions and policies in Latin America have been put in place to favor particular interest groups, who are the first to oppose reforms. Historical rights or some other arguments are used to maintain special privileges. But privileges at the cost of the rest of the population are neither fair nor efficient. At other times, the arguments are subtler, such as the threat that reforms pose to economic growth and even social progress. Policies must be promarket, not probusiness. Most of the time, what is good for markets is also good for business, but when differences emerge, well-functioning markets must be the goal. Meanwhile, arbitrary policies or expropriations should not be pursued. The insecurity of property rights severely handicaps investment. Thus a strong institutional framework is needed to advance reforms that stimulate growth and social progress. In many Latin American countries, corruption and weak rule of law hinder reforms.

Inequality and Institutions

Inequality in Latin America has been persistent, dating back to either colonization or the late 19th century, and resilient—it has survived many economic experiments and many growth strategies. Moreover, it creates distortions in policymaking that hamper economic growth. Classic cases are the introduction of unsustainable social policies or market distortions for the purposes of redistribution. Inequality reduces potential growth primarily because of its negative impact on the quality of economic policies.

In Latin America, inequality widened in the 1980s, remained stable for some countries and widened for others during the 1990s, and narrowed during the 2000s.[1] The evolution of income inequality parallels that of economic performance. Performance was poor in the 1980s, normal in the 1990s and early 2000s, and better afterward. Regardless of policies and politics, the trends are relatively homogeneous, and thus they support the view that high growth and low inflation are determinants of the decline in inequality in the region.

The evolution of income distribution in Latin America is presented in figure 6.1 for the seven largest countries, the LA-7.[2] From the mid-1980s to the early 2000s, inequality remained stable in some countries, while in others it increased. In all countries but Colombia, inequality fell during the last decade.

---

1. See De la Torre, Messina, and Pienknagura (2012), González and Martner (2012), and Lopez-Calva and Lustig (2012), among others.

2. International comparisons of inequality are difficult because countries are not fully comparable. In some countries, coverage is national; in others only big cities are covered. Moreover, adjustments are made to achieve consistency with other national figures. In Chile, strong assumptions are used to make household surveys compatible with national accounts. This adjustment would have systematically increased inequality as measured by the Gini coefficient by 7 percent (Bravo and Valderrama 2011).

Figure 6.1   Income distribution in Latin America, 1985–2010

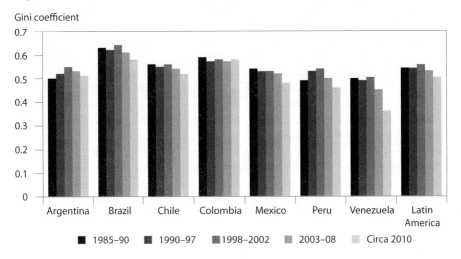

Note: The Gini coefficient is a measure of income distribution in a country. It ranges from 0 (perfect equality) to 1 (perfect inequality).

Source: Economic Commission for Latin America and the Caribbean.

The largest decline was in Venezuela, although whether it will last is questionable. Most remarkable, inequality did not increase during the global financial crisis. The last observations are for 2010, except for Brazil and Chile, where the data are for 2009, the worst year in terms of output. Macroeconomic resilience and income support for the poor during the recession played an important role in mitigating the social costs of the decline in output.

Little is known about specific policies to change income distribution significantly in the short run and on a long-lasting basis. Even the effects of growth are unclear. The evolution of inequality and income would follow the Kuznets curve, but the specific form of this relationship—for example, at which level of income inequality declines—is also unclear. This finding implies that at low income levels inequality increases as economies grow, then inequality reaches a maximum after which inequality declines as income grows. This is the famous inverted-U of Kuznets. However, the break point is country-specific and depends on many other factors influencing the evolution of inequality.

Some progress has been made recently, however, in understanding the factors underlying the decline in inequality in Latin America. This decline has been characterized by a decline in labor income inequality and therefore a decline in the skill premium.[3] The educational expansion and investment of the 1990s

---

3. The factors underlying the skill premium are beyond the scope of this discussion, but they may be related to improved terms of trade. As argued by De la Torre et al. (2012), the break in inequality in 2003 coincided with the onset of the terms of trade boom. As exchange rates appreciated, labor

and even earlier had then paid off. However, the effects of improved education do not affect measures of inequality overnight. As better-educated people gradually enter the labor force, this effect will gradually influence the overall measures of income inequality. Improvements in education are the most durable and effective way to reduce inequality and increase social mobility, but the distribution of human capital counts as well. The decline in inequality has also been a result of economic growth and stimulated by good macroeconomic conditions.

Social policies that provided cash transfers to the poor led to a decline in inequality. According to Lopez-Calva and Lustig (2012), the implementation of large-scale conditional cash transfer programs in Argentina, Brazil, Mexico, and Peru has been effective. Therefore, fiscal policy through conditional transfers directly affects income and its distribution, and it can alleviate the living conditions of the disadvantaged. For this reason, a strong fiscal policy must be in place to have permanent financing for permanent expenditures. The procyclicality of fiscal policy, discussed in chapter 4, is not only bad from a macroeconomic point of view but also unfavorable for social policy priorities. Tightening the budget during slowdowns usually affects social expenditure disproportionately. The progress in Latin America in recent years, together with the windfalls of the commodity price boom, has allowed effective social policies. Countries that have not built fiscal buffers for a fall in commodity revenues may have to face difficult policy choices as terms of trade decline. As already noted, relying on terms of trade has its limits. Terms of trade may remain high, but they will not continue to grow at the rate of the economy and social needs. It is quite likely that in the next years this boom will recede.

Finally, income distribution is perhaps the most important variable in terms of equity, but it is not the only relevant dimension. Improving the distribution of opportunities and correcting market distortions to level the playing field may bring the poor important benefits. Improving the functioning of markets, many times constrained by monopolistic behavior and uneven market relations due to asymmetric information, can have first-order effects on welfare and fairness. Many of the policies needed to advance in this area will have to deal with rooted vested interests that will oppose these reforms. Competition and consumer protection laws are important in this regard. Opaque political campaign finances open the door to political capture.

Institutions provide people with the incentives to devote their efforts and talents to different activities. According to Acemoglu and Robinson (2012), institutions can be inclusive or extractive. Inclusive economic institutions are those that "secure property rights and opportunities for not just the elite but for a broad cross-section of society." By contrast, extractive institutions are those "designed to extract incomes and wealth from one subset of society to

---

moved to the nontradable goods sectors, which are less skill-intensive, thereby reducing the skill premium.

benefit a different subset." Extractive institutions can generate growth but not in an enduring way.

Weak and extractive institutions have characterized Latin America since its days of colonization. Figure 6.2 shows one of the most pervasive features of Latin America, corruption. Except for Chile and Uruguay, and to a lesser extent Costa Rica, Latin American countries rank very poorly in terms of corruption, according to Transparency International's Corruption Perceptions Index. Corruption creates insecurity in property rights, induces rent-seeking behavior, and reduces the incentives for investment and productivity-augmenting activities. Corruption is also linked to drug trafficking, a major problem in some countries of the region.

On most indicators of institutional strength such as rule of law, ease of doing business, and competitiveness, Latin America ranks poorly, and the rankings resemble those for corruption. Chile, Uruguay, and Costa Rica are the exceptions in quality of institutions, and Chile, Colombia, Mexico, and Peru are the exceptions in ease of doing business.

Economic policies geared to efficiently reducing inequality and strengthening institutions are key to promoting growth. Improvements can be made in many country-specific areas. Avoiding the temptations of populism and kowtowing to special-interest groups are important to create an environment of inclusive institutions, which produces the appropriate incentives for widespread economic prosperity.

Macroeconomic Policies: Virtuous and Vicious Cycles

Good macroeconomic policies foster economic growth, which, in turn, promotes macroeconomic stability. Good terms of trade may facilitate this process, but a change in external conditions can reverse all gains. There is a virtuous cycle of growth, low inflation, and strong fiscal policy. However, that virtuous cycle can turn into a vicious cycle of instability and stagnation, as in figure 6.3.

High economic growth improves public finance by strengthening revenues, but also, in the other direction, sound fiscal policy fosters growth by, among other things, reducing sovereign risk and the cost of financing. In turn, sound fiscal policy does not require inflationary finance, contributing in this way to price stability. Finally, a low inflation rate and stability increase economic growth. This is a virtuous cycle, but low growth, weak public finance, and high inflation may turn out to be a vicious cycle of stagflation. This cycle can feed into the health of the financial system, producing something similar to what has been going on today in Europe, except for inflation, which is low.

Europe's monetary union has not proven to be a panacea, and the lack of exchange rate adjustments generates longer recessions. Flexible exchange rates are thus the preference noted in this book. However, belonging to a currency union is quite irreversible. The cost of exiting is probably much higher than the costs of gaining flexibility. The recent experience with the euro area shows the costs of rigidities and irreversibility on economic adjustment. In the euro

Figure 6.2   Corruption Perceptions Index, 2012

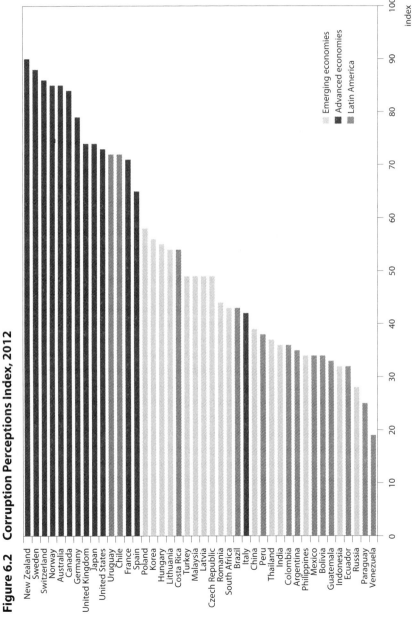

Note: Higher values indicate low perceived corruption.

Source: Transparency International.

Figure 6.3 The virtuous and vicious cycles of macroeconomic stability

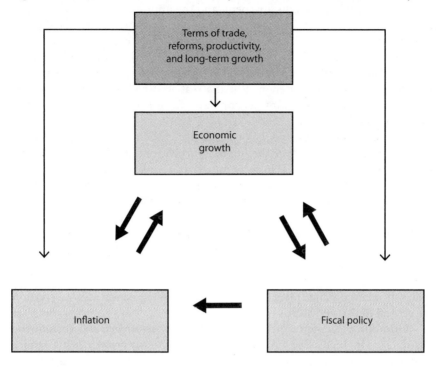

Source: Author's illustration.

area, the size of countries is not as heterogeneous as in Latin America. In addition, the most central and largest country in the euro area is also the richest and most stable economically and financially, unlike in Latin America. For this reason, the idea of creating a currency union in Latin America is a nonstarter. It is much more important to increase economic integration in the context of fairly open economies than to try to integrate macroeconomic policies.

High terms of trade, as illustrated in figure 6.3, may trigger the virtuous cycle. They increase growth through the impact of higher income on the domestic expenditure and the fall in the relative cost of inputs. They also improve public finances directly by the revenues earned from commodities and indirectly through higher growth. And finally, high terms of trade put downward pressures on inflation as the exchange rate appreciates. A deterioration in the terms of trade, however, can have damaging consequences for stability and growth.

That said, rising terms of trade can initiate a vicious cycle, which seems to have been the tragedy in Latin America during the debt crisis. An abundance of natural resources and the production of commodities can become a curse because positive terms of trade shocks can exacerbate procyclicality of the business cycle. The boom-bust cycle then becomes very pronounced. Government's windfall gains are spent, and the improvement in creditworthiness leads to overborrowing, private and public. From an institutional point of view, improvements in terms of trade also encourage rent-seeking behavior. And management of the exchange rate induces further inflows and a correction that must be even more intense. This time, however, the situation, in most countries at least, was different. But the real strength of countries will not be revealed until an important decline in terms of trade occurs, which could happen in the near term.

To avoid falling into the vicious cycle of terms of trade, countries need to adopt policies that reduce the impact of the external environment on the business cycle. Indeed, reducing the impact of terms of trade on short-term fluctuations and inflation is desirable to reduce fluctuations in employment and activity. As argued in earlier chapters, Latin America's greater resilience is built in part on the reduced impact of terms of trade on the domestic economy. However, reducing the impact of weak global conditions on the domestic economy means that in good times the strengths of the global economy are also dampened domestically. This is precisely how beneficial output stabilization works. As discussed throughout this book, inflation targets, prudent fiscal policy, flexible exchange rates, and sound financial regulation and supervision are central to this endeavor.

Promoting long-term growth is another way to trigger and sustain the virtuous cycle. Increasing productivity and long-term growth helps reduce inflation as potential output rises and thus inflation declines. It also contributes to public finances, reduces poverty, and is a necessary condition for sustained social inclusion.

Periods of genuine productivity and income catch-up, in contrast to overheating, have contributed in important ways to the conquest of inflation. Indexation and other forms of inertia become less relevant as the economy grows. As for wage inertia, if wages are indexed to past inflation and productivity is growing, it is possible to have real wage growth, indexation, and falling inflation, because the increase in wages does not translate into an increase in costs as productivity rises. In other words, as productivity grows, indexation may become a nonbinding constraint to reducing inflation. As low inflation consolidates because the deep causes of inflation have been removed, inertia becomes much less important.[4]

By contrast, when wages are indexed to past inflation but growth is low, reducing inflation becomes more difficult and slower to achieve. As nominal wages grow at the pace of past inflation, and productivity fails to grow, the

---

4. The disinflation in Chile in the 1990s can be attributed to strong public finance and to granting independence to the central bank. But the speed of disinflation, faster than originally expected, and the decline in the relevance of indexation can also be attributed to the rapid growth in productivity in the 1990s (De Gregorio 2004).

wage behavior feeds entirely into costs and prices and inflation becomes sticky. This scenario is at the core of the decline in inflation inertia in the region. It may, however, mask cosmetic reductions in inflation.

Eliminating the deep roots of inflation—the fiscal and monetary roots discussed in chapter 2—and productivity growth have fostered a decline in inflation in most countries in the region. Beyond the key role played by the central banks in conducting monetary policy within a flexible inflation targeting regime, the decline in inflation inertia has also contributed to this achievement. The task is now to avoid returning to inflation, and flexible inflation targeting regimes have proven to be a successful way of accomplishing this.

Macroeconomic and Financial Policies

Progress in macroeconomic and financial policies is fundamental to understanding the resilience of Latin America to the global financial crisis and the strong recovery that most of the region has been enjoying. Overall, advances in structural reforms have lagged in most countries of the region.

Macroeconomic Policies

One important policy lesson from the crisis is the need for macroprudential financial policies. They limit the vulnerability of the financial system to fluctuations in the business cycle. Macroprudential policies should aim to avoid excessive procyclicality from the financial system to the business cycle. A natural first reaction to the policy lesson just noted would be that there is no need to introduce new measures because of the resilience of Latin America's financial system to the crisis. However, it is in tranquil times that fragilities build up and policies to prevent crisis must be implemented. Equating resilience to immunity could aggravate the incubation of future problems. This is a sure recipe for booming asset prices and credit and the onset of fragility.

No matter how useful, macroprudential tools come with a risk: They are too broad and can be used for many purposes. As one policymaker put it, macroprudential policies could become a "license to kill." Indeed, today in the policy discussions of capital controls, controls are not mentioned. Rather, they are called macroprudential tools—it sounds better. It is true that some versions of capital controls are a form of macroprudential policy, but they are mostly used for exchange rate purposes.

Capital controls are far from a panacea. In the financial dimension, they must focus on the composition and volume of gross flows. Measures can be taken if the evolution of flows suggests increasing vulnerabilities because foreign borrowing is deemed to be excessive and volatile. However, when used as an exchange rate defense their effectiveness is more elusive, especially in financially open economies. As economies open, financial markets find ways to channel investment into the economy—but controls are not uniform for all types of flows. Still, their effectiveness is country- and context-specific.

It is important to remember that the use of capital controls is problematic when the deep root of appreciation is very large interest rate differentials, on the order of two digits. The false sense of security given by capital controls could lure authorities into overlooking the fact that they may not be the victims of a global currency war, but rather a local currency suicide.

As the toolbox of macroprudential regulation continues to grow, macroprudential tools may appear for exchange rates, inflation, and so forth, thereby creating confusion about what exactly are the appropriate policies for various circumstances. Misuse of the term *macroprudential* weakens the policy advice and makes international coordination more difficult. In spite of recent discussions, the area between capital controls and macroprudential regulation remains gray, and policymakers should be wary of a new period of financial repression in advanced economies triggered by the need to rebalance the public finances.

On the monetary side, flexible inflation targets have worked well in Latin America, a region that has the highest and most persistent inflation rates in the world. Inflation targets have helped anchor inflation and provide room for monetary policy, thereby playing an important role during the global financial crisis. Inflation targets are not a rigid scheme, and they can be complemented with other policies such as financial ones. They are fully consistent with exchange rate intervention, as long as the target does not become subordinate to an exchange rate objective.

Inflation targets have often been blamed for a narrow focus on stability. The significant monetary loosening during the global financial crisis revealed that employment and output are important inputs in monetary policy decisions. And yet challenges remain. Today, Latin America is moving closer to its potential level of activity. The tensions on the exchange rate front may produce a reluctance to tighten because of fear of appreciation. Replacing fear of floating with fear of tightening could be a problem. Fiscal policy may help, but the scope for tightening is limited. As noted in chapter 2, the retrenchment of fiscal expansion after the crisis has been only partial. There is heterogeneity in the region, and several countries are slowing down, which may require loose monetary policy.

Financial Policies

Countries can be classified into three categories: (1) financially closed, (2) financially open but fragile, and (3) financially open and resilient. The second category is the worst, because countries end up there typically because of opening the capital account in the context of weak domestic financial regulation and supervision. The best is the third type of economy, but unfortunately it appears that a country cannot achieve that status without crossing the second one. To avoid the second stage is the challenge.

Recent experience in Latin America indicates that being more financially integrated and open does not mean being more vulnerable. This finding adds a new complication to the discussion of financial stability. A process of financial integration does not necessarily lead to a collapse or fragility, as perhaps was thought some time ago.

Indeed, in their review of the effects of financial integration, Kose et al. (2006) argue that any positive effects are quite elusive. They give "qualified support" to the claim that developing countries benefit from financial integration, but they also add that "we find there is very little meaningful empirical support to underpin the more polemical claims of those who argue that capital account liberalization (as opposed to, say, inappropriately rigid exchange rate regimes) is the root problem underlying most developing country financial crises of the past fifteen years" (page 7).

As argued throughout this book, exchange rate rigidities have been important factors in crises in Latin America. Opening capital accounts in the context of a weak financial system is also a recipe for trouble. The massive evidence on financial integration and economic growth suggests that the beneficial effects of financial integration depend on thresholds. In particular, a financially open economy with strong macroeconomic and financial institutions and policies can reap the benefits of integration and be resilient.

An important concern in the region is the destabilizing effects of capital inflows. However, from the current account point of view recent experience shows there is no significant demand for foreign financing. But net inflows have been relevant. As discussed in chapter 5, their relevance stems to some extent from the fact that central banks have been accumulating reserves. Therefore, capital inflows from advanced economies to emerging markets may largely be the result of official demands for international reserves. This process may be changing, however, because the current account balances in Latin America and many emerging markets are deteriorating.

Current account deficits have traditionally been a concern of policymakers in the region, and it is not surprising. A large number of crises have been currency crises triggered by unsustainable deficits. Exchange rate misalignments (*atrasos cambiarios*) have been the underlying cause of this problem. Exchange rate flexibility is the most important policy for limiting the risk of external crisis. If the exchange rate is allowed to adjust when international conditions deteriorate, the adjustment becomes less costly. During a crisis, the responses of exchange rates in countries that float, as shown in chapter 3, reveal that the inflationary impacts are small and that there are no threats to financial stability.

Good terms of trade and good international conditions in the years before the global financial crisis were important in the performance of the Latin American region. They were also important to the recovery. Despite global financial turbulences, external conditions have remained sanguine: high terms of trade and easy financial conditions. However, the heterogeneity of terms of trade gains in the region, in view of its general resilience, shows that better macroeconomic frameworks and greater policy space were important to implementing expansionary policies.

Table 6.1   Growth performance in Latin America, 2009–14f (percent)

Country	2009	2010	2011	2012	2013f	2014f
Argentina	0.9	9.2	8.9	1.9	3.0	2.2
Brazil	−0.3	7.5	2.7	0.9	2.4	2.5
Chile	−1.0	5.8	5.9	5.6	4.2	4.3
Colombia	1.7	4.0	6.6	4.0	3.8	4.5
Mexico	−6.0	5.3	3.9	3.6	1.5	3.4
Peru	0.9	8.8	6.9	6.3	5.5	5.8
Venezuela	−3.2	−1.5	4.2	5.5	1.0	1.5

f = forecast

Sources: International Monetary Fund, *World Economic Outlook*, October 2013; JPMorgan; Consensus Forecasts; surveys of national central banks.

A Final Look at the Region

The countries in Latin America are growing at different speeds. After severe swings in activity during the 2008–09 crisis, most countries are approaching what would be for now their growth potential. This is the perfect time to consolidate macroeconomic and financial policy gains, to look at vulnerabilities, and to build the buffers and policy space needed to remain resilient. It is also a good time to recognize what has worked and identify the challenges that lie ahead in order to foster not only macroeconomic stability but also true social and economic progress.

Most emerging-market economies exhibited strong economic performance after the global financial crisis, but their pace of growth has begun to slow. This moderation has repercussions for commodity prices, which have been declining but still remain relatively high. Declining terms of trade and closing the output gap lead to inflationary pressures and a slowdown in activity. Indeed, the super commodity-emerging-market cycle seems to be coming to an end. Macroeconomic frameworks have improved in most countries, but they can only dampen, not avoid, a slowdown. Difficult times may be ahead.

Table 6.1 shows actual economic growth since the global financial crisis (2009–12) and estimated growth for 2013–14 for the seven largest Latin American countries. Growth has weakened in the region as has been happening in all emerging markets, which is not surprising. When macroeconomic policies are appropriate, as those applied in most emerging markets, economies recover faster than potential. There is a recovery bonus given that output is below full capacity. After the recovery has taken place growth normalizes at the pace of potential output growth. The table reveals that long-term growth across countries in the region may vary between 3 and 5 percent. More efforts have to be made in order to increase long-term growth, especially in the countries with the lowest income in the region.

During the crisis, performance was very dispersed. Consider the two largest countries in the region. Mexico was the hardest hit country because the crisis took place next door. Although oil is not a very important export item, it is quite relevant from the public finance point of view, and the crisis hit not only trade with the United States but also fiscal revenues. Economic prospects are improving. The case of Brazil is remarkable since during 2009–10 its relative performance was great but seems to have been more dominated by good cyclical conditions and macroeconomic impulse than genuine high long-term growth, which is more likely to be about 3 percent or even less. Indeed, inflation has been rising, despite low growth. As I discussed in chapter 2, it is not growth but the output gap that induces inflation. Hence, the resurgence of inflationary pressures is a sign that the economy has reached full capacity. The good performance in 2009–10 has ignored some more fundamental problems that need to be resolved to spur growth. A high and distortionary tax burden, industrial policy implemented through discretionary credit allocation, and significant trade distortions impair long-term growth.

The global economic situation in recent months is what the global adjustment should be delivering. The strong monetary expansion in advanced economies, implemented through nonconventional monetary policy after they reached the zero lower bound for monetary policy, is beginning to pay off, particularly in the United States. Its economy is gaining momentum, and there are more concrete signs that its quantitative easing is coming to an end. As argued at the end of chapter 3, the weakening of emerging-market currencies in relation to the US dollar should begin once the US recovery is under way, and that is exactly what has started happening since mid-2013. This process has been reinforced by the risk of a slowdown in China, triggered by financial tensions and difficulties in changing the patterns of growth to better meet domestic demand and softening of commodity prices. It is remarkable that today the capital inflow, overheating, and currency war rhetoric has been replaced by one of slowdown, tapering of quantitative easing, and financial turmoil in emerging markets.

To a rigorous observer the change of language of public officials in emerging markets may sound awkward. At the beginning of 2013 all the problems were blamed on loose monetary policy in advanced economies and the anticompetitive effects of the appreciation of emerging-market currencies. This changed with the announcement of the potential tapering of quantitative easing in May 2013, and the reversal of currencies led to a shift in sentiments. Currencies depreciated significantly, prompting the return of fear of turmoil. Nevertheless, first, this is exactly what should happen once advanced economies start performing better, while emerging markets should see an improvement in competitiveness. And second, current tensions are minor compared with what countries had to struggle with during late 2008 and early 2009, and economies that have preserved healthy macroeconomic and financial policy frameworks as well as enough policy space should be able to handle these tensions without major problems.

Indeed, the Latin American economies have implemented sound macroeconomic frameworks, and they have the policy space to contain negative external shocks. The big risk is the capacity to use fiscal policy and the cost this may entail for the future. As discussed in chapter 2, in emerging markets, and Latin America in particular, the full extent of the fiscal expansion was not eliminated after the crisis. If the pressure to increase social expenditures is added to the mix, the financing is essential; otherwise, well-deserved creditworthiness could be damaged.

Meanwhile, weakening economic growth is fertile ground for populism. Politicians impatiently search for shortcuts and measures that will deliver quick results, regardless of their long-term consequences. As the economies have progressed, massive demonstrations have been held from Brazil to Chile to demand fairer economic conditions. Not facing the real problems and choices and postponing solutions, or rushing in with populist answers, are risky not only to macroeconomic stability but also to long-term growth.

Whether the region's macroeconomic management has been successfully upgraded will be revealed in the next few years because the exceptional external environment the region has faced in recent years is deteriorating. The region has a unique opportunity to show that its well-deserved credit for successfully managing the global financial crisis is well grounded. And this should be the basis for tackling the much-needed reforms to foster economic growth and improve social conditions.

References

Abbas, S. Ali, Nazim Belhocine, Asmaa ElGanainy, and Mark Horton. 2010. *A Historical Public Debt Database.* IMF Working Paper WP/10/245. Washington: International Monetary Fund.

Abiad, Abdul, John Bluedorn, Jaime Guajardo, and Petia Topalova. 2012. Resilience in Emerging-Market and Developing Economies: Will It Last? In *World Economic Outlook* (October). Washington: International Monetary Fund.

Acemoglu, Daron, and James A. Robinson. 2012. *Why Nations Fail: The Origins of Power, Prosperity and Poverty.* New York: Crown Publishers.

Adler, Gustavo, and Camilo E. Tovar. 2011. *Foreign Exchange Intervention: A Shield Against Appreciation Winds?* IMF Working Paper WP/11/165. Washington: International Monetary Fund.

Adler, Gustavo, and Camilo E. Tovar. 2012. *Riding Global Financial Waves: The Economic Impact of Global Financial Shocks on Emerging-Market Economies.* IMF Working Paper WP/12/188. Washington: International Monetary Fund.

Adler, Gustavo, and Sebastián Sosa. 2013. *External Conditions and Debt Sustainability in Latin America.* IMF Working Paper WP/13/27. Washington: International Monetary Fund.

Adler, Gustavo, and Camilo E. Tovar. 2013. On the Effectiveness of Foreign Exchange Intervention—Evidence from Rules-Based Regime Changes. Mimeo. International Monetary Fund, Washington.

Aguiar, Mark, and Gita Gopinath. 2007. Emerging Market Business Cycle: The Cycle Is the Trend. *Journal of Political Economy* 115, no. 1: 69–102.

Ahrend, Rudiger. 2010. Monetary Ease: A Factor behind Financial Crises? Some Evidence from OECD Countries. *Economics: The Open-Access, Open-Assessment E-Journal* 4 (2010-12).

Aizenman, Joshua, and Jaewoo Lee. 2007. International Reserves: Precautionary vs. Mercantilist Views, Theory and Evidence. *Open Economies Review* 18, no. 2: 191–214.

Aizenman, Joshua, and Reuven Glick. 2008. Pegged Exchange Rate Regimes—A Trap. *Journal of Money Credit and Banking* 40, no. 4: 817–35.

Arcand, Jean-Louis, Enrico Berkes, and Ugo Panizza. 2012. *Too Much Finance?* IMF Working Paper WP/12/161. Washington: International Monetary Fund.

Baba, Chikako, and Annamaria Kokenyne. 2011. *Effectiveness of Capital Controls in Selected Countries in the 2000s.* IMF Working Paper WP/11/128. Washington: International Monetary Fund.

145

Bailliu, Jeannine, and Eiji Fujii. 2004. *Exchange Rate Pass-Through and the Inflation Environment in Industrialized Countries: An Empirical Investigation*. Working Paper 21. Bank of Canada.

Ball, Laurence, and Niamh Sheridan. 2005. Does Inflation Targeting Matter? In *The Inflation-Targeting Debate*, ed. B. Bernanke and M. Woodford. University of Chicago Press.

Barro, Robert J., and David B. Gordon. 1983. A Positive Theory of Monetary Policy in a Natural Rate Model. *Journal of Political Economy* 91, no. 4: 589–610.

Bergsten, C. Fred, and Joseph E. Gagnon. 2012. *Currency Manipulation, the US Economy, and the Global Economic Order*. Policy Brief 12-25. Washington: Peterson Institute for International Economics.

Bernanke, Benjamin S. 2010. Monetary Policy and the Housing Bubble. Speech at the Annual Meeting of the American Economic Association, Atlanta, GA, January 3.

Bernanke, Benjamin S. 2011. The Effects of the Great Recession on Central Bank Doctrine and Practice. Speech at the Federal Reserve Bank of Boston 56th Economic Conference, Boston, October 18.

Bernanke, Benjamin S., and Mark Gertler. 1999. Monetary Policy and Asset Price Volatility. In *New Challenges for Monetary Policy*. A Symposium Sponsored by the Federal Reserve Bank of Kansas City, Jackson Hole, Wyoming, August 26–28.

Betts, Caroline, and Michael B. Devereux. 2000. Exchange Rate Dynamics in a Model of Pricing to Market. *Journal of International Economics* 50, no. 1: 215–44.

BIS (Bank for International Settlements). 2010. *Triennial Central Bank Survey: Report on Global Foreign Exchange Market Activity in 2010* (December). Basel.

Blanchard, Olivier J. 1979. Speculative Bubbles, Crashes and Rational Expectations. *Economic Letters* 3, no. 4: 387–89. Washington: International Monetary Fund.

Blanchard, Olivier, and John Simon. 2001. The Long and Large Decline in US Output Volatility. *Brookings Papers on Economic Activity* 1: 135–64.

Blanchard, Olivier, and Jordi Galí. 2009. The Macroeconomic Effects of Oil Shocks: Why Are the 2000s So Different from the 1970s? In *International Dimensions of Monetary Policy*, ed. J. Galí and M. Gertler. Chicago: Chicago University Press.

Blanchard, Olivier, and Daniel Leigh. 2012. *Growth Forecast Errors and Fiscal Multipliers*. IMF Working Paper WP/13/1. Washington: International Monetary Fund.

Blinder, A., and R. Reis. 2005. Understanding the Greenspan Standard. In *The Greenspan Era: Lessons for the Future*. A Symposium Sponsored by the Federal Reserve Bank of Kansas City, Jackson Hole, Wyoming, August 25–27.

Bluedorn, John, Rupa Duttagupta, Andrea Pescatori, and Stephen Snudden. 2012. Commodity Price Swings and Commodity Exporters. In *World Economic Outlook* (April). Washington: International Monetary Fund.

Bordo, Michael D., Owen Humpage, and Anna J. Schwartz. 2012. *Epilogue: Foreign-Exchange-Market Operations in the Twenty-First Century*. NBER Working Paper 17984. Cambridge, MA: National Bureau of Economic Research.

Borensztein, Eduardo, José De Gregorio, and Jong-Wha Lee. 1998. How Does Foreign Direct Investment Affect Economic Growth? *Journal of International Economics* 45, no. 1: 115–35.

Borio, Claudio, and Mathias Drehmann. 2009. *Towards an Operational Framework for Financial Stability: "Fuzzy" Measurement and Its Consequences*. BIS Working Paper 284. Basel: Bank for International Settlements.

Bouakez, Hafedh, and Nooman Rebei. 2008. Has Exchange Rate Pass-Through Really Declined? Evidence from Canada. *Journal of International Economics* 75 (July): 249–67.

Bravo, David, and José Valderrama. 2011. The Impact of Income Adjustments in the Casen Survey on the Measurement of Inequality in Chile. *Estudios de Economía* 38, no. 1: 43–65.

Brunnermeier, Markus K. 2009. Bubbles. In *New Palgrave Dictionary of Economics*, ed. S. N. Durlauf and L. E. Blume. Palgrave McMillan.

Brunnermeier, Markus K., Andrew Crockett, Charles Goodhart, Avinash Persaud, and Hyun Shin. 2009. *The Fundamental Principles of Financial Regulation*. Geneva Reports on the World Economy 11. Geneva and London: International Centre for Monetary and Banking Studies and Centre for Economic Policy Research.

Bruno, Michael, and Stanley Fischer. 1990. Seigniorage, Operating Rules, and the High Inflation Trap. *Quarterly Journal of Economics* 105, no. 2: 353–74.

Bruno, Valentina, and Hyun Song Shin. 2012. Capital Flows and the Risk-Taking Channel of Monetary Policy. Paper presented at the 11th BIS Annual Conference, Lucerne, Switzerland, June 21–22.

Bruno, Valentina, and Hyun Song Shin. 2013. *Assessing Macroprudential Policies: Case of Korea*. NBER Working Paper 19084. Cambridge, MA: National Bureau of Economic Research.

Bufman, Gi, and Leonardo Leiderman. 1995. Israel's Stabilization: Some Important Policy Lessons. In *Reform, Recovery, and Growth: Latin America and the Middle East*, ed. Rudiger Dornbusch and Sebastian Edwards. Chicago: University of Chicago Press.

Bussière, Matthieu, and Tuomas Peltonen. 2008. *Exchange Rate Pass-Through in the Global Economy: The Role of Emerging Market Economies*. ECB Working Paper 951. Frankfurt: European Central Bank.

Ca' Zorzi, Michele, Elke Hahn, and Marcelo Sánchez. 2007. *Exchange Rate Pass-Through in Emerging Markets*. ECB Working Paper 739. Frankfurt: European Central Bank.

Caballero, Ricardo J., and Arvind Krishnamurthy. 2001. International and Domestic Collateral Constraints in a Model of Emerging Market Crises. *Journal of Monetary Economics* 48, no. 3: 513–48.

Caballero, Ricardo J., and Arvind Krishnamurthy. 2009. Global Imbalances and Financial Fragility. *American Economic Review Papers and Proceedings* 99, no. 2 (May): 584–88.

Cagan, Phillip. 1956. The Monetary Dynamics of Hyperinflation. In *Studies in the Quantity Theory of Money*, ed. Milton Friedman. Chicago: University of Chicago Press.

Calvo, Guillermo. 1998. Capital Flows and Capital Market Crisis: The Economics of Sudden Stops. *Journal of Applied Economics* 1: 35–54.

Calvo, Guillermo A., and Enrique Mendoza. 1998. *Empirical Puzzles of Chilean Stabilization Policy*. Working Paper 98-02. Durham, NC: Duke University, Department of Economics.

Calvo, Guillermo A., and Carlos Végh. 1999. Inflation Stabilization and BOP Crises in Developing Countries. In *Handbook of Macroeconomics*, volume C, ed. John Taylor and Michael Woodford. North Holland.

Calvo, Guillermo A., and Carmen Reinhart. 2002. Fear of Floating. *Quarterly Journal of Economics* 177: 379–408.

Calvo, Guillermo, Leonardo Leiderman, and Carmen Reinhart. 1996. Inflows of Capital to Developing Countries. *Journal of Economic Perspectives* 10, no. 2: 123–39.

Calvo, Guillermo, Alejandro Izquierdo, and Rudy Loo-Kung. 2012. *Optimal Holdings of International Reserves: Self-Insurance Against Sudden-Stops*. NBER Working Paper 18219. Cambridge, MA: National Bureau of Economic Research.

Campa, José Manuel, and Linda S. Goldberg. 2005. Exchange Rate Pass-Through into Import Prices. *Review of Economics and Statistics* 87 (November): 679–90.

Canales-Kriljenko, Jorge Iván, Luis I. Jácome, Ali Alichi, and Iván Luis de Oliveira Lima. 2010. *Weathering the Global Storm: The Benefits of Monetary Policy in the LAC5 Countries*. IMF Working Paper WP/10/292. Washington: International Monetary Fund.

Caputo, Rodrigo, Marco Núñez, and Rodrigo Valdés. 2008. Exchange Rate Analysis in Practice. *Economía Chilena* 11 (April): 61–91.

Cardenas, Mauricio, and Felipe Barrera. 1997. On the Effectiveness of Capital Controls: The Experience of Colombia During the 1990s. *Journal of Development Economics* 54, no. 1: 237–57.

Cavallo, Eduardo. 2007. *Output Volatility and Openness to Trade: A Reassessment.* Working Paper 604. Washington: Inter-American Development Bank.

Cecchetti, Stephen, and Enisse Kharroubi. 2012. Reassessing the Impact of Finance on Growth. Mimeo. Bank for International Settlements, Basel.

Cecchetti, Stephen G., Hans Genberg, John Lipsky, and Sushil Wadhwani. 2000. *Asset Prices and Central Bank Policy.* Geneva Reports on the World Economy 2. Geneva and London: International Centre for Monetary and Banking Studies and Centre for Economic Policy Research.

Central Bank of Chile. 2007. *Monetary Policy Report* (September). Santiago.

Central Bank of Chile. 2009. *Financial Policy Report* (first half). Santiago.

Central Bank of Chile. 2010. *Monetary Policy Report* (September). Santiago.

Central Bank of Chile. 2012. *Financial Stability Report* (second semester). Santiago.

Céspedes, Luis Felipe, and Andrés Velasco. 2011. *Was This Time Different? Fiscal Policy in Commodity Republics.* BIS Working Paper 365. Basel: Bank for International Settlements.

Céspedes, Luis Felipe, and Alessandro Rebucci. 2011. Macro-Prudential Policies in Latin America: A Survey. Mimeo. Inter-American Development Bank, Washington.

Chamon, Marcos, and Márcio Garcia. 2013. Capital Controls in Brazil: Effective? Efficient? Mimeo. International Monetary Fund, Washington.

CIEPR (Committee on International Economic Policy Reform). 2012. *Banks and Cross-Border Capital Flows: Policy Challenges and Regulatory Responses.* Washington: Brookings Institution.

Cifuentes, Rodrigo, Rodrigo Alfaro, Eduardo Olaberría, and Rubén Poblete. 2011. The Chilean Financial System and Macroprudential Policies. *Financial Stability Report* (First Semester). Santiago: Central Bank of Chile.

Čihák, Martin, Sònia Muñoz, Shakira Teh Sharifuddin, and Kalin Tintchev. 2012. *Financial Stability Reports: What Are They Good For?* IMF Working Paper WP/12/1. Washington: International Monetary Fund.

Claessens, Stijn, and Neeltje van Horen. 2012. *Foreign Banks: Trends, Impact and Financial Stability.* IMF Working Paper WP/12/10. Washington: International Monetary Fund.

Cline, William R. 2013. Capital Market Integration. In *The Evidence and Impact of Financial Globalization,* volume 3, ed. Gerard Caprio. Academic Press.

Corbo, Vittorio, and Klaus Schmidt-Hebbel. 2011. *The International Crisis and Latin America: Growth Effects and Development Strategies.* CASE Network Studies & Analysis no. 429. Warsaw: Center for Social and Economic Research.

Coulibaly, Dramane, and Hubert Kempf. 2010. *Does Inflation Targeting Decrease Exchange Rate Pass-Through in Emerging Countries?* Documents de Travail du Centre d'Economie de la Sorbonne 10049. Université Panthéon-Sorbonne (Paris 1).

Cowan, Kevin, and José De Gregorio. 2007. International Borrowing, Capital Controls and the Exchange Rate: Lessons from Chile. In *Capital Controls and Capital Flows in Emerging Economies: Policies, Practices and Consequences,* ed. S. Edwards. Chicago: National Bureau of Economic Research and the University of Chicago Press.

Cowan, Kevin, David Rappoport, and Jorge Selaive. 2007. *High Frequency Dynamics of the Exchange Rate in Chile.* Working Paper 433. Santiago: Central Bank of Chile.

Cowan, Kevin, José De Gregorio, Alejandro Micco, and Christopher Neilson. 2008. Financial Diversification, Sudden Stops and Sudden Starts. In *Current Account and External Finance,* ed. K. Cowan, S. Edwards, and R. O. Valdés. Santiago: Central Bank of Chile.

Crowe, Christopher, Giovanni Dell'Ariccia, Deniz Igan, and Pau Rabanal. 2011. *How to Deal with Real Estate Booms: Lessons from Country Experiences.* IMF Working Paper WP/11/91. Washington: International Monetary Fund.

Cubeddu, Luis, Camilo E. Tovar, and Evridiki Tsounta. 2012. *Latin America: Vulnerabilities Under Construction?* IMF Working Paper WP/12/193. Washington: International Monetary Fund.

Daude, Christian, Ángel Melguizo, and Alejandro Neut. 2011. Fiscal Policy in Latin America: Countercyclical and Sustainable? *Economics: The Open-Access, Open-Assessment E-Journal* 5, no. 14: 1–29.

Davies, H., and D. Green. 2010. *Banking on the Future: The Fall and Rise of Central Banking.* Princeton, NJ: Princeton University Press.

de Carvalho Filho, Irineu. 2010. Inflation Targeting and the Crisis: An Empirical Assessment. Mimeo (December). International Monetary Fund, Washington.

De Gregorio, José. 1992. Economic Growth in Latin America. *Journal of Development Economics* 39, no. 1: 59–84.

De Gregorio, José. 1993. Inflation, Taxation, and Long-Run Growth. *Journal of Monetary Economics* 31, no. 3: 271–98.

De Gregorio, José. 2004. *Productivity Growth and Disinflation in Chile.* NBER Working Paper 10360. Cambridge, MA: National Bureau of Economic Research.

De Gregorio, José. 2007. *Defining Inflation Targets, the Policy Horizon and the Output-Inflation Tradeoff.* Working Paper 415. Santiago: Central Bank of Chile.

De Gregorio, José. 2012. Commodity Prices, Monetary Policy, and Inflation. *IMF Economic Review* 60, no. 3: 600–633. Washington: International Monetary Fund.

De Gregorio, José. 2013 (forthcoming). Capital Flows and Capital Account Management. In *What Have We Learned? Macroeconomic Policy after the Crisis,* ed., George Akerlof, Olivier Blanchard, David Romer, and Joseph Stiglitz. Cambridge, MA. MIT Press.

De Gregorio, José, and Pablo Guidotti. 1995. Financial Development and Economic Growth. *World Development* 23, no. 3: 433–48.

De Gregorio, José, and Jong-Wha Lee. 2004. Growth and Adjustment in East Asia and Latin America. *Economía* 5, no. 1 (Fall): 69–134.

De Gregorio, José, and Andrea Tokman. 2007. Overcoming Fear of Floating: Exchange Rate Policies in Chile. In *Monetary Policy in Emerging Markets and Other Developing Countries,* ed. N. Batini. New York: Nova Science Publishers Inc.

De Gregorio, José, and Felipe Labbé. 2011. Copper, the Real Exchange Rate and Macroeconomic Fluctuations in Chile. In *Beyond the Curse: Policies to Harness the Power of Natural Resources,* ed. R. Arezki, T. Gylfason, and A. Sy. Washington: International Monetary Fund.

De Gregorio, José, Sebastian Edwards, and Rodrigo O. Valdés. 2000. Controls on Capital Inflows: Do They Work? *Journal of Development Economics* 63, no. 1: 59–83.

De Gregorio, José, Oscar Landerretche, and Christopher Neilson. 2007. Another Pass-Through Bites the Dust? Oil Prices and Inflation. *Economía* 7, no. 2: 155–96.

De la Torre, Augusto, Julian Messina, and Samuel Pienknagura. 2012. *The Labor Market Story Behind Latin America's Transformation.* LAC Semiannual Report, Regional Chief Economist's Office, Latin America and the Caribbean. Washington: World Bank.

Diaz-Alejandro, Carlos. 1985. Good-bye Financial Repression, Hello Financial Crash. *Journal of Development Economics* 19, nos. 1-2: 1–24.

Disyatat, Piti, and Gabriele Galati. 2007. The Effectiveness of Foreign Exchange Intervention in Emerging Market Countries: Evidence from the Czech Koruna. *Journal of International Money and Finance* 26, no. 3 (April): 383–402.

Dodd, Randall. 2009. Exotic Derivatives Losses in Emerging Markets: Questions of Suitability, Concerns for Stability. Mimeo. Financial Policy Forum.

Dominguez, Kathryn M. E., Yuko Hashimoto, and Takatoshi Ito. 2012. *International Reserves and the Global Financial Crisis.* NBER Working Paper 17362. Cambridge, MA: National Bureau of Economic Research.

Dornbush, Rudiger. 1976. Expectations and Exchange Rate Dynamics. *Journal of Political Economy* 84, no. 6: 1161–76.

Dornbusch, Rudiger. 2000. *Keys to Prosperity: Free Markets, Sound Money and a Bit of Luck.* Cambridge, MA: MIT Press.

Dornbusch, Rudiger, and Sebastian Edwards. 1991. *The Macroeconomics of Populism in Latin America.* Chicago: National Bureau of Economic Research and University of Chicago Press.

Dornbusch, Rudiger, and Alejandro Werner. 1994. Mexico: Stabilization, Reform and No Growth. *Brookings Papers on Economic Activity* 1: 235–315. Washington: Brookings Institution.

Dornbusch, Rudiger, Federico Sturzenegger, and Holger Wolf. 1990. Extreme Inflation: Dynamics and Stabilization. *Brookings Papers on Economic Activity* 2: 85–156. Washington: Brookings Institution.

Edwards, Sebastian. 1999. How Effective Are Capital Controls? *Journal of Economic Perspectives* 13, no. 4: 65–84.

Edwards, Sebastian. 2007. The Relationship between Exchange Rates and Inflation Targeting Revisited. In *Monetary Policy under Inflation Targeting*, ed. Frederic Mishkin and Klaus Schmidt-Hebbel. Santiago: Central Bank of Chile.

Edwards, Sebastian. 2010. *Left Behind: Latin America and the False Promise of Populism.* Chicago: University of Chicago Press.

Edwards, Sebastian, and Alejandra Cox-Edwards. 1991. *Monetarism and Liberalization: The Chilean Experiment*, 2d ed. Chicago: University of Chicago Press.

Edwards, Sebastian, and Roberto Rigobon. 2009. Capital Controls, Exchange Rate Volatility and External Vulnerability. *Journal of International Economics* 78, no. 2: 257–67.

Engel, Charles. 1999. Accounting for U.S. Real Exchange Rate Changes. *Journal of Political Economy* 107, no. 3: 507–38.

Engel, Charles. 2003. Expenditure Switching and Exchange-Rate Policy. *NBER Macroeconomics Annual 2002*, volume 17. Cambridge, MA: National Bureau of Economic Research.

Esaka, Taro, and Shinji Takagi. 2012. *Evidence from the Experience of Japan with Short-Term Capital Inflows in the 1970s.* Discussion Paper in Economics and Business 12-03. Graduate School of Economics and OSIPP, Osaka University.

Fatás, Antonio, Prakash Kannan, Pau Rabanal, and Alasdair Scott. 2009. Lessons for Monetary Policy from Asset Price Fluctuations. In *World Economic Outlook* (October). Washington: International Monetary Fund.

Fernandez-Arias, Eduardo. 1996. The New Wave of Private Capital Inflows: Push or Pull? *Journal of Development Economics* 48, no. 2: 389–418.

Fernandez-Villaverde, Jesús, and Juan Rubio-Ramirez. 2007. *How Structural Are Structural Parameters?* NBER Working Paper 13166. Cambridge, MA: National Bureau of Economic Research.

Fischer, Stanley. 1993. The Role of Macroeconomic Factors in Growth. *Journal of Monetary Economics* 32, no. 3: 485–512.

Fischer, Stanley. 2012. The Washington Consensus. In *Global Economics in Extraordinary Times: Essays in Honor of John Williamson*, ed. C. Fred Bergsten and C. Randall Henning. Washington: Peterson Institute for International Economics.

Fjanzylber, Eduardo, and Andrea Repetto. 2009. Instrumentos Alternativos para la Protección Social. In *A Medio Camino: Desafíos de la democracía y del desarrollo en América Latina* [Mid Way: Challenges of Democracy and Development in Latin America], ed. Fernando H. Cardoso and Alejandro Foxley. Santiago, Chile: CIEPLAN.

Forbes, Kristin J. 2007. One Cost of the Chilean Capital Controls: Increased Financial Constraints for Smaller Traded Firms. *Journal of International Economics* 71, no. 2: 294–323.

Frankel, J., and G. Saravelos. 2010. *Are Leading Indicators of Financial Crises Useful in Assessing Country Vulnerability?* NBER Working Paper 16047. Cambridge, MA: National Bureau of Economic Research.

Fratzscher, Marcel. 2011. *Capital Flows, Push versus Pull Factors and the Global Financial Crisis.* ECB Working Paper 1364. Frankfurt: European Central Bank.

Frenkel, Jeffrey A., Carlos Végh, and Guillermo Vuletin. 2013. On Graduation from Fiscal Procyclicality. *Journal of Development Economics* 100, no. 1: 37–47.

Fuentes, Miguel. 2007. *Pass-Through to Import Prices: Evidence for Developing Countries.* Documento de Trabajo 320. Instituto de Economía, Pontificia Universidad Católica de Chile.

Gagnon, Joseph E., and Jane Ihrig. 2004. Monetary Policy and Exchange Rate Pass-Through. *International Journal of Finance and Economics* 9 (October): 315–38.

Galí, Jordi. 2013 (forthcoming). Monetary Policy and Rational Asset Price Bubbles. *American Economic Review*.

Galí, Jordi, and M. Gertler. 1999. Macroeconomic Modelling for Monetary Policy Evaluation. *Journal of Economic Perspectives* 21, no. 4: 25–45.

Galí, Jordi, and Luca Gambetti. 2009. On the Sources of the Great Moderation. *American Economic Journal: Macroeconomics* 1, no. 1: 26–57. American Economic Association.

Gallego, Francisco, Leonardo Hernández, and Klaus Schmidt-Hebbel. 1999. *Capital Controls in Chile: Effective, Efficient?* Working Paper 59. Santiago: Central Bank of Chile.

García, Pablo, and Claudio Soto. 2006. Large Hoarding of International Reserves: Are They Worth It? In *External Vulnerability and Preventive Policies*, ed. R. Caballero, C. Calderón, and L. F. Céspedes. Santiago: Central Bank of Chile.

García-Escribano, Mercedes, and Sebastián Sosa. 2011. *What Is Driving De-dollarization in Latin America?* IMF Working Paper WP/11/10. Washington: International Monetary Fund.

Gavin, Michael, and Roberto Perotti. 1997. Fiscal Policy in Latin America. *NBER Macroeconomics Annual* 12: 11–70. Cambridge, MA: National Bureau of Economic Research.

Gavin, Michael, Ricardo Hausmann, Roberto Perotti, and Ernesto Talvi. 1996. *Managing Fiscal Policy in Latin America.* Working Paper 326. Washington: Inter-American Development Bank, Office of the Chief Economist.

Ghosh, Atish R., Jonathan D. Ostry, and Charalambos G. Tsangarides. 2012. *Shifting Motives: Explaining the Buildup in Official Reserves in Emerging Markets since the 1980s.* IMF Working Paper WP/12/34. Washington: International Monetary Fund.

Ghosh, Atish R., Jun Kim, Mahvash S. Qureshi, and Juan Zalduendo. 2012. *Surges.* IMF Working Paper WP/12/22. Washington: International Monetary Fund.

Gonçalves, C., and J. Salles. 2008. Inflation Targeting in Emerging Economies: What Do the Data Say? *Journal of Development Economics* 85: 312–18.

González, Ivonne, and Ricardo Martner. 2012. Overcoming the "Empty Box Syndrome": Determinants of Income Distribution in Latin America. *CEPAL Review* 108: 7–25.

Gopinath, Gita, and Roberto Rigobon. 2008. Sticky Borders. *Quarterly Journal of Economics* 123, no. 2: 531–75.

Gourinchas, Pierre-Olivier, and Maurice Obstfeld. 2012. Stories of the Twentieth Century for the Twenty-First. *American Economic Journal: Macroeconomics* 4, no. 1: 226–65. American Economic Association.

Gürkaynak, R. 2005. *Econometric Tests of Asset Price Bubbles: Taking Stock.* Federal Reserve Board Finance and Economics Discussion Series 2005-04. Washington: Federal Reserve Board.

Habermeier, Karl, Annamaria Kokenyne, and Chikako Baba. 2011. *The Effectiveness of Capital Controls and Prudential Policies in Managing Large Inflows.* IMF Staff Discussion Notes SDN/11/14. Washington: International Monetary Fund.

Hahm, Joon-Ho, Hyun Song Shin, and Kwanho Shin. 2012. *Non-Core Bank Liabilities and Financial Vulnerability.* NBER Working Paper 18428. Cambridge, MA: National Bureau of Economic Research.

Hall, Pamela. 2011. *Is There Evidence of a Greenspan Put?* Swiss National Bank Working Paper 2011-6. Berne: Swiss National Bank.

Hammond, Gill. 2012. *State of the Art of Inflation Targeting—2012.* Handbook no. 29. London: Centre for Central Bank Studies, Bank of England.

Hott, Christian, and Terhi Jokipii. 2012. *Housing Bubbles and Interest Rates.* Swiss National Bank Working Paper 2012-7. Berne: Swiss National Bank.

Hyvonen, Markus. 2004. *Inflation Convergence across Countries.* Discussion Paper 2004-04. Sydney: Reserve Bank of Australia.

IDB (Inter-American Development Bank). 2005. *Unlocking Credit: The Quest for Deep and Stable Bank Lending.* Economic and Social Progress in Latin America: 2005 Report. Washington.

IDB (Inter-American Development Bank). 2008. *All That Glitters May Not Be Gold: Assessing Latin America's Recent Macroeconomic Performance.* Washington.

IDB (Inter-American Development Bank). 2012. *The World of Forking Paths: Latin America and the Caribbean Facing Global Economic Risks.* 2012 Latin American and Caribbean Macroeconomic Report. Washington.

IMF (International Monetary Fund). 2008. *Global Financial Stability Report* (October). Washington.

IMF (International Monetary Fund). 2012a. External Balance Assessment (EBA): Technical Background of the Pilot Methodology. Mimeo (August 3). Washington.

IMF (International Monetary Fund). 2012b. Taking Stock: A Progress Report on Fiscal Adjustment. *Fiscal Monitor* (October). Washington.

IMF (International Monetary Fund). 2012c. *World Economic Outlook* (April). Washington.

IMF (International Monetary Fund). 2012d. *World Economic Outlook* (October). Washington.

IMF (International Monetary Fund). 2013a. *World Economic Outlook* (April). Washington.

IMF (International Monetary Fund). 2013b. *World Economic Outlook* (October). Washington.

Jácome, Luis, and Francisco Vázquez. 2008. Is There Any Link Between Legal Central Bank Independence and Inflation? Evidence from Latin America and the Caribbean. *European Journal of Political Economy* 24, no. 4: 788–801.

Jácome, Luis I., Erlend W. Nier, and Patrick Imam. 2012. *Building Blocks for Effective Macroprudential Policies in Latin America: Institutional Considerations.* IMF Working Paper WP/12/183. Washington: International Monetary Fund.

Jeanne, O., and R. Rancière. 2006. *The Optimal Level of International Reserves for Emerging Market Countries: Formulas and Applications.* IMF Working Paper WP/06/229. Washington: International Monetary Fund.

Jeanne, Olivier, Arvind Subramanian, and John Williamson. 2012. *Who Needs to Open the Capital Account?* Washington: Peterson Institute for International Economics.

Jinjarak, Yothin, Ilan Noy, and Huanhuan Zheng. 2012. *Capital Controls in Brazil—Stemming a Tide with a Signal.* Working Paper 12-13. University of Hawaii.

Kamil, Herman. 2008. *Is Central Bank Intervention Effective Under Inflation Targeting Regimes? The Case of Colombia.* IMF Working Paper WP/08/88. Washington: International Monetary Fund.

Kamil, Herman. 2012. *How Do Exchange Rate Regimes Affect Firms' Incentives to Hedge Currency Risk? Micro Evidence from Latin America.* IMF Working Paper WP/12/69. Washington: International Monetary Fund.

Kamil, Herman, and Kulwant Rai. 2010. *The Global Credit Crunch and Foreign Banks' Lending to Emerging Markets: Why Did Latin America Fare Better?* IMF Working Paper WP/10/102. Washington: International Monetary Fund.

Kiguel, Miguel A. 1989. Budget Deficits, Stability, and the Monetary Dynamics of Hyperinflation. *Journal of Money, Credit and Banking* 21, no. 2: 148–57.

Kim, Chang-Jin, and Charles R. Nelson. 1999. Has the U.S. Economy Become More Stable? A Bayesian Approach Based on a Markov Switching Model of the Business Cycle. *Review of Economics and Statistics* 81, no. 4: 608–16.

King, Mervyn. 2012. Twenty Years of Inflation Targeting. Stamp Memorial Lecture, London School of Economics, October 9.

Kose, M. Ayhan, and Eswar S. Prasad. 2010. *Emerging Markets: Resilience and Growth Amid Global Turmoil.* Washington: Brookings Institution Press.

Kose, M. Ayhan, Eswar Prasad, and Marco Terrones. 2009. Does Openness to International Financial Flows Raise Productivity Growth? *Journal of International Economics* 28, no. 4: 554–80.

Kose, M. Ayhan, Eswar Prasad, Kenneth Rogoff, and Shang-Jin Wei. 2006. *Financial Globalization: A Reappraisal.* IMF Working Paper WP/06/189. Washington: International Monetary Fund.

Krugman, Paul R. 1987. Pricing to Market When the Exchange Rate Changes. In *Real-Financial Linkages Among Open Economies,* ed. Sven W. Arndt and J. David Richardson. Cambridge, MA: MIT Press.

Lane, Philip R., and Gian Maria Milesi-Ferretti. 2007. The External Wealth of Nations Mark II. *Journal of International Economics* 73, no. 2: 223–50.

Levine, Ross. 2006. Finance and Growth: Theory and Evidence. In *Handbook of Economic Growth,* ed. Philippe Aghion and Steven Durlauf. New York: Elsevier North-Holland.

Lopez-Calva, Luis F., and Nora Lustig. 2012. Explaining the Declines in Inequality in Latin America: Technological Change, Educational Upgrading and Democracy. In *Declining Inequality in Latin America: A Decade of Progress?* ed. Luis F. Lopez-Calva and Nora Lustig. Washington: Brookings Institution Press and United Nations Development Program.

Magud, Nicolas E., Carmen Reinhart, and Kenneth S. Rogoff. 2011. *Capital Controls: Myth and Reality—A Portfolio Balance Approach.* NBER Working Paper 16805. Cambridge, MA: National Bureau of Economic Research.

Marazzi, Mario, and Nathan Sheets. 2007. Declining Exchange Rate Pass-through to U.S. Import Prices: The Potential Role of Global Factors. *Journal of International Money and Finance* 26, no. 6: 924–47.

Marcel, Mario, Mabel Cabezas, and Bernardita Piedrabuena. 2012. *Recalibrando la Medición del Balance Estructural en Chile* [*Recalibrating the Measurement of the Structural Balance in Chile*]. IDB Publications 73838. New York: Inter-American Development Bank.

Mendoza, Enrique G. 1995. The Terms of Trade, the Real Exchange Rate, and Economic Fluctuations. *International Economic Review* 36, no. 1: 101–37.

Mihaljek, Dubravko, and Marc Klau. 2008. Exchange Rate Pass-Through in Emerging Market Economies: What Has Changed and Why? In *Transmission Mechanisms for Monetary Policy in Emerging Market Economies.* BIS Papers 35 (December). Basel: Bank for International Settlements.

Miller, Marcus, Paul Weller, and Lei Zhang. 2001. *Moral Hazard and the US Stock Market: Analyzing the Greenspan Put.* CSGR Working Paper 83/01. University of Warwick.

Mishkin, Frederic, and Klaus Schmidt-Hebbel. 2007. Does Inflation Targeting Make a Difference? In *Monetary Policy under Inflation Targeting,* ed. F. Mishkin and K. Schmidt-Hebbel. Santiago: Central Bank of Chile.

Montoro, Carlos, and Liliana Rojas-Suárez. 2012. *Credit at Times of Stress: Latin American Lessons from the Global Financial Crisis.* BIS Working Paper 370. Basel: Bank for International Settlements.

Nogueira Jr., Reginaldo Pinto. 2006. Inflation Targeting, Exchange Rate Pass-Through and "Fear of Floating." Mimeo. University of Kent.

Obstfeld, Maurice. 2009. International Finance and Growth in Developing Countries: What Have We Learned? *IMF Staff Papers* 56, no. 1 (April): 63–111. Washington: International Monetary Fund.

Obstfeld, Maurice, and Kenneth Rogoff. 1995. The Mirage of Fixed Exchange Rates. *Journal of Economics Perspectives* 9, no. 4 (Fall): 73–96.

Obstfeld, Maurice, and Kenneth Rogoff. 2000. New Directions for Stochastic Open Economy Models. *Journal of International Economics* 50, no. 1: 117–53.

Obstfeld, Maurice, Jay C. Shambaugh, and Alan M. Taylor. 2010. Financial Stability, the Trilemma, and International Reserves. *American Economic Journal: Macroeconomics* 2, no. 2: 57–94. American Economic Association.

Ostry, Jonathan D., Atish R. Ghosh, Karl Habermeier, Luc Laeven, Marcos Chamon, Mahvash Qureshi, and Annamaria Kokenyne. 2011. *Managing Capital inflows: What Tools to Use?* IMF Staff Discussion Note SDN/11/06. Washington: International Monetary Fund.

Prasad, Eswar S. 2012. Role Reversal in Global Finance. In *Achieving Maximum Long-Run Growth*. A Symposium Sponsored by the Federal Reserve Bank of Kansas City, Jackson Hole, Wyoming, August 25–27.

Prasad, Eswar S., Kenneth Rogoff, Shang-Jin Wei, and M. Ayhan Kose. 2003. *Effects of Financial Globalization on Developing Countries: Some Empirical Evidence*. IMF Occasional Paper 220. Washington: International Monetary Fund.

Rajan, Raghuram. 2005. Has Financial Development Made the World Riskier? In *The Greenspan Era: Lessons for the Future*. A Symposium Sponsored by the Federal Reserve Bank of Kansas City, Jackson Hole, Wyoming, August 25–27.

Reinhart, Carmen M., and Kenneth S. Rogoff. 2009. *This Time Is Different: Eight Centuries of Financial Folly*. Princeton, NJ: Princeton University Press.

Rose, Andrew K., and Mark Spiegel. 2011. Cross-Country Causes and Consequences of the Crisis: An Update. *European Economic Review* 55, no. 3: 309–24.

Sargent, Thomas J., and Neil Wallace. 1981. Some Unpleasant Monetarist Arithmetic. *Quarterly Review* 5, no. 3: 1–17. Federal Reserve Bank of Minneapolis.

Sargent, Thomas J., Noah Williams, and Tao Zha. 2009. The Conquest of South American Inflation. *Journal of Political Economy* 117, no. 2: 211–56.

Smith, Penelope A., and Peter M. Summers. 2002. *Regime Switches in GDP Growth and Volatility: Some International Evidence and Implications for Modeling Business Cycles*. Working Paper 21/02. Melbourne Institute of Applied Economic and Social Research, University of Melbourne.

Sorezcky, Avihay. 2010. *Did the Bank of Israel Influence the Exchange Rate?* Discussion Paper 2010.10. Bank of Israel.

Spilimbergo, Antonio. 1999. *Copper and the Chilean Economy, 1960-98*. IMF Working Paper WP/99/57. Washington: International Monetary Fund.

Stein, Jeremy C. 2013. Overheating in Credit Markets: Origins, Measurement, and Policy Responses. Speech delivered at the Federal Reserve Bank of Saint Louis, February.

Stock, James H., and Mark W. Watson. 2003. Has the Business Cycle Changed? Evidence and Explanations. In *Monetary Policy and Uncertainty: Adapting to a Changing Economy*. A Symposium Sponsored by the Federal Reserve Bank of Kansas City, Jackson Hole, Wyoming, August 28–30.

Takhtamanova, Yelena F. 2010. Understanding Changes in the Exchange Rate Pass-Through. *Journal of Macroeconomics* 32, no. 4: 1118–30.

Tapia, Matías, and Andrea Tokman. 2004. Effects of Foreign Exchange Intervention under Public Information: The Chilean Case. *Economía* 4, no. 2 (Spring): 215–56.

Taylor, John B. 1993. Discretion versus Policy Rules in Practice. *Carnegie-Rochester Conference Series on Public Policy* 39: 195–214.

Taylor, John B. 1998. Monetary Policy and the Long Boom: The Homer Jones Lecture. *Review* (November): 3–12. Federal Reserve Bank of St. Louis.

Taylor, John B. 2000. Low Inflation, Pass-Through, and the Pricing Power of Firms. *European Economic Review* 44, no. 7: 1389–408.

Taylor, John B. 2010. Getting Back on Track: Macroeconomic Policy Lessons from the Financial Crisis. *Review* 92, no. 3 (May/June): 165–76. Federal Reserve Bank of St. Louis.

Tirole, Jean. 1982. On the Possibility of Speculation Under Rational Expectations. *Econometrica* 50, no. 5: 1163–82.

Tovar, Camilo E., Mercedes García-Escribano, and Mercedes Vera Martin. 2012. *Credit Growth and the Effectiveness of Reserve Requirements and Other Macroprudential Instruments in Latin America.* IMF Working Paper WP/12/142. Washington: International Monetary Fund.

Truman, Edwin M. 2003. *Inflation Targeting in the World Economy.* Washington: Institute for International Economics.

Truman, Edwin M. 2011. Three Evolutionary Proposals for Reform of the International Monetary System. Remarks delivered at the Bank of Italy's Conference in Memory of Tommaso Padoa-Schioppa, December 16.

Valdes-Prieto, Salvador, and Marcelo Soto. 1996. Es el Control Selectivo de Capitales Efectivo en Chile? Su Efecto sobre el Tipo de Cambio Real [Are Selective Capital Controls Effective in Chile? Effects on the Real Exchange Rate]. *Cuadernos de Economía* 33, no. 98: 77–108.

Vega, Marco, and Diego Winkelried. 2005. Inflation Targeting and Inflation Behavior: A Successful Story? *International Journal of Central Banking* 1, no. 3: 153–75.

Williamson, John. 1990. What Washington Means by Policy Reform. In *Latin American Adjustment: How Much Has Happened?* ed. John Williamson. Washington: Institute for International Economics.

Winkelried, Diego. 2011. Exchange Rate Pass-Through and Inflation Targeting in Peru. Mimeo. Central Reserve Bank of Peru.

Woodford, Michael. 2003. *Interest and Prices.* Princeton, NJ: Princeton University Press.

About the Author

José De Gregorio, visiting fellow at the Peterson Institute for International Economics, is full professor in the Department of Economics at the Universidad de Chile. He was governor of the Central Bank of Chile from 2007 until 2011. Before that he was vice-governor from 2003 and member of the bank's board from 2001. During 2000 and 2001, De Gregorio was minister of the combined portfolios of economy, mining, and energy.

Between 1997 and 2000 he was professor and head of postgraduate programs at the Center of Applied Economics at the University of Chile. He also served on the executive of the Latin American Doctoral Program in Economics. From 1994 to 1997, he was coordinator of economic policy at the Ministry of Finance, Chile. From 1990 to 1994 he worked as an economist in the research department of the International Monetary Fund (IMF). He has been a visiting scholar at the IMF and the World Bank and visiting professor at the Anderson School, University of California, Los Angeles. He is on the board of and advisor to several private companies. He is also a consultant to international organizations.

De Gregorio has received a number of honors and awards, including Central Banker of the Year in Latin America for 2008, awarded by *The Banker*, a member of the *Financial Times* editorial group. He was also named Distinguished Industrial Engineer of 2007 by the Industrial Engineering–Universidad de Chile Alumni Association and Economist of the Year by the newspaper *El Mercurio* in 2011, among others.

He has a degree in civil engineering and a master's degree in engineering from the University of Chile, where he received the Marcos Orrego Puelma award for the best graduate of his year. He obtained a PhD in economics from

MIT in 1990. He has published two books and more than 100 articles in international academic reviews and books on issues including monetary policy, exchange rates, international finance, and economic growth. He has served as a referee and member of editorial boards for several academic journals. He is also a member of the Executive Committee of the Latin American and Caribbean Economic Association.

Index

ratio of banking credit to, 90–91, 91*f*
volatility of, leverage and, 95*f*, 95–96
global financial crisis (2008)
  banks and, 88–94
  causes of, 72–76
  economic growth during, 1, 3*f*, 7*f*, 11
  economic growth since, 142, 142*t*
  exchange rates during, 50–53, 51*f*
  financial stability and, 85
  fiscal policy during, 40–42, 41*f*, 43*f*
  housing prices before, 74*f*, 74–75
  inflation during, 32–33
  international reserves during, 63–68, 64*f*,
    65*f*
    versus Asian crisis, 65–67, 66*t*
  macroeconomic policy since, 143–44
  monetary policy during, 38–40, 39*f*, 42, 43*f*
  versus other crises, 12–13
  recovery dynamics, 96, 142–43
  risks from, 4–5
good luck, 3–4, 14, 18–24, 44
government expenditure, 41, 42*f*
Great Moderation, 44–45, 95
Greenspan, Alan, 72, 76
Greenspan put, 76, 86, 91
Group of Seven (G-7)
  debt levels, 35, 35*f*
  private credit in, 90–91, 91*f*

headline inflation, 30–31
heterodox programs, 26
housing prices, 72–76, 74*f*, 96–97
hyperinflation, 24–25

impossible trinity, 49
inclusive institutions, 134–35
income inequality, 10, 132–34, 133*f*
inflation, 24–28
  during 1980s, 24, 25*f*
  causes of, 24–26
  in emerging-market economies, 31–32,
    32*f*–33*f*
  exchange rates and, 26–27, 29, 47–49, 53–56
  fiscal policy and, 24–25, 34–36, 82–83
  forecasting, 30
  macroeconomic stability and, 17–18,
    138–39
inflation bias, 26
inflation inertia, 26–29, 33, 45, 138–39
inflation targeting, 28–29
  after Asian crises, 10
  asset price bubbles and, 76–78
  capital flows and, 119–21
  current data (2012), 28, 28*t*

effectiveness of, 34, 39–40, 45
exchange rates and, 47–48, 53–56, 60–62
financial stability and, 87
monetary policy with, 25, 29–34, 120
resilience and, 13, 18, 140
institutional factors, 134–35, 136*f*
Inter-American Development Bank, 21, 92
interest groups, 132
interest rates, 22–24, 23*f*
  in advanced economies, 75–77
  capital controls and, 124–26
  financial stability and, 85–87
  during global financial crisis, 39*f*, 39–40
  Taylor rule, 29–30, 72–77
  variables used in setting, 30–31
international environment, 17–45. *See also*
    specific factor
  financial integration (*See* financial
    integration)
  macroeconomic policy and, 138
  resilience and, 3–4, 18, 44–45, 138–41
International Monetary Fund (IMF)
  euro area bailouts, 4
  inflation targeting and, 28
  World Economic Outlook (WEO), 1*n*, 12*n*,
    19–20, 24
international reserves, 47–70
  capital flows and, 104–106, 110–13, 126–27
  exchange rates and, 58–63, 104–106
  global adjustments and, 68–70
  during global financial crisis, 63–68, 64*f*, 65*f*
    versus Asian crisis, 65–67, 66*t*
  role of, 14, 48, 58–59
intervention addiction, 60
Inti plan (Peru), 26
Ireland, 73
irrational exuberance, 76
Israel
  capital flows, 110, 111*f*
  exchange-rate-based stabilization, 27*n*,
    61–62

Japan, 121*n*

Keynesian approach, 36
Kirchner, Néstor, 10
Korea, 80*n*, 123–24
Kuznets curve, 133

LA-7 economies, 1–2. *See also specific country*
  current economic data (2012), 5, 6*t*
  debt levels, 35, 35*f*
  economic growth, 7–10, 8*f*, 9*f*
    versus other emerging-market

Other Publications from the
Peterson Institute for International Economics

WORKING PAPERS

* = out of print

75 **Curbing the Boom-Bust Cycle: Stabilizing Capital Flows to Emerging Markets**
John Williamson
July 2005   ISBN 0-88132-330-6

76 **The Shape of a Swiss-US Free Trade Agreement**   Gary Clyde Hufbauer and Richard E. Baldwin
February 2006   ISBN 978-0-88132-385-6

77 **A Strategy for IMF Reform**
Edwin M. Truman
February 2006   ISBN 978-0-88132-398-6

78 **US-China Trade Disputes: Rising Tide, Rising Stakes**   Gary Clyde Hufbauer, Yee Wong, and Ketki Sheth
August 2006   ISBN 978-0-88132-394-8

79 **Trade Relations Between Colombia and the United States**   Jeffrey J. Schott, ed.
August 2006   ISBN 978-0-88132-389-4

80 **Sustaining Reform with a US-Pakistan Free Trade Agreement**   Gary Clyde Hufbauer and Shahid Javed Burki
November 2006   ISBN 978-0-88132-395-5

81 **A US–Middle East Trade Agreement: A Circle of Opportunity?**   Robert Z. Lawrence
November 2006   ISBN 978-0-88132-396-2

82 **Reference Rates and the International Monetary System**   John Williamson
January 2007   ISBN 978-0-88132-401-3

83 **Toward a US-Indonesia Free Trade Agreement**   Gary Clyde Hufbauer and Sjamsu Rahardja
June 2007   ISBN 978-0-88132-402-0

84 **The Accelerating Decline in America's High-Skilled Workforce** Jacob F. Kirkegaard
December 2007   ISBN 978-0-88132-413-6

85 **Blue-Collar Blues: Is Trade to Blame for Rising US Income Inequality?**
Robert Z. Lawrence
January 2008   ISBN 978-0-88132-414-3

86 **Maghreb Regional and Global Integration: A Dream to Be Fulfilled**
Gary Clyde Hufbauer and Claire Brunel, eds.
October 2008   ISBN 978-0-88132-426-6

87 **The Future of China's Exchange Rate Policy**
Morris Goldstein and Nicholas R. Lardy
July 2009   ISBN 978-0-88132-416-7

88 **Capitalizing on the Morocco-US Free Trade Agreement: A Road Map for Success**
Gary Clyde Hufbauer and Claire Brunel, eds
September 2009   ISBN 978-0-88132-433-4

89 **Three Threats: An Analytical Framework for the CFIUS Process**   Theodore H. Moran
August 2009   ISBN 978-0-88132-429-7

90 **Reengaging Egypt: Options for US-Egypt Economic Relations**   Barbara Kotschwar and Jeffrey J. Schott
January 2010   ISBN 978-088132-439-6

91 **Figuring Out the Doha Round**   Gary Clyde Hufbauer, Jeffrey J. Schott, and Woan Foong Wong
June 2010   ISBN 978-088132-503-4

92 **China's Strategy to Secure Natural Resources: Risks, Dangers, and Opportunities**   Theodore H. Moran
June 2010   ISBN 978-088132-512-6

93 **The Implications of China-Taiwan Economic Liberalization**   Daniel H. Rosen and Zhi Wang
January 2011   ISBN 978-0-88132-501-0

94 **The Global Outlook for Government Debt over the Next 25 Years: Implications for the Economy and Public Policy**   Joseph E. Gagnon with Marc Hinterschweiger
June 2011   ISBN 978-0-88132-621-5

95 **A Decade of Debt**   Carmen M. Reinhart and Kenneth S. Rogoff
September 2011   ISBN 978-0-88132-622-2

96 **Carbon Abatement Costs and Climate Change Finance**   William R. Cline
July 2011   ISBN 978-0-88132-607-9

97 **The United States Should Establish Permanent Normal Trade Relations with Russia**   Anders Åslund and Gary Clyde Hufbauer
April 2012   ISBN 978-0-88132-620-8

98 **The Trans-Pacific Partnership and Asia-Pacific Integration: A Quantitative Assessment**   Peter A. Petri, Michael G. Plummer, and Fan Zhai
November 2012   ISBN 978-0-88132-664-2

99 **Understanding the Trans-Pacific Partnership**   Jeffrey J. Schott, Barbara Kotschwar, and Julia Muir
January 2013   ISBN 978-0-88132-672-7

100 **Foreign Direct Investment in the United States: Benefits, Suspicions, and Risks with Special Attention to FDI from China**
Theodore H. Moran and Lindsay Oldenski
August 2013   ISBN 978-0-88132-660-4

101 **Outward Foreign Direct Investment and US Exports, Jobs, and R&D: Implications for US Policy**   Gary Clyde Hufbauer, Theodore H. Moran, and Lindsay Oldenski, Assisted by Martin Vieiro
August 2013   ISBN 978-0-88132-668-0

102 **Local Content Requirements: A Global Problem**   Gary Clyde Hufbauer, Jeffrey J. Schott, Cathleen Cimino, Martin Vieiro, and Erika Wada
September 2013   ISBN 978-0-88132-680-2

BOOKS

IMF Conditionality*   John Williamson, ed.
1983   ISBN 0-88132-006-4

Trade Policy in the 1980s*   William R. Cline, ed.
1983   ISBN 0-88132-031-5

Subsidies in International Trade*   Gary Clyde Hufbauer and Joanna Shelton Erb
1984   ISBN 0-88132-004-8

International Debt: Systemic Risk and Policy Response*   William R. Cline
1984   ISBN 0-88132-015-3

Trade Protection in the United States: 31 Case Studies*   Gary Clyde Hufbauer, Diane E. Berliner, and Kimberly Ann Elliott
1986   ISBN 0-88132-040-4

Toward Renewed Economic Growth in Latin America*   Bela Balassa, Gerardo M. Bueno, Pedro Pablo Kuczynski, and Mario Henrique Simonsen
1986   ISBN 0-88132-045-5
Capital Flight and Third World Debt*
Donald R. Lessard and John Williamson, eds.
1987   ISBN 0-88132-053-6
The Canada-United States Free Trade Agreement: The Global Impact*   Jeffrey J. Schott and Murray G. Smith, eds.
1988   ISBN 0-88132-073-0
World Agricultural Trade: Building a Consensus*   William M. Miner and Dale E. Hathaway, eds.
1988   ISBN 0-88132-071-3
Japan in the World Economy*   Bela Balassa and Marcus Noland
1988   ISBN 0-88132-041-2
America in the World Economy: A Strategy for the 1990s*   C. Fred Bergsten
1988   ISBN 0-88132-089-7
Managing the Dollar: From the Plaza to the Louvre*   Yoichi Funabashi
1988, 2d ed. 1989   ISBN 0-88132-097-8
United States External Adjustment and the World Economy*   William R. Cline
May 1989   ISBN 0-88132-048-X
Free Trade Areas and U.S. Trade Policy*
Jeffrey J. Schott, ed.
May 1989   ISBN 0-88132-094-3
Dollar Politics: Exchange Rate Policymaking in the United States*   I. M. Destler and C. Randall Henning
September 1989   ISBN 0-88132-079-X
Latin American Adjustment: How Much Has Happened?*   John Williamson, ed.
April 1990   ISBN 0-88132-125-7
The Future of World Trade in Textiles and Apparel*   William R. Cline
1987, 2d ed. June 1999   ISBN 0-88132-110-9
Completing the Uruguay Round: A Results-Oriented Approach to the GATT Trade Negotiations*   Jeffrey J. Schott, ed.
September 1990   ISBN 0-88132-130-3
Economic Sanctions Reconsidered (2 volumes)
Economic Sanctions Reconsidered: Supplemental Case Histories
Gary Clyde Hufbauer, Jeffrey J. Schott, and Kimberly Ann Elliott
1985, 2d ed. Dec. 1990   ISBN cloth 0-88132-115-X
                                  ISBN paper 0-88132-105-2
Economic Sanctions Reconsidered: History and Current Policy   Gary C. Hufbauer, Jeffrey J. Schott, and Kimberly Ann Elliott
December 1990   ISBN cloth 0-88132-140-0
                                  ISBN paper 0-88132-136-2
Pacific Basin Developing Countries: Prospects for the Future*   Marcus Noland
January 1991   ISBN cloth 0-88132-141-9
                    ISBN paper 0-88132-081-1
Currency Convertibility in Eastern Europe*
John Williamson, ed.
October 1991   ISBN 0-88132-128-1

International Adjustment and Financing: The Lessons of 1985-1991*   C. Fred Bergsten, ed.
January 1992   ISBN 0-88132-112-5
North American Free Trade: Issues and Recommendations*   Gary Clyde Hufbauer and Jeffrey J. Schott
April 1992   ISBN 0-88132-120-6
Narrowing the U.S. Current Account Deficit*
Alan J. Lenz
June 1992   ISBN 0-88132-103-6
The Economics of Global Warming
William R. Cline
June 1992   ISBN 0-88132-132-X
US Taxation of International Income: Blueprint for Reform   Gary Clyde Hufbauer, assisted by Joanna M. van Rooij
October 1992   ISBN 0-88132-134-6
Who's Bashing Whom? Trade Conflict in High-Technology Industries   Laura D'Andrea Tyson
November 1992   ISBN 0-88132-106-0
Korea in the World Economy*   Il SaKong
January 1993   ISBN 0-88132-183-4
Pacific Dynamism and the International Economic System*   C. Fred Bergsten and Marcus Noland, eds.
May 1993   ISBN 0-88132-196-6
Economic Consequences of Soviet Disintegration*   John Williamson, ed.
May 1993   ISBN 0-88132-190-7
Reconcilable Differences? United States-Japan Economic Conflict*   C. Fred Bergsten and Marcus Noland
June 1993   ISBN 0-88132-129-X
Does Foreign Exchange Intervention Work?
Kathryn M. Dominguez and Jeffrey A. Frankel
September 1993   ISBN 0-88132-104-4
Sizing Up U.S. Export Disincentives*
J. David Richardson
September 1993   ISBN 0-88132-107-9
NAFTA: An Assessment   Gary Clyde Hufbauer and Jeffrey J. Schott, rev. ed.
October 1993   ISBN 0-88132-199-0
Adjusting to Volatile Energy Prices
Philip K. Verleger, Jr.
November 1993   ISBN 0-88132-069-2
The Political Economy of Policy Reform
John Williamson, ed.
January 1994   ISBN 0-88132-195-8
Measuring the Costs of Protection in the United States   Gary Clyde Hufbauer and Kimberly Ann Elliott
January 1994   ISBN 0-88132-108-7
The Dynamics of Korean Economic Development*   Cho Soon
March 1994   ISBN 0-88132-162-1
Reviving the European Union*
C. Randall Henning, Eduard Hochreiter, and Gary Clyde Hufbauer, eds.
April 1994   ISBN 0-88132-208-3
China in the World Economy   Nicholas R. Lardy
April 1994   ISBN 0-88132-200-8
Greening the GATT: Trade, Environment, and the Future   Daniel C. Esty
July 1994   ISBN 0-88132-205-9

Witness to Transformation: Refugee Insights into North Korea   Stephan Haggard and Marcus Noland
January 2011   ISBN 978-0-88132-438-9
Foreign Direct Investment and Development: Launching a Second Generation of Policy Research, Avoiding the Mistakes of the First, Reevaluating Policies for Developed and Developing Countries   Theodore H. Moran
April 2011   ISBN 978-0-88132-600-0
How Latvia Came through the Financial Crisis   Anders Åslund and Valdis Dombrovskis
May 2011   ISBN 978-0-88132-602-4
Global Trade in Services: Fear, Facts, and Offshoring   J. Bradford Jensen
August 2011   ISBN 978-0-88132-601-7
NAFTA and Climate Change   Meera Fickling and Jeffrey J. Schott
September 2011   ISBN 978-0-88132-436-5
Eclipse: Living in the Shadow of China's Economic Dominance   Arvind Subramanian
September 2011   ISBN 978-0-88132-606-2
Flexible Exchange Rates for a Stable World Economy   Joseph E. Gagnon with Marc Hinterschweiger
September 2011   ISBN 978-0-88132-627-7
The Arab Economies in a Changing World, 2d ed.   Marcus Noland and Howard Pack
November 2011   ISBN 978-0-88132-628-4
Sustaining China's Economic Growth After the Global Financial Crisis   Nicholas R. Lardy
January 2012   ISBN 978-0-88132-626-0
Who Needs to Open the Capital Account?   Olivier Jeanne, Arvind Subramanian, and John Williamson
April 2012   ISBN 978-0-88132-511-9
Devaluing to Prosperity: Misaligned Currencies and Their Growth Consequences   Surjit S. Bhalla
August 2012   ISBN 978-0-88132-623-9
Private Rights and Public Problems: The Global Economics of Intellectual Property in the 21st Century   Keith E. Maskus
September 2012   ISBN 978-0-88132-507-2
Global Economics in Extraordinary Times: Essays in Honor of John Williamson   C. Fred Bergsten and C. Randall Henning, eds.
November 2012   ISBN 978-0-88132-662-8
Rising Tide: Is Growth in Emerging Economies Good for the United States?   Lawrence Edwards and Robert Z. Lawrence
February 2013   ISBN 978-0-88132-500-3
Responding to Financial Crisis: Lessons from Asia Then, the United States and Europe Now   Changyong Rhee and Adam S. Posen, eds
October 2013   ISBN 978-0-88132-674-1
Fueling Up: The Economic Implications of America's Oil and Gas Boom   Trevor Houser and Shashank Mohan
January 2014   ISBN 978-0-88132-656-7
How Latin America Weathered the Global Financial Crisis   José De Gregorio
January 2014   ISBN 978-0-88132-678-9

SPECIAL REPORTS

1   Promoting World Recovery: A Statement on Global Economic Strategy*   by 26 Economists from Fourteen Countries
December 1982   ISBN 0-88132-013-7
2   Prospects for Adjustment in Argentina, Brazil, and Mexico: Responding to the Debt Crisis*   John Williamson, ed.
June 1983   ISBN 0-88132-016-1
3   Inflation and Indexation: Argentina, Brazil, and Israel*   John Williamson, ed.
March 1985   ISBN 0-88132-037-4
4   Global Economic Imb alances*   C. Fred Bergsten, ed.
March 1986   ISBN 0-88132-042-0
5   African Debt and Financing*   Carol Lancaster and John Williamson, eds.
May 1986   ISBN 0-88132-044-7
6   Resolving the Global Economic Crisis: After Wall Street*   by Thirty-three Economists from Thirteen Countries
December 1987   ISBN 0-88132-070-6
7   World Economic Problems*   Kimberly Ann Elliott and John Williamson, eds.
April 1988   ISBN 0-88132-055-2
    Reforming World Agricultural Trade*   by Twenty-nine Professionals from Seventeen Countries
1988   ISBN 0-88132-088-9
8   Economic Relations Between the United States and Korea: Conflict or Cooperation?*   Thomas O. Bayard and Soogil Young, eds.
January 1989   ISBN 0-88132-068-4
9   Whither APEC? The Progress to Date and Agenda for the Future*   C. Fred Bergsten, ed.
October 1997   ISBN 0-88132-248-2
10   Economic Integration of the Korean Peninsula   Marcus Noland, ed.
January 1998   ISBN 0-88132-255-5
11   Restarting Fast Track*   Jeffrey J. Schott, ed.
April 1998   ISBN 0-88132-259-8
12   Launching New Global Trade Talks: An Action Agenda   Jeffrey J. Schott, ed.
September 1998   ISBN 0-88132-266-0
13   Japan's Financial Crisis and Its Parallels to US Experience   Ryoichi Mikitani and Adam S. Posen, eds.
September 2000   ISBN 0-88132-289-X
14   The Ex-Im Bank in the 21st Century: A New Approach   Gary Clyde Hufbauer and Rita M. Rodriguez, eds.
January 2001   ISBN 0-88132-300-4
15   The Korean Diaspora in the World Economy   C. Fred Bergsten and Inbom Choi, eds.
January 2003   ISBN 0-88132-358-6
16   Dollar Overvaluation and the World Economy   C. Fred Bergsten and John Williamson, eds.
February 2003   ISBN 0-88132-351-9
17   Dollar Adjustment: How Far? Against What?   C. Fred Bergsten and John Williamson, eds.
November 2004   ISBN 0-88132-378-0

WORKS IN PROGRESS

Confronting the Curse: The Economics and Geopolitics of Natural Resource Governance
Marcus Noland and Cullen Hendrix

China's Rise as Global Direct Investor: Policy Implications   Daniel H. Rosen and Thilo Hanemann

Inside the Euro Crisis   Simeon Djankov

Managing the Euro Area Debt Crisis
William R. Cline

Breaking Barriers: Toward Economic Integration between India and the United States   C. Fred Bergsten and Arvind Subramanian

Toward Free Trade and Investment between China and the United States
C. Fred Bergsten and Gary Clyde Hufbauer

DISTRIBUTORS OUTSIDE THE UNITED STATES

Australia, New Zealand,
and Papua New Guinea
D. A. Information Services
648 Whitehorse Road
Mitcham, Victoria 3132, Australia
Tel: 61-3-9210-7777
Fax: 61-3-9210-7788
Email: service@dadirect.com.au
www.dadirect.com.au

India, Bangladesh, Nepal, and Sri Lanka
Viva Books Private Limited
Mr. Vinod Vasishtha
4737/23 Ansari Road
Daryaganj, New Delhi 110002
India
Tel: 91-11-4224-2200
Fax: 91-11-4224-2240
Email: viva@vivagroupindia.net
www.vivagroupindia.com

Mexico, Central America, South America,
and Puerto Rico
US PubRep, Inc.
311 Dean Drive
Rockville, MD 20851
Tel: 301-838-9276
Fax: 301-838-9278
Email: c.falk@ieee.org

Asia *(Brunei, Burma, Cambodia, China,*
Hong Kong, Indonesia, Korea, Laos, Malaysia,
Philippines, Singapore, Taiwan, Thailand,
and Vietnam)
East-West Export Books (EWEB)
University of Hawaii Press
2840 Kolowalu Street
Honolulu, Hawaii 96822-1888
Tel: 808-956-8830
Fax: 808-988-6052
Email: eweb@hawaii.edu

Canada
Renouf Bookstore
5369 Canotek Road, Unit 1
Ottawa, Ontario KlJ 9J3, Canada
Tel: 613-745-2665
Fax: 613-745-7660
www.renoufbooks.com

Japan
United Publishers Services Ltd.
1-32-5, Higashi-shinagawa
Shinagawa-ku, Tokyo 140-0002
Japan
Tel: 81-3-5479-7251
Fax: 81-3-5479-7307
Email: purchasing@ups.co.jp
For trade accounts only. Individuals will find
Institute books in leading Tokyo bookstores.

Middle East
MERIC
2 Bahgat Ali Street, El Masry Towers
Tower D, Apt. 24
Zamalek, Cairo
Egypt
Tel. 20-2-7633824
Fax: 20-2-7369355
Email: mahmoud_fouda@mericonline.com
www.mericonline.com

United Kingdom, Europe
(including Russia and Turkey), **Africa,**
and Israel
The Eurospan Group
c/o Turpin Distribution
Pegasus Drive
Stratton Business Park
Biggleswade, Bedfordshire
SG18 8TQ
United Kingdom
Tel: 44 (0) 1767-604972
Fax: 44 (0) 1767-601640
Email: eurospan@turpin-distribution.com
www.eurospangroup.com/bookstore

Visit our website at:
www.piie.com
E-mail orders to:
petersonmail@presswarehouse.com